Loyalty and Disloyalty

The history of morality

When I was 14 or 15 my grandfather said something that has stayed with me for all the years since his death. He spent his life mining coal in Haydock, a Lancashire village on the eastern edge of St. Helens, where I was born in 1952. He said 'you can learn all there is to know about life without going any further than Billinge' another village, on the northern edge of St. Helens. Well I went off to University, became a Structural Engineer, and lived in the Midlands and then the South West for awhile, but after the 1970s were over came back to where I started. He was right, that tough old man, I could have figured it all out without moving away, see what you think…

Loyalty and Disloyalty

The history of morality

David Knowles

Arena Books

First published simultaneously in Great Britain & the USA in 2013 by Arena Books

Arena Books
6 Southgate Green
Bury St. Edmunds
IP33 2BL

www.arenabooks.co.uk

Distributed in America by Ingram International, One Ingram Blvd., PO Box 3 LaVergne, TN 37086-1986, USA.

David Knowles, 1952 -
Loyalty and Disloyalty: *The history of morality*

        British Library cataloguing in Publication Data. A Catalogue record for this book is available from the British Library.

ISBN 978-1-909421-21-9

BIC classifications: JFM, HPX, JFCA, HRAM1, HPX.

Printed & bound by Lightningsource UK

For Maria

Else tomorrow a stranger will say with masterly good sense precisely what we have thought and felt all the time, and we shall be forced to take with shame our own opinion from another.

Ralph Waldo Emerson

Foreword

The theme of what follows is simple enough I hope. Close your eyes for a moment and imagine yourself to be living in a group of early *Homo sapiens*. We can only guess what they were really like, but think of them as a cruder version of a group of native foragers we still see left here and there in the world today. To orientate you in time and place picture them about 150,000 years ago in the East African Rift Valley, from there we can go back in time as well as come forward.

My questions is this: since our moral responses seem likely to have first appeared amongst us in the ancient hunter-gatherer groups of our early human and pre-human acestors, why do we not refer to these groups when trying to figure out moral problems? Why instead do we plunge in with society as it stands today in all its modern complexity?

So that is what I've done, gone back before coming forward again. There are various side effects to this approach, but I will mention just one and then let's get on. I could have called this book 'The Boundaries of Morality' because being aware of our moral beginnings delineates a list of items beyond those boundaries.

Amongst other things, we will take a trip along the edges of these boundaries and if what I propose is eventually seen to be true let's set out now where this is likely to lead us. It will mean that all those, well meant and not so well meant, attempts by humans over many centuries to define morality without reference to the original human and also pre-human groups in which it was formed, are doomed to either complete failure or at best to only partial success.

PART 1 – covers the Contract made between those first group members.

PART 2 – looks at a number of things subsequently, and confusingly, included under the heading of morality, which are actually beyond its boundaries.

PART 3 – follows the progression of the Contract through time.

PART 4 – discusses human rights and some more boundary issues.

CONTENTS

Foreword

PART 1 – THE CONTRACT

PART 2 – BEYOND THE CONTRACT

PART 3 – THE CONTRACT THROUGH TIME

PART 4 – HUMAN RIGHTS and FORGIVENESS

Appendices

Part 1

The Contract

1. Introduction

Once upon a time, back when life began to appear on this little planet, came the first of six long threads that still run through our lives today. These threads can serve us well as an introduction to how ancient, but continuous, are the phenomena that fall within the remit of philosophy.

The oldest of these that we can still find and recognise in ourselves today is Pleasure-Pain, this first thread must have appeared 2,000 to 3,000 million years ago, with the birth of the very first life forms.

1. PLEASURE-PAIN. Not Pleasure and Pain, because Pleasure-Pain are part of the same continuum. Tiny life forms move towards areas of their environment that suit them best; mild acid good – alkali bad, fresh water good – salty water bad, and for others vice versa. Either way they flourish and proliferate in the environments most suited to them. All living creatures are drawn towards Pleasure and at the same time are repelled by Pain.

In us humans this is extended further and can be physical, emotional or intellectual pleasures. Thus humans come to use the word good to identify Pleasure, and the word bad for Pain, but all those millions upon millions of years ago there is just Pleasure-Pain, and nothing else.

Procreation by the splitting and copying of cells is not a thread in human life, because we breed offspring via sexual reproduction, and so of the threads that influence our behaviour Power is next, with Sex third on the list.

2. POWER arrives when some life forms, conglomerates of cells, consume others, swallow up the nearby single cell organisms, yummy, yummy, tasty. Being a successful predator is good, is Pleasurable – I survive and you don't.

Then a gap in time, 1000 million, maybe 2000 million years who knows certainly not me.

3. SEX appears next, umm double tasty, even more Pleasurable. Now if I am big and strong my Power keeps others off my patch, where my potential sexual partners are, double yummy, sex is double good – I procreate and you don't.

Then another long gap ... let's say one that brings us up to 100 million years ago or so.

4. Reason appears and the KNOWLEDGE that results. A bird learns how to drop and crack a nut, later a hominid learns how to make a tool, as chimps do today. Later still another discovers fire, or makes a spear, builds a hut, or plants a seed, domesticates an animal, or tans a hide, fashions a plough, invents the wheel, the printing press... Knowledge has arrived on planet earth, and it is good, because it enhances Pleasure and aids survival. For us humans it becomes as big as any of the three before, but something bigger still is coming soon.

In awhile, in terms of geological time, another kind of good is coming, a kind of good so special we call it by another name – we call it Right. Beware, beware Power thy nemesis awaits thee, already hidden, where, where? Like Herod, you cry where? Why hidden in thy loins of course where else could it hide? In your loins and in the loins of the object, and objects, of your desire.

5. And for this fifth phenomenon, appearing somewhere in the last few million years we come to use the word MORALITY – to cover those things we feel are either Right or Wrong.

And this, as we shall see, becomes intimately involved with the sixth and final thread we're interested in.

6. For the sixth we come to METAPHYSICS, which is not an everyday kind of word. I use it here to stand for all our theories about what things 'mean'. With the advent of humans, abstract and theoretical questions have arrived inside the heads of a certain life form on this earth, and the first answers are called Metaphysics-religion.

Metaphysics covers all our theories about what our lives mean, all our ideas about what lies under the surface of things, why the Sun-God rises and sets, why the Rain-God sometimes comes and other times doesn't. It is not a very surprising development, following on as it eventually does from reason and Knowledge, especially with the increasing size and complexity of the human brain. The word Metaphysics covers all theoretical speculation and so gives rise to all religious, philosophical and later all scientific theories too.

Morality and Metaphysics-religion come tumbling after one another, so close together, these children of their four long lived ancestors.

Predecessors that until recent times have had the field all to themselves. Why should they give ground to these upstarts called Morality and Metaphysics-religion?

Oh but they do, in us humans they give a lot of ground, not everything by any means, but a lot. Let's try to figure out how much they give, and where and when they give, then give again, as Power and Sex try to reassert themselves, not least upon the back of Knowledge, then change again, and again, all the way to the present.

Every human on this planet dislikes being dominated by others. This is also true of other creatures too, as they battle for survival and take their place in the story of evolution. This then seems like a solid starting point, it is something we humans all share, with other animals as well as amongst ourselves. It is a feeling we all share, and is thus the basis for a commonality of experience, amongst us all. A dislike of being dominated by others.

One hears of some who enjoy being dominated during sex, but that is a sexual aberration and so applies in that context only. It is thus limited in time and place and does not extend to the whole of their lives. No one enjoys being downtrodden and dominated on a continuous and continual basis, day after day, week after week, year after year, ad infinitum.

Yet at the same time no human can 'go it alone'. By which I mean that for their survival *Homo sapiens* are always to be found living in groups of their fellows. There are hermits of course, sometimes they survive isolated from the community they were born into, other times they play a religious role in nearby communities. Either way they rely upon being left in peace, but are still under the protection of a nearby community. Neither do they have the wherewithal to support a full life, in particular a spouse and family. They are thus eccentrics, and that is fine, I'm pretty eccentric myself, but even these need group protection and so must live on the edge of a group, rather than alone in total solitude.

Incidentally it would appear that these hermits dislike being dominated so much that they choose to live separated from those, within a group, who might dominate them.

And so I put it to you that every human on this planet hates to be dominated, but at the same time is forced by the necessity of survival to live in groups with others. Groups where there is a tendency for certain members of the group to dominate other members. In the animal groups we see around us we call the most dominant of all by the terms Alpha Male and Alpha Female, and indeed we often transfer these terms to some of our human groups or organisations, with good reason. We see certain people as being more dominant than others are.

3

This is our philosophical starting point, so let's take a look at these groups.

Since we must start at the beginning, or rather try to figure out what point in time we might reasonably refer to as the beginning of moral philosophy, right at the outset we must go further back. In the Foreword I asked you to imagine us about 150,000 years ago, because back then it is generally accepted that the first *Homo sapiens* lived in small groups, probably of about 50 to 100 individuals (Ridley, 1993). I gave you this date because, before that time we were no longer strictly speaking classifiable as humans, we were pre-human.

To begin though we must also encompass a time further away from the present, back to our immediate predecessor *Homo erectus*, the most general term used for pre-humans.

2. Loyalty to the Group

*H*omo erectus was around from about 300,000 to 1,800,000 years ago. My proposition is that what we humans now call morality, the fifth of the six threads, developed from a certain facet of these creature's social lives, from them and from those that followed them, early *Homo sapiens*.

It seems probably that they gathered themselves in similar groups to the humans they preceded. Groups of 50 to 100 living under the pressure of evolutionary survival, in other words gathered together for the 'greatest good/happiness (pleasure as opposed to pain) of the greatest number'. Gathered thus so that more of them would survive to procreate, populate and thereby increase the strength of their group. This continuation of and increase of the group, would in turn help to ensure the future continuing survival of the group and thus in turn the individuals within it.

Actually this seems likely to be true of many other 'group dwelling' animals; they like us, band together because there is safety in numbers. They like us, have formed themselves into packs for the greatest good and chance of survival of the greatest number.

This principle of the 'greatest happiness of the greatest number' is from a branch of moral philosophy called Utilitarianism. And quite a few philosophers think that it is the basis of human morality – but it has a rival, the Contract theory. Well two rivals actually, there is also religious revelation, or Divine Command as it is sometimes called. However we won't be spending a lot of time on that, just enough to do it the justice it deserves.

I should stop a moment here and, so as not to give the impression at the outset that I am anti-religion, say a word or two about my own religion. For most of my life I've got a lot out of religion, and expect to continue to do so to my dying day. So much so that when at the age of 19 I perceived some less than satisfactory aspects of the Church of England version of Christianity that I had up to then avidly followed, I spent the next few years trawling through the world's religions for additional inspiration. Before too long I came across Buddhism and realised it was so flexibible one could actually combine it with Christianity.

Well I could anyway – it works for me as they say. And since it has always seemed to me that ones religion is a private matter (save for these few words to explain myself), it is really no business of anyone's if I have a personalised combination of Buddhism and Christianity, wherein if I disagree with something in one, I simply invoke the other. There are one or two other ingredients in there as well, but as I say they are no business of anyone else's.

So, after that brief interruption let's return to Utilitarianism for a moment. Since the 'greatest happiness (pleasure as opposed to pain) of the greatest number' is a fair description of the evolutionary principle behind the formation of the first human Groups, whereas the Contract represents relationships between the individuals in those groups (after they have been formed), they are two different principles. It is therefore odd that these two different entities vie for the title of the basis of human morality, and this is something we will be looking into in Chapters 9, 23 and 24.

First though we must tackle the Contract, so that once we have a handle on this, we can branch out and see where it leads us. Incidentally the hominids we are going to concern ourselves with, probably existed in a world without words, or if they did have words they were certainly not of the range and subtlety of words today. We will address this shortly, along with the definitions of some other words in Chapter 5. For the moment it will suffice for us to be aware that in many contexts the term 'greatest happiness of' is synonymous with the term 'greatest good of', where good means pleasure as opposed to pain, and does not necessarily mean morally good.

One can see that early humans and pre-humans probably did gather themselves into groups for protection, just as animal groups do today, from the elements and from creatures with big sharp teeth and very fast legs. But 'gathered together' is the correct term, these are individuals, not ants, termites or bees with their swarm intelligence. These are individuals that the course of evolution, over all those millions of years, when the first four threads were developing, has fashioned into selfish individuals. Look after number one, eat, drink, run, hide, catch, evade, survive, and take Pleasure in procreation.

Now, for the good of the group, they must compromise, now they must change, now they must become team players, now they must give consideration to others, must help others to survive alongside themselves. And soon, as more of this new type survive and flourish in the team, they must sometimes think of others more than they think of themselves.

What? This flies in the face of the whole of evolution – look after you know who, and the rest of you look to yourselves.

Well yes and no.

Parenting for example, in many species parents selflessly spend time and energy on their young, including sometimes sacrificing their lives to protect their offspring. So evolution does include examples of creatures willing to sacrifice themselves for others. Not all parents are like those plants, fish or insects that spew out millions of seeds and eggs to be carried away in every direction placing reliance upon the statistical chance that some will survive.

So these individual pre-humans now gathering in groups are capable of change, capable of changing from being selfish individuals to being unselfish team players. Of course they are – these are pre-human parents, and like so many other life forms are cable of dying for their offspring. Now all they have to do to become a tight knit group is become capable of sometimes sacrificing themselves for other group members who are not their close blood relatives. Do humans do this? Oh yes.

Where do we find today, in our huge societies, that feeling of 'the Group' and the special strength and Pleasure we have in the feeling of belonging, the feeling of unquestioning loyalty to the Group above all else? Male gang culture obviously, young men not finding a fit or even perhaps any employment in the huge society around them drift into gangs, into primate groups, and find there a fit, a niche and a special ancient Pleasure not found or felt elsewhere.

They even create what we might call fake wars, with nearby rival gangs, so that they can re-visit the way of life long gone in which loyalty to the group was everything. Treat all inside the group fairly and with full respect, but for those outside the same within Group rules need not apply.

Or in full scale wars between nations.

Is it any wonder soldiers can never recapture the intense camaraderie of human beings together under fire when they leave the army? Is it any wonder that many search for something to replace it all their lives, without success? This camaraderie is the stuff of our birth as humans, a call back to that first grassy plain and the Ancient Group that stood on it. Thou shalt trust thy comrade with thy life. This is the revolutionary law of the later primates, the law that blew away millions upon millions of years of one strand of evolution based upon self, self, self, any left self again, this is the stuff that made us what we are.

Made us human, part selfish animal, part selfless friend.

Men who have fought together in wartime often remark on the special bond formed between them and their comrades in arms, such friendships formed during the Second World War are still alive thirty, forty, fifty and sixty years on. That bond is formed by what people went through together, formed by each one of them not wanting to let his fellows down, not wanting to lose the respect of his comrades under fire. Not wanting to be anything other than a fully paid up member of the team, and feeling good (Right) about it, feeling good about being respected, feeling good about being human, feeling good about being a member of the team.

Not feeling good about the horrible hell of war, of times spent in terror under fire, surely the feeling good can only come from the comradeship,

7

from Loyalty-to-the-Group. Feeling good about being willing to give up everything including life itself for the man next to you, and knowing that he feels the same way towards you.

This situation truly is a special time, a pure, almost experimental case; to the front is the enemy, a separate group, to the rear are the generals some of whom these men respect, many of whom they don't. And even further to the rear are their families, the homes, towns, relatives, children and lovers they have left behind, some of whom they love and some of whom they don't.

Their whole lives are concentrated for the months or years of the war, into this special pack – their front line comrades. For a short time there are no divided loyalties, no claims from wives against the tyranny of mother-in-laws, no squabbling children crying about who's picking on them, no boss to work so hard to please while colleagues seem to please themselves and get away with it.

For now there is a pack of comrades, comrades who will give their lives for you, and you for them, and nothing ever feels so good again.

Because this is the same troop that leaves its village in the dark before the dawn thousands upon thousands of years ago – to hunt. To face strong fast animals with crude weapons, with improved verbal communications, with increased cunning from their special brains, and ... with ... trust in each other.

They go to drive part of a herd over a cliff, to trap and kill, to spear the slowest, to stand together by the kill and drive off other predators, carrion feeders, vultures, thieves of all kinds, including other groups of hominids, by sticking close together. By knowledge, by planning yes, but these are of only theoretical use if you cannot ... trust those next to you.

Trust them not to let you down.

Trust that they, like you, desire the mutual respect of others more than they desire life itself. Trust that they will give their life for yours.

Behold the birth place of morality in modern garb, no wonder that they never find the same again, in oh so complicated Civvy Street. Civilian life, that messy intermeshing clash of conflicting overlapping loyalties that is the expanded modern world.

But we are also individuals, and some of us are more selfish than others, and some of us notice that others of us work harder and some of us work less hard than others. We notice that some seem better team players than others do, some of us seem never to be around when work or danger threatens, but to always be around at meal times. We realise that there are some of the group that we would happily die for, and we are pretty sure they feel the same way about us too.

And so we trust them, and we distrust others.

LOYALTY AND DISLOYALTY

There is thus a tension within the Group, a constant itch, a feeling that some team members are maybe not pulling their weight as much as others. A feeling that some are not doing their Duty, a feeling that there is a (as yet unwritten) Contract between us Group members and that some are reneging on this Contract. To be Disloyal is a crime, and if we go back far enough I put it to you that it is THE ONLY CRIME.

It is the Contract that is the great rival to Utilitarianism for the soul of human morality. I have used the word 'soul', really for nothing more than dramatic effect, but let's take the opportunity to remind ourselves that religion does have a part to play. Not here though, not yet, it is a later part. As will be seen in Chapter 15 we are presently discussing a time way back before humans had any concept of religion.

When they didn't trade with each other the only contact between groups would be border skirmishes during territorial disputes, not dissimilar perhaps to those we find in modern chimp groups. There will also have been some natural leakage between groups when young males and or females leave one group, or are driven out by them, due to food shortages or lack of breeding opportunities. We can see this amongst packs of other animals to this day, such 'deserters' either join nearby groups who are short of labour and breeding stock, or in their wanderings come across and recruit other outcasts. Eventually they either form new groups, or they die young and alone.

In this world in which, like many other creatures, pre-humans are found gathered in groups, one of the most important attributes of each group member would be Loyalty-to-the-Group. Would it not? And thus one of the greatest failings of any group member in the eyes of others in the group would be a lack of loyalty? One could say that every act that each group member looks at and denigrates, as being Wrong, is an act of Disloyalty. It is the Duty of each Group member to be a Loyal Group member, and this is the whole of the Contract. It is thus also at this time the whole of Morality.

Yes, you've guessed, I'm not a Utilitarian.

It is disloyal to other group members to be a traitor and side with an enemy group

It is disloyal to other group members to steal from one of them. (To steal from members of other groups is at this time fine and acceptable – is in fact worthy of praise.)

It is also disloyal to other group members to hit them when this is unprovoked.

It is disloyal to other group members to rape them.

It is disloyal to other group members to insult or hurt them in any way, even emotionally, if unprovoked.

It is disloyal to other group members to torture them.

It is disloyal to other group members to have illicit hidden sex with their spouse behind their back.

It is disloyal to other group members to lie to or about them.

It is disloyal to other group members to blackmail them.

It is disloyal to other group members to...

On and on and on, every Wrong you can think of likely to be present then is an act of Disloyalty. *Unfortunately morality isn't quite as simple as this, but we'll discuss the exception called the human 'sex in public prohibition' later (in Chapter 8).*

Meanwhile we are all in this team together and for any of us to break ranks is Wrong, our survival depends upon this law. This one law, the law of laws, the only law, in this time long before modern words existed.

So I put it to you that, *except for the human sex in public prohibition,* every Wrong you can think of, applicable now in modern times, is still at heart an act of Disloyalty-to-the-Group, even though we no longer live in such small tight knit communities. Whether it is finding some money in the street that a fellow group member has dropped and quietly pocketing it, or embezzlement on a gargantuan scale practised by members of huge companies. Whether it is tax evasion, or acts committed in the torture chamber of a murderous dictatorship. Whether it is failing to help a child sprawled face down and exhausted drowning in a pool of water because an enemy group is chasing us, or failing to stand and fight alongside a comrade in arms in a theatre of modern warfare.

Disloyalty, disloyalty, disloyalty is the wrong of wrongs, is in fact the root of all Wrongs.

HYPOCRISY

At this juncture, having introduced the principle of disloyalty, we should also introduce and address the concept of hypocrisy. We hate hypocrites because they manipulate us into behaving one way, while they do the opposite themselves – they fool us, and they betray us. Many times in our disputes and moral arguments we accuse others of hypocrisy. So let's have a look at the concept of hypocrisy, what is it and who does it because it lies at the core of the Contract.

Of course people are hypocrites, from what we have been saying they are bound to be – to an extent, and as with altruism (in Chapter 31), it is the 'to an extent' that is important. They are bound to be because we each have a personal battle to keep our hypocrisy down to the bare minimum. A few Saints manage to banish it altogether, the rest of us never really do. And the reason for this is simple – we are set upon a road to hypocrisy from the moment of our birth. Born like all life forms fighting for life, fighting for breath, for food, for water, for air, for sufficient attention and care from our parents so that our little selves will survive. Born 'selfish', because to be born otherwise is to be born with a much reduced chance of survival.

But...

Humans survive by teamwork, and to work as a team you must also be willing to share. Creatures must think primarily of themselves in order to survive – but human creatures must, at the same time think of others, so that the whole group, the whole team also survives – because without the team you're dead. Here, in this dichotomy lies the elusive hidden core of so many moral dilemmas. First yourself, but almost equally the team.

It is this 'almost' that is the seedbed of hypocrisy. We are all hypocrites the question is – how big? We are all 'pretending' to be totally committed to the team, but we are really committed to ourselves plus the team. We tend to talk more morally than we actually behave, and tend to spot this habit more in others than in ourselves, and then we get angry and call those others hypocrites. Sometimes this is justified, when those we call hypocrites are incapable of doing anything more than pay the vaguest lip service to the team.

Those we correctly call hypocrites are the ones who talk, loudly and a lot, as though they put the team equal first, but really they always put themselves and their needs and desires way way out front. When we see through them, we despise them for it, and we call them hypocrites.

They say one thing, but do another.

They say share, but do self.

The important thing to realise is that we all of us do this to some extent. Evolution has made us that way, all creatures look to themselves first, in order to survive. Our moral dilemma on becoming team players is to keep this 'to some extent' down to a minimum.

We all behave less morally (more selfishly) than we should, while at the same time espousing the importance of Morality. But some of us do this far more than others, some are always secretly looking after themselves while trying to kid the rest of us they are making personal sacrifices for the team. They are liars, they are the special kind of liar who live a lie about their own motives, and they are the ones we specifically brand hypocrites.

SAINTS
Those we call Saints are the opposite of those we call hypocrites, they don't just share, and don't ever share grudgingly. They give what little they have with Pleasure to others of the group. They give beyond the call of duty, the call of 'think of other team members almost as much as you

think of yourself'. They think of others at least equally and often – oh no wonder they receive our incredulous admiration, even our adoration, no wonder – often they think of others more than they think of themselves.

They fly in the face of the natural world, in the face of the whole world of 'look after yourself at all costs', survive, come what may, survive. They turn nature on its head – well not quite, as we will see later (in Chapters 30 to 33) their behaviour is 'just' an incredibly selfless version of something we do find in nature.

They are morality at its strongest, no they are beyond morality. These are the ones who contemplate, believe in and are actually capable of granting unlimited forgiveness. *We will address this particular aspect of sainthood being beyond morality specifically in Chapter 33.* Meanwhile note please that Saints are not necessarily religious, though they often are, but certainly not of one religion only, all religions produce Saints (as well as their opposites). Nor are they necessarily those the Catholic church choose to grant sainthood to, we are using the concept in its generic form, to mean those who are totally selfless – all the time.

On one level they are fools. Idiots to be taken advantage of. Call them what you will, they do not care. They don't give a damn they are saints. They care only to give and give, more and more – they take our breath away.

Names?

What do they care what names we puny nothings call them?

They are those who live in poverty, and give their lives up working for others, for the poor, and enjoy it. They are those who stay behind to help when the rest of us flee, and go first to the places where only human misery survives.

They are the opposite of the leech, the opposite of the hypocrite who thinks only of self and self again, the opposite of the group's freeloader who thinks it is clever to 'get one over' on others. They are Saints, they are those who spirit Jews away from Nazis, no matter what the personal risk. They spirit Jews away from Nazis while the rest of us look the other way.

They are the unselfish, and not just occasionally unselfish like the rest of us aspire to be, but the totally unselfish, the selfless. And they are very few in number.

COMPLICATIONS

Now, almost straightaway we are going to encounter complications. But stop here, wait a moment, breathe in again and feel the closeness of your long dead predecessors, living in their long dead Ancient Groups. Try to feel how it was, how it will have been – in the beginning.

Complications even from the start. For example, 'he pushed me first when I was ahead of him in the food queue, what you saw me do to him was only a response to his insulting attitude, his act of Disloyalty to me, a loyal, trustworthy and hard working comrade'. Or maybe 'she slapped my child when he had done nothing at all to her child, so she got a slap from me in response'.

Note this anger.

It is this anger that, long before modern spoken or any written word at all exists, expresses the Contract between each of the individual members of the Group, it is … one for all and all for one. It is anger at those who do Wrong, it is anger at perceived acts of Disloyalty.

Or sometimes it is 'too close to call' when we understand both points of view, and we quietly take soundings amongst our fellows. Gossip – she says she's been wronged, but isn't she one who is never to be found when there's work to be done? Doesn't he always hang back when danger threatens? I don't feel I can trust this person, I don't feel that they do their Duty. Whereas the other party to this disagreement is brave, works so hard and always does her share, in short is trustworthy in my experience.

Oh it's never been easy, this judging lark, not easy from the start, but wait till you see what there is still to come.

Later, as groups become much much bigger and inter relate with other groups much more closely, there will be complication upon complication upon complication. But nonetheless, for now, I say again, feel the breath of your human and pre-human ancestors, feel their breath on the back of your neck, feel the presence of those Ancient Groups now hidden from us forever.

3. Other Groups

After the time of minimal contact between Groups, there will have come a time when inter-group trade developed. Evidence of this is found in artefacts unearthed in one area, made from stone found only in another (Ridley, 1997). As this developed, just as happens with traders today, individuals in one group will have come to have personal relationships with individuals in other groups. And it is at this time that the term Loyal/Disloyal, as a complete and sufficient definition of morality, was first compromised, in this time long before written words.

As a system of trade and regular contacts developed, everything is in place for this to be the moment when one of our trading partners accuses one of Our Group, the leading male's brother for example, of cheating him. For him to do this of course we must all share, both the other group and ours, must hold the concept 'to be fair' in common. And when, because he knows his brother only too well, an apology is made to the trading partner, one of the most momentous changes in human pre-history has occurred.

This ancestor of yours, and mine because no matter what your lineage we are going so far back that this ancestor of mine will be your ancestor too. This ancestor of ours does a wonderful thing, he has the courage and integrity to say that his brother and fellow group member is in the Wrong, he has the steadfastness to say it is Wrong to cheat, to not play fair with, our trading partner. He has always dealt fairly with us and we have traded with him quite some years now, he is a person we can … a person we can … trust.

But with this judgement he has transferred his assessments of Right and Wrong from being only within Group to now applying also to those in other groups. And with this one act, repeated time and again between group after group, with this one act the Contract has gone international, has gone from being solely and only within Group, to now being applied also to relationships between individuals in different groups as well.

Apart from the very many complications this brings it also presents us with a problem of nomenclature, because now every act that is Wrong is no longer wholly and solely an example of Disloyalty to ones fellow group members. Behold the first moral conundrum, well the second actually. The first, as we have touched upon, has always been and will always be in any given situation whether or not to be selfish. Whether or not to put oneself and one's own needs and desires first, or to sacrifice oneself to some extent (and to what extent) for the sake of the Group.

LOYALTY AND DISLOYALTY

The First Dilemma...

In many circumstances and environments those who look after number one survive and procreate, producing progeny who being similarly selfish in their turn also survive and procreate. But when pre-humans come to live in groups and to depend more for survival on loyalty to the group, then more of the progeny of those who are willing to make sacrifices for the group survive. Thus by a relatively simple change of circumstance, acts of occasional selflessness become an important attribute instead of a recipe for genetic oblivion, such is the haphazard path of evolution. And so the first moral dilemma is always and will always be; in this situation I face, shall I react in a selfish or a selfless manner, or somewhere in between?

The Second Dilemma...

Meanwhile let's get back to dilemma number two, that moment hidden now from us forever in the darkness of pre-history, when a member of one group becomes disgusted by the way a trusted trading partner from another group is being treated, or cheated. This feeling is the same feeling as when one of Our Group is treated unfairly, is hit, stolen from, raped or killed by another member of Our Group, this anger is the same anger felt then.

The anger felt towards those who by their actions are Disloyal to Our Group or one of its members, by not treating them fairly, is now also transferred. We feel angry that a member of Our Group is now mistreating someone who has always been fair when trading with us. This transfer of anger probably comes about as it still does today, because we see this same member of Our Group behaving in the same unfair way to trusted members of our own Group – and we feel just as angry with him now even though his actions this time are between group, rather than within Group.

Note these words 'fairly' and 'trusted', subtle words probably not invented then, but appropriate to their feelings, they are words that up till now have had no meaning outside Our Group. One only treats fairly (by returning in kind what is due to them) those with whom one has a relationship, those who are part of the co-operative we call Our Group. We have no relationship with anyone outside Our Group, they are beyond, they are part of the world that Our Group has bonded together to protect itself from. Yet now we have developed relationships with other group members and are feeling the same anger at the treatment of a member of another group that we feel when one of our own is treated badly.

We have learned to trust this other in our trading with him, and perhaps to find him more trustworthy than some in our own group. Trust is the glue that binds Our Group together, and yet here is a member of another group who we feel we can trust more than we trust some members of our own group.

Of course we do.

This was bound to happen as soon as groups started to come into regular trading contact, in addition to 'marital' contact with each other. Now, instead of being in a constant state of suspicion, guarding their borders in a virtual state of war, relationships have developed across group boundaries. Every group has amongst its members some more trustworthy than others, some selfish, some unselfish and others unselfish to such an extent that we think of them as selfless. It is at this time that morality, the code of trust and reciprocity that until now has been formed and encompassed by Loyalty to fellow group members, goes inter-group and thereby goes international for the first time ever. Mark this day; mark this historical long drawn out 'moment' lost forever to us, because on this 'day' human morality changed.

Things were complicated up to this time within Group, the never ending ebb and flow of who did what to whom, who cheated and who played fair in accepting the dangers and workload of the group. Who shirked his or her duties, but still wanted a share of group rewards. Who amongst us is always trustworthy, who only sometimes and who virtually never, who are the freeloaders amongst us and who the ones who will lay down their lives in a crisis. Who are the ones we trust so much that they bring tears of joy to our eyes when we talk of them, or spend time with them, and who are the ones who almost always leave us spluttering with rage at their selfish venality. And how should we Right these Wrongs?

And we haven't included there the pressure to be more loyal to your immediate nuclear family than to members of the extended families that form Our Group. Oh there are many complications from the start, but once morality jumps to also applying between groups, the complications really take off, now the curve threatens to go exponential.

What turns that threat into a completely out of control explosion? Well it seems to me to be when societies become enormous, when Our Group comes to consist of millions upon millions of people instead of a hundred or so. We'll look at that more closely later on, but first pause and note that in our efforts to find the basic ground of human morality we can no longer use only the term Disloyalty, it is lost to us now, along with all its perfect accuracy. One cannot be loyal to every other human from every other group one interfaces with, nor can one be loyal to millions upon millions in your own diverse and vastly extended group as one could be to a hundred or so.

What is it we say to ourselves when we side with our trading partner against one of our own group members? We say that our trading partner has been treated 'unfairly', that they 'did not deserve' to be mistreated and misused thus. Why did they not deserve to be so treated – because they have always been fair, straight and honest in their dealings with us. We'll come to definitions soon, but meanwhile note these words they are the foundation, the cornerstone of all that follows.

Oh we've crossed a boundary all right, and there's no going back. So at this point let's remember what the Contract is. It is how the gene for co-operation develops in us, how we humans came, seemingly in the face of evolution, to gain a special kind of pleasure by sharing, by sometimes sacrificing ourselves for others. For as we will see, it is via the ancient mechanism of Pleasure that acts of selflessness arise from amongst our underlying selfishness. Group loyalty is the specific Pleasure derived when our ego says to us 'you are an unselfish person' because 'you are willing to share, you are willing to sacrifice yourself for others'. Not all the time, most of us don't allow ourselves to be used as doormats, but some of the time, provided we are not 'taken advantage of', provided we are shown the 'respect' we feel we 'deserve' and have 'earned'.

It is the group, the group, all this is via the mechanism of the group. *As an aside notice that because the individuals in these groups have coalesced into 'the Group', who hunt and collect food together, for mutual protection to help them survive against the rigours of the world outside the Group. It is therefore an erroneous line of reasoning, as one hears some attempt, to import the evolutionary mechanism of the 'survival of the most fit' back into the internal workings of the group. These groups have been formed for the specific contrary purpose, to offer shelter, to try to reduce the effects of nature 'red in tooth and claw' on the lives of those within it.*

Certainly though we can see that some in the Group may tend to assert themselves inside the group in the same way as they would have done if they had to live alone amongst harsh and debilitating nature. And thus aggression within the group is a genetic fact of life pulling in one direction, just as our ability to 'sometimes make sacrifices on behalf of others' for the good of the team, is a genetically inherited pull in the opposite direction.

The group is all, The group is king, and then that ancestor of ours performs that great and terrible act.

He shows the same consideration to the member of another group as he is duty bound by bonds of loyalty to show to members of his own group. Let loose the dogs of war, or rather let loose the dogs of peace – because this consideration is an act that cements friendships between groups, instead of cementing war. He considers this member of another group to be trustworthy, and so treats him with the same respect he treats all those others he trusts in his own Group. He is the first anti-racist, because up until now it has been 'my Group right or wrong', no matter what one of us has or hasn't done to the wogs in the group next door.

All these terms: rights, entitlements, fairness, taken advantage of and respect, are clearly, and perhaps only, meaningful when related to a Contract. An unwritten Contract formed by our emotions, by the feeling that to share in the spoils and advantages of the group, we must be loyal to the group. We must pull our weight, do our fair share of the work and not desert our comrades when danger threatens, and thus we will gain the respect we feel we deserve, that we feel we have earned. And if after our honest efforts we are not given this respect, it is then that we feel we are being 'taken advantage of'.

How are we not given respect?

Those who break the Contract that we are so assiduous in keeping disrespect us, either when they push us out of the way to grab a larger share of whatever is on offer, or when they are lazy or hang back when danger threatens, thus by commission and omission. In fact by any form of Disloyalty, any form of betrayal, of the Group, of its members and of its purposes. Including for example by 'cosying up' to one of our leaders and asking for favours in return for sycophantic flattery. As we see and know only too well to this day, there are many forms of Disloyalty to the ethos of one for all and all for one; Disloyalty to the concept of 'a fair share'.

But when unwritten and almost non-verbal (seen in rudimentary form in chimp, wolf and other animal packs), how is this contract made and monitored? How else could it be but by an emotional reaction amongst the creatures forming the group? A reaction, an outburst that shouts – stop, not fair, not fair, not fair! They need not use the actual words, they need only grab back (often violently) the larger share that has been taken, or push forward those who hang back when work or dangers are upon us.

And thus the Contract; made and cemented long before modern words are in existence. Words that, in the interests of accurate communications, we now use to define the Contract, in the much extended form it still exists in today.

The Contract is the fellow feeling that binds each group together, they swear to be loyal (by their actions) each of them to each fellow group member, and thereby the group will be loyal to each individual member in return. We are in this together, we all survive and prosper together, or we will all go under together. At this time the definition of every 'right action' is that it is a loyal action, and every wrong action is a disloyal one. To be Disloyal to the Group, in any way, is to break the code.

This is the unwritten contract that could not be, need not be, and never was, originally written down. And then our ancestor, with his wonderful and yet terrible integrity, goes and transfers it between groups too.

OTHER GROUPS

And from now on we need another word, we need another concept to accurately summarise this Contract extended across group boundaries. It has become something other than a Contract, because the Contract was between the Group, it has become Morality. Or more accurately, this is the word we in our time of detailed words, come to apply to it.

We are thus presented with a problem of terminology, now every act that is Wrong is no longer an example of Disloyalty to ones fellow Group members. This has happened long before there is in the world the precise language that we use today, but nonetheless trying now to look back and using what we find there to come forward again, we can no longer use the word Disloyalty for every immoral act. We sit here, in this modern time of so many words, in need of another concept, another summarising term. We have been robbed, robbed of our single neat all encompassing word, the word that precisely defined morality at its birth.

We have inside ourselves, the same emotional reaction to right and wrong, contract keeping and contract breaking, as we did all those many thousands of years ago. And it is this emotional reaction to right and wrongdoing that is the genetically instilled moral contract we all still share. It is this reaction we must follow through the twists and turns of human history if we are to accuarately follow morality as it wends its way through time, through our time, the time of the humans.

4. Bullying & Manipulation

A famous Professor of Philosophy A. J. Ayer, dismissed the whole subject of morality on the basis of these feelings, on the basis that all our moral pronouncements are emotional reactions and therefore no different than saying Boo or Hooray, and thus also worth nothing more than saying that. Morality – nothing more, nothing more than that? You stopped halfway Professor, that Boo/ Hooray is only half the story, the real question is – Boo/ Hooray about what exactly?

That Boo/ Hooray is the basis of the moral contract, in the days before we could write or maybe even speak with precision, it was then the whole of Morality, that's 'all'. And so my proposition is; Boo to those we see as being Disloyal within the group and Hooray for those who are Loyal hard working trustworthy members of the group. Then with that proviso yes Professor I agree, you're right, that is 'all' there is to Morality.

This split then, between acts and behaviours that are Disloyalty to others in the group, compared to acts that are Loyal towards the group, is the same as the split between acts that are immoral and behaviour that is moral. This split is the basis of morality, or rather is the Basic Morality. The Basic Morality, from which all later versions are cultural add-ons, as we shall see. Sometimes these are added as a result of different ethnic or cultural responses to physical conditions and social problems, sometimes following religious revelations, or simply because of the cumbersome size of the huge modern groups we call countries. However they come about, they result in diversity, as opposed to that which we all hold in common, namely anger at those who fail to be Loyal to the Group.

To handle the complications of the increasing size of the groups we now call societies, and the relationship of 'our Group' with other groups around them, we need an enhanced vocabulary. Loyalty and Disloyalty are not enough anymore. Listen to all these terms we have been using, don't disrespect me, my rights, entitlements, fairness, what I am owed and so forth and so forth. What do all these terms have lying behind them, what other generic term can we find lurking here as an extension of Disloyalty-Loyalty? It will never be a perfect term, because Disloyalty to one's group is, one might say, the original sin – *we will come to the inadequacies of that confusing little three letter word in Chapter 9*. What term or terms then are generic enough to cover, if not all, then at least most of the same ground as the morally definitive and all encompassing term Disloyalty-Loyalty?

Well many acts we would designate as Disloyal to one's fellow group members are also what we would commonly call the bullying of one's fellow group members. And thus also many acts of resistance to those who do wrong towards others could be called anti-bullying acts. So why don't we try using the terms Bullying and Anti-bullying?

The concept Bully/Anti-bully might be a term we could use instead of Disloyal/Loyal, no wait not in place of, I propose the concept 'to bully another' to augment the underlying originating and morally definitive term 'to be Disloyal'. My dictionary defines bullying as the intimidation or persecution of weaker people. I put it to you that the simple and commonly understood concept of bullying is a possible term, albeit less accurate than Disloyal/Loyal, that we can nonetheless use when we are faced with the need to extend human morality beyond the group.

Let's see how it fits.

Included in the usual definition of bullying is also when 'unjustified, unfair and uncalled for' attacks are made by one upon another. This is when attacks that are ostensibly in response to previous attacks are actually overkill rather than a tooth for a tooth, these are thus responses that fail the test of reciprocity. Depending upon circumstances an eye for an eye is not bullying, but two eyes for an eye always is.

It is Anti-bully when we say ... thou shalt not torture
It is Anti-bully when we say ... thou shalt not kill
It is Anti-bully when we say ... thou shalt not rape
It is Anti-bully when we say ... thou shalt not blackmail
And so forth, along the same lines...

Bully/Anti-bully (B/A-b) is not perfect, but is close enough for us to use, as long as we keep in mind that it is a substitute for the originating term. As long as we grant it some leeway and remember that we are trying to come up with a word now, in this time of many words, for something that first appeared amongst us long ago in the time of hardly any words.

Part of this leeway involves the issue of marginal bullying:

It is about Bullying-manipulation when we say ... thou shalt not bear false witness – tell lies to or spread slander about another Group member

It is about Bullying-manipulation when we say ... thou shalt not cheat your trading partner

It is about Bullying-manipulation when we say ... thou shalt not cheat on your sexual partner

It is about Bullying-manipulation when we say ... thou shalt not steal.

Although when we see one creature consistently steal another's food, we would call that bullying I think. It is just that these days we have so many possessions, that thefts of some of these artefacts are not usually fatal.

21

No substitution though is possible, it can only ever be Disloyalty when we say:

Thou shalt not avoid paying tax ... thy due proportion of the costs of the Group.

Thou shalt not find money in the street ... and quietly pocket it for oneself, because this is to be disloyal to a fellow group member.

Thou shalt not betray thy Group in times of war ... this is treason.

Thou shalt not treat your parents with disrespect ... for they are the closest to you in the Group.

Thou shalt not be a Peeping Tom ... because this is to be disloyal, is to secretly take advantage of another member of the Group.

The concept 'to bully or to bully-manipulate' is a useful, even powerful, moral term, but it is a secondary term, a concept one step on and so one step away from its origin – the concept 'to be disloyal'. We each hate to be dominated, especially inside the group after taking refuge there, in fact to be dominated inside the group is the 'final insult' as it were.

Thus my proposal is Bully/Anti-bully, with the added modification of bullying-manipulation, as an extension of Disloyal/Loyal – bearing in mind the long history we humans have survived through. My proposal is that Bully/Anti-bully can take us forward from our beginnings, to help us get morality in perspective since it went international and since our societies became so huge that the term Loyal/Disloyal is now doubly lost to us.

Or, trying to look at things the other way round for a moment, we could put the act first and follow this with its generic categorisation:

Thou shalt not bully by killing ... is definitely bullying.

Thou shalt not bully by committing adultery ... bullying-manipulation by the use of a lie, not really in line with our everyday use of the term 'to bully'.

Thou shalt not bully by stealing ... is bullying, because as we've just said, to repeatedly steal food in the wild can be to condemn to death your fellow group member.

Thou shalt not bully by telling lies ... bullying-manipulation again.

Thou shalt not bully by raping ... definitely bullying.

Thou shalt not bully by torturing ... bullying in its worst form.

Thou shalt not bully by blackmailing ... this is possibly bullying-manipulation, but pretty close to our use of the term 'to bully'.

Thou shalt not bully by using emotional blackmail ... the bullying-manipulation, often by close friends or family, the subtle manipulation of those close to us.

Thou shalt not bully by insulting … pernicious insults can be used to persecute others and so this is a form of bullying. *Thus the subtlest form of bullying is to 'cut someone dead' as the old fashioned phrase has it. To ignore them as though they don't deserve to be acknowledged as a valid fully paid up member of the Group.*

Manipulation: we sometimes push, or hustle, others into doing what we want, rather than what they want. Sometimes we do it as managers of others, because we see it as being for the 'good of the firm' and for the 'good of the individual concerned'. We sometimes intimidate people a little 'for their own good', and provided it is for their own good, then it isn't bullying and we don't call it so. Instead we use non-pejorative terminology such as pushing someone who is dithering into doing something.

For example by positioning them into having to jump head first into the deep end of our joint project, and low and behold they swim just fine, and if they don't we are there to jump in and rescue them. On the other hand I find no undue stretching involved in saying that to manipulate someone for our own 'selfish' reasons is to bully them, albeit in a none physical way.

We can use the term Disloyal only up to the first time that my brother-in-law, or trading partner from the group next door, accuses my brother of striking him for no reason. From this point in our history my brother's aggression is no longer an asset in defending Our Group, but instead becomes a liability, the moment when for the first time ever in human history 'being in the wrong' means more than some aspect of 'being disloyal'.

As a result we are trying to produce appropriate terminology that sums up a feeling present amongst us, probably for the best part of a half million years, certainly a quarter million before the present. A time long before modern societies existed. We shouldn't really be surprised should we that this exercise presents us with some difficulties? In fact, when you think of it like that, it is surprising how close we have come with one commonly used everyday little word – bullying.

It seems to me that a mistake of moral philosophy has been the failure, in addition to seeing moral problems in our own time, to also put the moral questions we face into the perspective of our original Ancient Groups. Those groups are where morality and we ourselves originated, to ignore them is a foolish oversight.

Thus, for the moment, I rest the initial part of my case – admitting that the use of the additional term bully-manipulate is unavoidable as a direct result of projecting a small modern five-letter word back to the time of our pre-human ancestors. Back to that time when Disloyalty towards the fellow members of one's Group was the definition of every crime in the book, but there was no book.

5. Definitions

As we just observed the dictionary defines a bully as a person who intimidates or persecutes others, and we can add to this all those whose response to aggression consists of overkill instead of proportionality. We now need to extend this definition further and also clearly define our usage of some other words. This dictionary has been written recently in 'the time of many words', so we must take a moment to consider our projection backwards to the root grown deep in our genetic make-up, back to 'the time of no words' or 'the time of very few words'.

Back then, at its beginning, before there was any concept of between group relationships, a bully was 'a person who intimidated or persecuted a weaker fellow group member', while to intimidate members of other groups was instead 'justified aggression', in order to discourage them from encroaching onto our hunting grounds.

To be accurate we must look at every reasonable use of 'persecution or intimidation'. For example we can easily see that torture, rape and murder are all forms of bullying and are in fact what we might call ultra-bullying. The reason we don't use the term bullying for these foul acts is because we have the words torture, rape and murder. Words that describe the exact form of bad behaviour we wish to refer to, and condemn it far more accurately than a vague and general term such as bullying. Not only are the individual words more accurate, they are also enshrined within the law as specific criminal activities.

BULLYING
We all know what bullying is, because the emotional reaction to it is built into us from birth. However for accuracy, for the pedantic amongst us, for the codified morality and the lawyers who administer it, and for completeness:

* Bullying is the unprovoked hurting, intimidation or persecution of a weaker or smaller person, or section of society. It is the domination of one by another.

* Bullying can be the torture and murder of thousands or millions by a brutal dictator, or it can be persistent insults, disrespect and minor manipulative behaviour between close members of some tight knit community.

* Any response to an act of aggression (ie an act of bullying), is itself

Bullying only if it is disproportionate to the provoking act, hence the need for restraint and the concept of 'reasonable force'. *When some little twerp is cheeky enough at school to slap a bigger and older boy, if the response is to bloody his nose and seriously hurt him instead of giving him a hard slap back and a warning, then that older boy has bullied him. We all understand what bullying is, even when in this example the little twerp was the supposed 'aggressor'.*

- Bullying-manipulation is non-physical. It is the use of various levels of psychological pressure to force someone to do something that they would not otherwise do, for the manipulator's benefit. It is also the manipulation of others by the use of a lie.

DEFINITIONS – common words that occur in our moral discussions:

Good/Bad and Right/Wrong: if we define happiness as the surfeit of pleasure over pain that every last one of us seeks, this in turn defines the difference between the words Good and Right.

Pleasures in general are felt as being Good, whereas our moral acts are felt as being Right.

We perhaps say casually that a particular event, a change of career, felt 'right', but what we mean, and should say strictly speaking, is that the change felt 'good'. Right should really be reserved for moral issues but instead the word Right spills over from the moral to the general sphere, or conversely we place Good opposite to Evil, and befuddle the issues and ourselves in this way also.

Since Evil is ultimate bullying, ultra-Wrong, its opposite should be strictly called ultra-Right, not Good – which is a far more general observation on our many varied pleasures.

To have sex with our life partner, or to see a film and go to a restaurant, or go on holiday feels good, because sexual (or other sensual) pleasure is non-moral. It is pleasure compared to pain. Yet afterwards we might say (mistakenly), 'that holiday felt right' – how easily are words, and thereby important meanings, jumbled up.

Right (loyal and non-bullying behaviour) is the opposite to Wrong (disloyal and bullying actions), and therefore it would be more accurate to say this is a Right person, and that a Wrong person, than this is a Good person and that a Bad person. When we say this person is a good tennis player or that one is good looking, we are being specific about non-moral attributes, therefore the use of good is correct, but when we say Gandhi was Good we confuse things.

We know what we mean when we say it; Gandhi was a morally good person. But it would be clearer to say that Gandhi was a Right person,

Gandhi was Right, but not in the sense of being correct, rather than incorrect – a further linguistic complication.

Correct/Incorrect: things are made worse by this use of the word right (and wrong) in the sense of correct and incorrect. Which is the reason why saying this is a Right person and that is a Wrong person sounds strange to us. It's too late to change and re-train ourselves but, as we sit here together for philosophical purposes, we must use our words with care and be sure of what we speak.

Good is derived from the Pleasure-Pain mechanism, whereas the word Right (as opposed to correct) is derived from Morality.

Selfish/Unselfish: is an important concept in the lexicon of Bully /Anti-bully and we all pretty much understand what these words indicate. To accuse someone of being selfish is pejorative of course, but not in the same way as to accuse him or her of being a bully. Selfishness is an accusation levelled at someone about themselves and their conduct that does not quite involve their conduct towards others as much as the accusation of bullying does. The idea behind the continuum from selfish through unselfish and beyond to selfless (running say from Hitler to Mother Teresa) is clearly relative to our relationships to others. If one were the only person left on the planet, then the concept 'to be selfish' would completely disappear.

But, unlike bullying, we can sometimes be selfish 'in a good way', whereas there is no such thing as 'bullying in a good way'. Bullying is always Wrong. As soon as we 'bully someone for their own good' we immediately change our terminology, and correctly say that 'we pushed them into something', and are now vindicated by the eventual happy results.

Selfish conduct can also sometimes be 'good for us' as individuals, for example we are advised to be selfish in order to look after ourselves after an illness. Cancer patients are told to be selfish, to make time for themselves, go to the theatre, concerts, go out painting pictures in the country, etc, whatever activity they enjoy and so will help them to gain strength and aid their recovery.

Thus selfishness is the root from which Disloyalty and thus Bullying actions spring, and we are rightly wary of those we see as selfish for fear that they will use and misuse us. But selfishness is not bullying and is therefore 'only' the seedbed of disloyalty and bullying, and thus it lies just over the other side of a borderline.

- Thus bullying is always based upon selfishness and is the opposite of sainthood, which is always selfless.

27

Duty: what is 'our duty'? Is it not essentially to 'be fair' to others in Our Group? To 'refrain from bullying' them and to be hard working and loyal, or at least refrain from being disloyal to them? Yet how can any of us be 'loyal' to 60, 200, 500 or 1000 million people?

No wonder then that today we are faced with such a confusing and overlapping series of responsibilities and loyalties, so much so that we can't be loyal to everyone in the whole country that is now 'Our Group'. Such 'loyalty' is meaningless. Such loyalty is now part of personal friendships, or part of much smaller localised or 'shared interest' groups.

And because we can't be loyal to a hundred million people our emotional reaction to wrongdoing has now become the criteria of 'thou shalt not bully' any of those hundred million. Rather than, 'you shall be loyal' to all those hundred million. Going further – how can we be loyal to the whole expanding world population? How can we be loyal to group after group after group, stretching further and further away into the distance?

Being fair: isn't it reasonable to categorise 'being fair' as 'being anti-bully'? There are many other words, some of which we have already touched on, along these same lines: a 'fair share', the 'rights' I am 'entitled to', that which I have 'earned', which I 'deserve', I am deserving of 'respect' don't 'disrespect' me. I don't propose to go laboriously, and boringly, through each word because it is obvious from the explanations above that all these terms relate to loyal and non-bullying membership of the group.

Is it not therefore the case that all our specific rights, earned by us doing our Duty are nothing other than our one single sole and all encompassing right, the right for this Loyalty to be returned, the Right not-to-be-bullied? And can this come from anywhere else other than the Ancient Group to whom, by our actions, we first swore loyalty to all those many years ago.

- Thus all human rights are actually detailed parts of one single right only, the Right not-to-be-bullied, and in particular the right not to be bullied by your own government.

RACIAL PREJUDICE

As soon as groups start to exchange artefacts with other groups and keep in contact with those who marry outside the group, then the issue of racial prejudice appears amongst us. Do I always support my fellow group members because they are racially the same as me? Even when my Group is behaving badly? Or should I do the Right thing, the moral thing, and support the one who is being bullied, whether he's of my (racial) group or not? Shall I cast my vote against the bully because he's in the Wrong? Against the bully no matter whether he's a member of my Group or not?

This 'moment' when morality jumped, from being within Group to applying between groups as well is the boundary of racial prejudice that we're still struggling with today. Actions against and/or inflammatory speeches inciting hatred or violence based upon racial differences are a legitimate limitation on free speech, because to be prejudiced is, according to the dictionary, to be biased and unjust. Biased against what, prejudiced and unjust according to what standard?

We have seen the standard, it is the one and only commonly shared moral code, it is the Basic Morality of: thou shall judge thy fellows by Bully/Anti-bully, judge them by the fairness of their actions, not by the colour of their skin.

The phrase defines itself.

Once these funny foreigners were outside Our Group, were potential enemies in the constant uneasy tension between neighbouring groups, but now the principle of Bully/Anti-bully has been extended. Racial prejudice is the 'left over' barrier that once divided the isolated groups within which morality first developed.

We are still at that boundary and some of us, the right wing of us, still hanker after the old days, they crave a return to the other side of that boundary. In some ways they were simpler days I suppose, but things are actually going the other way, the world is now smaller than it has ever been. We know more about and come into contact with more and more 'others' than we have ever done. And so morality stands against all those who make statements based upon, "my racial or religious group first, be they Right or Wrong".

No other stance has been logical or moral since that 'day' of 'days', since the day-of-integrity, oh so many hundreds of thousands of years ago, the day when that ancestor of mine and yours apologised to his trading partner for what his brother had done.

6. Who is Bullying whom?

With all this in mind, let's backtrack a little. Originally, in those Groups of morality's inception, many acts of Disloyalty were also acts of Bullying, acts that we would recognise today and use the term bullying to describe. These are unfair and unprovoked acts of aggression in a variety of situations, visited by one group member upon another.

Thus even from the time of the Ancient Groups Bully/Anti-bully was a major sub-category of the fundamental defining principle of Disloyalty/Loyalty. My proposition is that we should bring this sub-category to the fore because it accurately describes a large majority of cases of Disloyalty between groups and within the massive groups we now call countries.

Furthermore using this principle defines and separates those issues that are moral issues from those entities that have often been confusingly included under the heading of morality, but are actually from a different source. As a result of which we confuse ourselves, adding one of a number of needless layers of additional confusion onto the central unavoidable confusion that we shall come face to face with on the last page of this Chapter.

When we try to look back to our pre-human ancestors half a million or so years ago, and for that matter how life is played out in the raw animal world around us now, we see that the 'bully' is king. In this world the strong, the bully, rules in a natural order of things that has existed for millions of years. When the pack makes a kill, then the biggest of the bullies, the bully amongst bullies, eats first, eats best, eats longest. In the mating season he mates first, mates many, mates longest.

In this context the word bully is meaningless, because bullying is the only order of things. One shall rule, the biggest, fastest, most aggressive, most powerful shall rule the small, the slow, the weak. There is no question of morality because this is all there is; God is on the side of the big battalions. Then gradually, stage by stage, step by step something different happens, and evolution takes a turn down a different road.

The first hint that morality is beginning to appear amongst humans seems likely to have been when someone, some pack member, complains about rough treatment. Maybe he complains about the leading male, or maybe he complains to him, we'll never know, but as we'll see in due course the former is more likely. However it happens, harsh treatment at the hands or teeth of another, is resented and labelled unfair. It is at some time voiced out loud, for the first time ever, "I am a loyal pack member,

a loyal member of the team, and to treat me thus is not fair, it is Unjust."
Except they will have used less subtle words.

What we now call morality appears on this planet, when some pre-human individual in a social group, a vanquished rival for pack leader status perhaps, or an out of favour youngster denied a share of the kill, instead of cowering back and quietly returning to his allotted place in the pecking order to await a further opportunity, still goes, but as he does so whispers to his neighbours "not fair". Then soon afterwards cries out; "foul play, injustice! Stop, stop! STOP BULLY STOP!"

From this anger commences the whole of what we should properly call morality, all sense of just and unjust, fair and unfair, Right and Wrong. It is a cry for help from the dominated, against the dominator, within the group. I see moral issue after moral issue, I see on one side the oppressor and on the other, the oppressed. I see no good spirits versus evil demons, only human behaviour, only right versus might. I see freedom versus repression, the dominated and the dominator, over and over, again and again.

That oft repeated challenge is the seed, but there is something else that seals it. After all a whole series of creatures suffer such humiliations, there must be another factor as well, something that imparts the final impetus that produces morality.

The 'moment' of not fair plus something else.

Ah yes, the moment when someone else agrees with the accuser when another being says, I agree that wasn't Right you have been treated badly, you have been, you have been … Wronged. They agree and in addition they are able to communicate that agreement to others. At that moment, the moment of agreement, the word 'Wrong' comes into existence, and for the first time ever on planet earth, the word 'Right' sits in opposition to it. In this time, before the subtlety of modern words, when anger is our sole response – to Wrongdoing.

They turn to other members of their social group, and some maybe most nod their heads, nod their increasingly clever primate heads in assent, we concur. Heads with special 'bigger brains' new upon this earth now make a judgement, a new kind of judgement. You have been wronged. These are heads with longer memories than this planet has ever seen before.

Prior to this myriad numbers of creatures nurse their sense of hurt alone, as we see animals doing today for however long, or short, it lasts, but in some kind of pre-human social pack, that feeling comes to be shared. They agree and perhaps drive off a bully and protect the weak, or they stick together and plot, mutinous because their leader, their Alpha Male is too harsh, too much of a bully. Now being strongest is not enough, not enough on its own anymore. Now you have to consider the feelings of others. For the first time fascism has been questioned, these mutinous plotters have invented politics.

What is Justice? The great Socratic question, what is Doing Right?
Plato's question, the most famous question in all philosophy.
Justice is when the weak, the repressed, the bullied, strike back at their oppressor, strike back at the Bully with an eye for an eye, strike back with reciprocity, and no more. That is Justice – problem solved.
There is no 'justice' throughout most of the animal world, only murder, rape and theft, the law of the jungle, with occasional stand offs and compromises. Outside the Group bullying still reigns supreme, reigns because there is no concept of bullying, no concept of an alternative. Until, for the first time ever, some pre-human shouts, or rather grunts the equivalent of – foul play!
No, no, not fair! Stop bully stop!
Shouts out "I have been Wronged", and someone else agrees. Then it is that, somewhere lost in the darkness of pre-history, that which we should properly call morality is born.
Morality starts as a negative, morality is so strong, so sure of itself in the negative; thou shalt not. 'Thou shalt not' is so much easier to sum up than 'thou shalt'. Why – because acts of Disloyalty are far easier to point to than different degrees of Loyal (selfless) behaviour. Especially when your vocabulary is limited. Torture for example can thus be seen and condemned as the ultimate repression. 'I repress you by holding you at my mercy, to do with you as I will'; ultimate power, ultimate repression is the definition of evil. Human behaviour, not things that go bump in the night, let's stop shifting the blame.
We all have to die, but we don't all have to be tortured. Torture is worse than death. If it weren't then there would be no such concept as a fate worse than death, no such thing as a mercy killing, a release from misery and lingering pain by death. We never torture as a favour, but we do kill as a favour. Torture is the ultimate crime, the ultimate oppression in the great and endless battle of freedom versus repression.
Torture, something so cruel, something so bad, we call it evil. To hold another in your Power, to do with them as you will, to inflict pain, to desist, for awhile, then to inflict pain again. Pain, fear, rape, to force entry, to hold another at your mercy, and to have no mercy, torture, to enjoy, the feeling of Power misused, to enjoy the helplessness, the suffering of another, to inflict more, more, and then a little more.
I put it to you that good and evil are derivative terms, that the root terms beyond these surface labels are the basis of all human morality; Right versus Wrong is freedom versus repression. Freedom-from-bullying

we should say for the sake of accuracy. This is the freedom we are talking of, not freedom-as-license to do whatever we wish. Good and evil are words from old time religion, they have no existence except as freedom and repression, bullied and bully, right versus might, Morality versus Power.

Let me put to you the case of the scolded-comforted child. A young girl has been naughty, she has been bullying her little brother, and the mother or father is angry and scolds big sister, and big sister cries. For a few minutes the parent leaves her alone, so that the lesson sinks in, but within a very short time, Mum or Dad is picking the child up to console and comfort her.

In the space of only a few minutes discipline has been administered, hopefully useful communication made, and love provided as a balance. What has happened here? What has happened here, but also why at such speed? What changes in the world of moral judgements so quickly, that one moral reaction is turned on its head within minutes, seconds even?

The little brother was a victim of his bigger sister, but now the sister is the 'victim', of the parent. We humans rush to the aid of the one who is hurt, and vent our anger upon the aggressor, and then, hey presto, the circumstances change. At speed this response judges a situation and acts, because of the action the situation changes dramatically, it judges again and acts again. This time the exact opposite response, supportive instead of critical, loving instead of censoring.

Instantly reversing a moral decision, the parent takes pity, and forgives, and sustains an ongoing relationship. Sends a message of admonition, and at the same time the message that all the little person in the Wrong needs to do is to mend her ways, to behave more considerately towards her little brother, behave more morally. Stop bullying him and all will be well.

No wonder the various lumbering summaries made by the many well-intentioned and less well-intentioned kings, politicians and law makers can't keep up. No wonder the law is so full of holes, loose ends and iniquities for slimy lawyers to exploit. No wonder we are often confused, angry and puzzled over injustices and Wrongs not Righted. No wonder we talk of the spirit compared to the letter of the law.

The 'spirit of the law' is the chaotic, switching, ever changing B/A-b basis of morality that emanates from inside each one of us, we want things to be fair, we want things to be Right. The law, the codified morality could administer discipline, and then it would simply watch while big sister cried, unable and unwilling to do anything since the child's reaction to being disciplined was hurt and resentment, which is logical and therefore there's nothing further to be done. The parent's action though is something far more sophisticated, it forgives, and more importantly, it forgives at speed. It forgives but the admonition still stands.

We should note here that when we write down many of our laws we are confirming that the issue so prohibited is considered by the majority of the community to be an act of bullying and/or disloyalty towards other group members. The other laws we write, and that are exceptions to this, are laws based on Utilitarianism. Wearing car seat belts or helmets while riding a motor bike for example are Utilitarian laws, and are sometimes considered paternalistic. It is confusing when some are both, for example the recent ban on smoking in bars, restaurants and certain other public places. The ban is mainly against bullying smokers blowing their smoke into the atmosphere around non-smokers, but it is also an encouragement to the smoker to pack in the habit, for the sake of their own health.

Meanwhile when does the parent stop being an administrator of justice and become an overbearing ogre instead? A difficult issue, because until that moment it seems clear that the parent is administering a superior and more fair morality than the slower codified morality. Yes – until the moment the parent steps over this hidden boundary, the individual can often leave the codified morality trailing behind. The law is an ass, and so only at this tipping point does the law come into its own. What is this tipping point, what is this hidden boundary?

Can it be anything other than the moment when the parent becomes overbearing? The moment when the parent goes so far that she herself becomes a bully?

Wouldn't you say?

From your own experiences of human affairs?

Thus we all agree that bullying (Disloyalty to others in the group) is Wrong, what we disagree about is who we think is bullying whom. That is so important I'll take the liberty of saying it again; black or white, male or female, young or old, left wing or right, we all agree that bullying is Wrong, what we disagree about is who we think is bullying whom.

The right wingers amongst us think the individual is being bullied by the masses, and the left thinks the downtrodden peasants are being bullied by the individuals in Power. This is the basis of morality, it is the Basic Morality, and it is something every human on this earth agrees about and in fact lives by, even though they may often mistakenly believe that it emanates from somewhere or something else.

So with this as our weapon, with this as our philosophical tin opener as it were, lets set to work on all the tins…

7. Incest

There are two phenomena that we must address next, due to their habitually being included under the heading of morality, the first of these is incest. There is one crime, and only one, that we can be sure precedes Disloyalty as a Wrong amongst our pre-human ancestors. And we can also see below why and how quickly it must have become subsumed within the category Disloyalty-to-a-fellow-Group-member.

Incest between close blood relatives, that is with your brother or sister, mother or father, son or daughter is forbidden. We can see this in our observations of the sex lives of many animals beside ourselves, and we can be fairly sure that in evolutionary terms this is because the resulting genetic defects in the offspring frequently leads to health problems and their early death. They die and so do not pass on their tendency towards sex-with-close-relatives, and instead those who have an aversion to sex with their nearest and dearest survive and breed. Thus the vast majority of us, bred from this stock, also have the aversion we call the incest taboo.

This is not just true of humans, it has been observed (Wolf and Durham, 2004) that many other animals, are specifically not sexually attracted to their closest blood relatives, compared to the attraction demonstrated towards others outside the immediate family. The males of many species, when given a choice of females never choose their sister or even cousin over an unrelated female, thus it has an ancient lineage. An aversion to incest must have been around for at least as long as mammals have been, that's 200 million years. Pretty old compared to the age of *Homo sapiens,* 150,000 years for modern humans.

The incest taboo is a biological fact, and without doubt precedes Disloyalty, because its existence clearly precedes humans and pre-humans too. Nonetheless, and especially when others are not readily available, sex is so strong an urge that it can override our biological aversion. Thus incest is not by any means uncommon, but there are different kinds of cases and our condemnation tends to vary accordingly, which is interesting.

1. First (infrequent) case.
Occasionally, a brother and sister do seem to love each other genuinely and also sexually, and provided this arrangement is entered into freely by both parties then it is not a Disloyal-bullying wrong. It is still incest, but we view it as less reprehensible, as long as the couple have no children together, since the assumption is that such children will have a higher than

average likelihood of being handicapped. Most of us perhaps shrug our shoulders and are willing to turn a blind eye to this infrequent case.

But at the same time we also ask ourselves, are there really any such cases? Or is it not true that there is always an element of duress by the stronger more dominant partner in the relationship? Be it physical duress or emotional blackmail, certainly pressure of some kind? Surely one of the partners is less willing to break the genetically instilled incest taboo than the other? In which case, no matter the ancient and different biological basis from which incest originally springs, the leading partner is a bully.

2. Second case.

This thought leads us to the more common case. Most cases of incest are clearly B/A-b wrongs in addition to the taboo itself because there is usually a dominant, often older, partner who coerces, pesters and frequently bullies the younger 'partner' into having sex. This is often a trusted family member who misuses his (it's usually a him isn't it) special position of trust. He who should be a protector of the young family member turns instead into the one they need protection from.

He is not unlike the dictator, the modern Alpha Male, who is supposed to be the protector of his flock against the aggression of other groups. Instead he and his henchmen become the ones the flock need protection from, but we'll come to these foul mass bullies later.

3. Third case.

The all too frequent case where the younger 'partner' is a child under the legal age of consent. Then the bullying father or older brother is also a paedophile as well, a second layer of bullying laid onto the first, a vile double misuse of Power laid on top of the prehistoric incest taboo itself.

These are the varying circumstances of incest are they not? And without doubt the second two cases always involve bullying, and we're pretty suspicious of even the first case. Little wonder then that incest is rapidly subsumed by early humans and pre-humans into the general category of Wrong that we now firstly classify as Disloyalty and then extend as bullying due to subsequent changes in social circumstances. In fact incest is always an act of Disloyalty, because we need only use the concept of bullying when we apply morality between those who are not closely related.

This is the first confusion (of others to follow), but it is not a difficult one, because although the incest taboo originates from a different source, virtually every case of it is an act of Disloyalty-bullying by the dominant partner.

We can see then that incest, despite its different root, is to all intents and purposes Disloyalty, but at the same time because of its different root we cannot quite place it in the same class as the numerous other examples of Disloyalty we have briefly looked at up till now.

Why split hairs, when virtually every instance of incest is a *de facto* case of bullying Disloyalty? Well firstly for the sake of accuracy, we are engaged upon trying to carefully delineate the boundaries of the term morality. And secondly not so much for the case of the incest taboo itself, but more to get us into good habits, particularly for the subject we must address next, the peculiar human sex-in-public prohibition.

In Part 2 we will come to some illegitimate impostors that should not be associated with the word morality at all, but to finish Part 1 we must next tackle the confusion that has a foot in both camps, now that is confusing. Not to worry, that's life, and once we have grasped this particular nettle we are at our first boundary, in many ways the boundary of boundaries. The boundary between The Contract (which consists of both Bully/Anti-bully morality/incest and the sex-in-public-prohibition), and those things beyond The Contract, the importuning entities massed along its borders clamouring for attention. Often these are non-moral but still reasonably important matters, gathered at the edge of morality, along lines of demarcation that we must become aware of and never forget, if we are to use the term 'moral' with any precision.

8. The Sex-in-Public Prohibition

Some time in the last 5 million years, since we branched off from the common ancestor we shared with the Chimpanzees our sexuality changed in a number of ways, and one in particular has played a large part in our confusion over the word morality. It is perhaps the chief reason that the term has become such a catchall.

Unlike incest however this change can be no older than 5 million years, because our chimp relatives don't share it with us. Thus this first major confusion appears amongst us on a similar time scale to the phenomenon of Disloyalty itself, whereas all the other confusions that follow in Parts 2 and 4 are laid on afterwards.

It seems probable though that even if Sex-in-public had been like incest, millions upon millions of years older than Disloyalty-to-the-Group, we would still have mixed it up with Disloyalty-bullying and called them both morality. From now on we must do better, morality is a word we use for 'disloyalty that includes bullying and bullying-manipulation', and so it should be used for nothing else. As we shall see the sex-in-public prohibition is without doubt part of the Contract between us, but it is a needless and unhelpful confusion to call it by the same shorthand name of 'morality' that we also use for the phenomenon of Disloyalty-bullying.

It is from a different source, and so the reason we call it by the same name is the reason we shall see so often displayed in the chapters that follow – for the convenience of condemnation. It is much simpler and also much more punchy to shout 'that is immoral', than to shout 'that is a contravention of the sex-in-public prohibition'.

Humans have no 'in heat' season.
Unlike most animals, which mate only at certain times of the year, instead human females are sexually receptive all year round. (Diamond, 1992).

Humans have sex long after the female is capable of conceiving.
No other animal, as far as I understand matters, continues to have sex when they are no longer fertile.

Humans have sex in private.
Animals have sex in front of others, but humans greatly prefer privacy. In fact we do not just 'greatly prefer' it's more of a 'must have' privacy. We seem to be unique in this in the whole of the natural world (Diamond, 1997)

Sex you will recall from Chapter 1 is the third evolutionary thread in terms of age, the third ancient influence on our behaviour. Surprisingly, or maybe not, if we humans were made differently in this one regard, then we would be entirely spared this particular confusion.

The facts noted above are just that, facts of human sexual behaviour, uncontested biological facts that are independent of any religion, racial group or sub-group, creed or culture. Common human behaviour that we all share. And it is this last fact, the unusual fact of humans requiring privacy which dictates that to have sex in public in full view of others in your Group is considered Wrong. It is thus labelled a moral wrong, when it should be called 'the other Contractual Wrong along with Disloyalty-bullying, bullying-manipulation and incest'. Whew, not surprising that we have long ago slipped into the habit of calling it a moral wrong is it?

Before we take another step we need to be clear about what we're saying. Please note that there is a world of difference between sex 'in public places' and sex 'in full public view', the former one might do when drunk or for a dare when no one much is around, the latter is rarer than hen's teeth. This is because, to be accurate when comparing ourselves to other animals, we must clearly stipulate that this public act of sex does not take place on the high street at night with only a few drunken revellers around. Instead it is undertaken in broad daylight in front of Marks and Spencer, with ones parents or ones children along with other members of the group, stood watching, as an aside to their normal errands and business of the day.

Anyone think they could manage that?

Could be aroused and consummate, with Pleasure, under those circumstances? No, as I say none of us does, but other animals do just that. Anyone heard of or seen humans in any group that anthropologists or others have studied having sex in front of the rest of the group in broad daylight like that? We are not talking about in the dark sensual corners of some communal native hut here.

No one cares much either way if, in the privacy of their own home a couple have sex, for the Pleasure of it, at any time of the year, day or night, nor if they continue to do so long after the female is fertile. But how would their fellow shoppers react if this same couple were to have sex along the high street on a nice warm Saturday morning in early May? They would take exception to it, they would protect the eyes of their beloved children, and they would label it obscene.

We will come to the word obscene in Chapter 10, it is a much used and over-used word that adds its own extra layer of confusion onto confusions already caused by the peculiar biological twist of the human sex-in-public prohibition.

They take exception, not because they have been physically hurt in any way, but because this couple have offended against a code, the unanimous predilection humans have for privacy in sexual matters. If we were any other animal: chimp, elephant, deer, dog, cat, or horse, sheep or cattle there would be no issue, because they have sex in front of each other all the time.

SEXUAL PRIVACY

We all share this unique aspect of human sexual behaviour, in other words we all agree on this, just as we all agree that bullying and bullying-manipulation is Wrong, even though, like incest, the sex-in-public prohibition comes from a different source than Disloyalty. We all agree to such an extent that no one does it.

No one does it, not because they will be arrested, but because in the circumstance of full public view, they would have no Pleasure in it. They feel insufficient sexual arousal to consummate in the public circumstances described, circumstances in which no other animal would turn a hair, yet we humans cannot manage it and instead have to 'get a room'. Is there any other part of the Contract that we are so unable to break? I think not, so we don't just 'agree' as we do about bullying, we are not capable of disagreeing on this important contractual matter.

However, despite being the underlying nub of the issue, not having sex-in-public is not what we argue about. What we argue so ferociously about is the extent to which simulated sex in public is permissible, what we argue about is pornography. What we argue about is where harmless and thus acceptable titillation stops and where some form of simulated sexual imagery is so explicit that many of us feel it is tantamount to a contravention of the sex-in-public prohibition.

If two humans have sex in their front garden in full public view, no matter how sweet it is in private, we all of us, no matter our religion, colour or culture, label it Wrong. It is the way we are made and so it seems reasonable to therefore include the Sex-in-public prohibition as part of The Contract, alongside Disloyalty (bullying and bullying-manipulation). This is The Contract made between all members of The Group, in all human groups without exception, and it is thus the Basic Contract from which all others flow. This brings us to one side of our first and most confusing boundary, and we shall shortly re-visit it from the other side, in Chapters 10 and 11 covering obscenity and pornography: simulated sex-in-public. Meanwhile here though we will concentrate on that part of it that cannot but be included in The Contract, actual sex-in-public.

There are various evolutionary theories (Diamond, 1992), but no general agreement, as to why humans are so different in this regard, so let's press on, observing from whence the concept obscenity arises, from our predisposition for sex in private, rather than in full view of the rest of the group. From sex-in-private, not from anything written in the Analects, Bible, Koran, Talmud, Gita or Dhammapada – it is a physiological bent of the human lineage common to us all.

There is no right to freedom of sex in public as there is to freedom of public speech, because no bully has taken away our right to public sex. We don't want to do it, and 'they' don't want to see it.

And those deviant few who do enjoy sex in public places?

Tough, either control yourself or be prepared for the consequences. But there aren't any such deviants, because those who seek that alleged thrill have sex in a public place, but not in full public view. No tart with her tits hanging out or stud if that's the male equivalent, make a habit of having sex in full public view amongst the shoppers on a Saturday morning, no matter how intoxicated by their own youthful sexuality they are. No even they, the sexy young beasts of the group, prefer to 'get a room'.

We humans, like many other forms of life, are sexually excited and stimulated by the sight of the sex act even when we see animals doing it. But at the same time we humans, and only us, have an equally strong reaction that sex between two humans should always be undertaken in private. How odd we are in this regard, we enjoy a bit of titillation, but can't bring ourselves to do it in full public view ourselves. And then we invented pornography.

Having no 'in-heat-season' and 'sex-continuing-after-fertility' are mere asides, just facts of our genetic make-up, interesting peculiarities of human sex, compared to the sex lives of other creatures. But the fact of the human sex-in-public prohibition brings with it arguments and spin-offs galore. We all agree that a couple having sex in their front garden is Wrong because they should do it in private. What we disagree about is the many aspects of simulated sex-in-public that fall just short of live sex-in-public. We find it Wrong, we find it obscene, for a couple to 'inflict' the sight of them having sex upon us. But we also find it prudish and hypocritical to say so because we rather enjoy sex ourselves – in private.

No wonder we're confused.

CONFUSION

The sight of others having sex turns us on, but at the same time we turn away when we think of ourselves as voyeurs. What a pickle we are in.

No other life form can ever think of itself as a voyeur, because sex-in-public is the norm. What a peculiar, and peculiarly human dilemma, and what problems and confusions it brings. Our sex drives enjoy and are stimulated by the sight of the sex act, in the same way that we see other animals are, yet we are also forced by the direction of our genetic development to turn away from the sight of a couple having sex in public.

It's a peculiar trap, maybe life would be simpler if we had sex in front of one another and reacted to it in the same way other social mammals do, as something perfectly normal, but we don't. The fact is that this is our situation, and it leads to a lot of disagreements about which of those things that come under the title of pornography are on the harmless titillation side of the line, and which are so graphic as to be on the prohibited side.

As soon as we say that we are embarrassed by the sight of sex-in-public, we label ourselves (and others label us) as prudes. But this is inaccurate because we are not necessarily prudish in the bedroom, but nonetheless hurriedly look away from a couple we see locked together in a never-ending public kiss. Hence the expression 'get a room', and the people who shout that are anything but prudes, they are out on the tiles having a rip roaring time.

We enjoy sex, not only that, we also enjoy a bit of sexual titillation, we enjoy the Pleasure of arousal. Pornography is not sex in public in front of the rest of the group, and equally clearly it was not an issue at all for us anytime before the last 3000 years, prior to our ability to draw, then to write and act in plays. In fact it wasn't much of an issue until a few hundred years ago, and especially even more recently with the invention of photography, film and the internet, which has so greatly extended the scope of writing, drawing and painting.

The sex act when portrayed is just that a portrayal via a secondary medium. So a proponent of porn could make the case that anything on film is not real live sex. In which case the only immoral 'art' would be real live sex on the stage in a theatre, the vast majority of soft porn is simulated sex in which penetration does not occur, therefore a film of simulated sex is not actual sex and so is not immoral. Hmm...

Even so one would think that hard core pornography, showing actual penetration is the depiction of real sex and so is in contravention of the sex-in-public prohibition. Or some would say why not ban all depictions of sex. For the moment this is where we will leave the subject, we are here together to highlight philosophical questions and hopefully some answers, not discuss details of legislation. It would seem that there are some aspects of pornography that are so graphic that they amount to sex-in-public rather than being simulated sex. Therefore even though they are on film and so not live, they are still a contravention of this peculiar twist of human evolution.

Whatever conclusions a society reaches regarding pornography, the issue of primary philosophical importance is that we should stop dumping the

Sex-in-public prohibition and Disloyalty-bullying into the same basket and calling that basket morality. That basket should actually be called The Contract. At present this blind unthinking dumping has created a situation of utter confusion wherein the word moral is all things to all men, and women (Scanlon, 2000). Establishing the boundaries of morality is surely a prerequisite to any understanding of morality?

Since they are different 'wrongs' from different sources either the Sex-in-public prohibition is morality or Disloyalty-bullying is. They can't both be, and to continue to use the same term for two different things is philosophical and social madness. As already stated my vote is that we continue to call matters of Disloyalty-bullying moral matters, but that we call the Sex-in-public prohibition, just that: the Sex-in-Public Prohibition.

Even if it takes us a hundred years to re-train ourselves we must start now. Henceforth when we condemn hard core, or any other aspect of pornography that we think goes too far, to be accurate we must say that it is in contravention of the sex-in-public prohibition, rather than calling it immoral.

As mentioned, calling something immoral has far more rhetorical force than giving it another, albeit more accurate, name. All one can say about that is, yes it does, and as we shall see this is one of the reasons why people have the deplorable habit of labelling a whole range of things they object to as immoral. And in the process they, sometimes deliberately and other times accidentally, exacerbate our confusion – here endeth The Contract.

Part 2

Beyond The Contract

9. Self-governance, Sin and Skilfulness

In discussing self-governance, or skilfulness as the Buddha calls it, we are addressing the area of autonomy each of us has as a free human being, so we will start as most youngsters do, with masturbation. Obviously there is no Disloyalty involved in this common act, nor is there a bully or a bullied, so masturbation cannot be immoral.

What then is it?

Rather than call it natural (which I'm sure it is) and thereby dismiss the attitude of old time religion out of hand, let's look at it for a moment. Someone masturbating cannot possibly be behaving immorally, because no one else is involved.

Is someone snorting cocaine behaving immorally? Not if they are only hurting themselves alone. Yes if they are hurting their friends, or spouse, parents or children. The moment their habit hurts someone else, including someone they steal money from, or should be turning up to work with or for, they are behaving immorally.

It is for the hurt to others that we call such habits morally wrong, and for what the drug pusher does as he bullies and bully-manipulates by getting others hooked, but not for what addicts do solely to themselves.

That is something else – behaving stupidly maybe.

When someone falls victim to a debilitating drug habit or masturbates to the exclusion of an adult sexual relationship, there is surely something unwise in their conduct, yet it cannot be immoral.

The Buddha calls such actions unskilful.

They exhibit a lack of personal wisdom, and no matter what the underlying psychological reasons these habits can often lead next to immoral behaviour. The drug addict begins to increasingly 'put upon' his friends, spouse and other relations, and hence we counsel against 'being unskilful', we counsel that such things are unwise.

Wife swapping is another example, or partner swapping as we should call it. Provided both parties agree to this 'bit of fun' then it cannot be immoral. It is immoral only if one partner is pressurised into it, bully-manipulated as we have now learned to say. There is an argument that one partner is almost always pressured into taking part, and all such cases are immoral. Not because of the alleged salacious nature of the enterprise, but because one of the four involved is being bullied.

It is unskilful and not immoral when all involved take part freely. It is unskilful because of the potential for jealousy, hurt and resultant anger which can then result in an immoral act, an act that is designed to hurt others, be it bullying or bullying-manipulative. Thus being unskilful, lacking in self-governance, is often potentially immoral.

SIN

This is a concept by no means exclusive to Buddhism, the seven deadly sins of Christianity, indeed the whole Christian concept of sin, deals in the same coin – the potential to behave immorally. Many of us though, including many Christians, tend to miss out the word potential in our condemnation. Anger, lust, avarice, gluttony, sloth, pride, envy, none of these seven deadly human attitudes are immoral in the way that torture, rape or murder is, but they can, when we are in the grip of them, lead to immorality.

Lord knows there are times when it is right to be angry, as Jesus was that day in the Temple. Right to be briefly proud, and natural to lust, a time (when totally exhausted) that it is good to rest to the point of slothfulness, even a time when envy can spur us forward into making a greater effort with our own lives. But when these attitudes take us over, we have been unskilful, we have taken a step towards an immoral act. An act that hurts others, a Disloyal act that bullies others.

'SINNING' BY THOUGHT

In Matthew 5.27 Jesus says that sinning by thought is as bad as sinning by deed, "I say to you that every one who looks at a woman lustfully has already committed adultery with her in his heart". Well I say to you, that this sinning by thought being as bad as by deeds, is an enormous mistake, a mistake that lies at the heart of the difference between skilfulness and morality. It is a council of perfection that we must call time on.

'Sinning' by deed is to hurt someone, to bully someone, to oppress someone, and is therefore immoral. 'sinning' by thought is to be only unskilful and is to demean only oneself, and though unwise, can never be immoral, as long as one never carries out one's fantasies.

Religions offer advice about skilfulness and about the best routes to happiness, as do psychologists, psychiatrists, self-help books and the like, but when a religious teacher offers it, there is a tendency for it to be seen as moral advice. But skilfulness is not morality, it sits on the other side of a boundary. It is potential immorality.

I prefer the Buddha's terminology on this issue; the concept of sin is a Christian disaster zone.

SOCIAL SKILFULNESS

Which brings us to questions of group or social skilfulness, and the paternalistic legislation that sometimes follows. Prohibition in the United States was social skilfulness, for much bad behaviour, pain, poverty and suffering is caused by our over indulgence in alcohol. The personal over indulgence is unskilful, the resultant bad behaviour, pain and suffering of others is immoral.

This is not new, it seems probable that the Ancient Groups did not just deliberate about moral matters, they will have wrestled also with other decisions concerning the welfare of the group. 'The winter is barely over, but the camp is partly flooded, we could strike camp now and head for the high land, the damp has already killed one baby. By leaving now we would arrive early in the upper pasture and get the best pickings, but it will probably be cold there still another month, one or two of the old ones might die on the journey.'

UTILITARIAN DECISIONS
Questions that weigh alternatives: how many of the group might die down here compared to striking camp early, are often decided on a Utilitarian basis – by weighing the greatest happiness (greatest good – greatest pleasure as opposed to pain), of the greatest number. Decisions such as these, in this particular case about the group-as-a-whole, are about the survival of the group and are not about Disloyalty.

Why then do we not call these types of decisions by the term Utilitarian instead of lumping them in under the good old heading of morality as we so often do? If we are to use the term morality for acts of Disloyal-bullying then to use it also for Utilitarian decisions leads us into error. When in this context we say that a wrong decision was made (to move camp), we mean an incorrect decision that was to the eventual detriment of the group. We do not mean a morally wrong (evil or reprehensible) decision, ie an act of bullying disloyalty.

We should therefore call these decisions Utilitarian decisions, founded on the underlying principle behind the formation of the Ancient Groups, as discussed in the first pages of Chapter 2. Without adding on to them the epithet 'moral'. My preference is to call them half-moral, as explained on the first page of Chapter 23, and they are not just whole group dilemmas, they do apply to problems facing individuals, as we will see in Chapter 24 as well as 23, when we look at Utilitarianism again. Even when they are dilemmas facing individuals, the technique of the greatest happiness principle is still derived from the principle behind the formation of the group, rather than from Disloyalty, the principle that controls the tensions within the group.

Since these are different principles we should not call them both by the name morality. As in the last chapter, choose one to be called morality. It seems to me that when we are angry and shout 'that's immoral' we are usually pointing at acts of Disloyalty-bullying causing tension within the group, hence my preference. If the majority think otherwise then fine swap it round if you wish, but not both. Surely to call ourselves philosophers and then use the same term for two different, albeit closely related, entities is lamentable?

'Or should we stay and harvest the spring fruits down here this year, as we sometimes have, but if we do who will stay to dry and store them in the heat of summer. How many should be left to do the work, and should we leave warriors to protect them, or do we need them all for the upland hunt? Will it be dangerous to split our forces, there is still bad blood between us and our neighbours across the river?'

Humans face many questions, imponderable and difficult concerning the welfare of the group, but though they lie along morality's boundary, they are not primarily moral questions. Some questions are almost scientific, matters of Knowledge, number four of the six threads that run through our lives. Applying the knowledge from previous experience as to whether an early flood means a good year for the spring fruits, or whether a harsh winter and sudden thaw usually precedes good grazing in the mountain pastures.

And these can lead to moral issues.

Let us suppose that a method of manipulating plants is discovered and this will enhance food production but with environmental risks. Let's say that its proponents state; "it would be immoral not to develop this science, because with it we can feed the hungry of the world".

When faced with these difficult questions, it can be useful to go back to first principles. Try it, I seat myself quietly down and project myself back as best I can, back to those early days, those days when morality had not long been with us. Back to an idealised time of my imagination, back to the first Ancient Groups, back to a time when things were a little less complicated. Suppose one of the Group discovered a new source of food, a fungi or a vegetable, or maybe a way of cooking to make something previously inedible, now edible.

DUTY

It is not his or her cleverness or the time spent developing the idea that is the moral element here, it is how willingly he or she shares it with the group. Because without the group, without the support of our fellows, each of us is alone, alone against the elements, alone against the big cats that hunt this land, alone without speed, without big teeth, alone without the pack as our support. Surely therefore this clever member of Our Group has a Duty to share.

The new invention sounds like a good cause but the moral element here is about one thing and one thing only, Trust, unselfishness, sharing what you have with others, sharing what the extended family group has with all its members.

The moral element is sharing all the food in the world now.

Or, if you are going to come up with a new way of producing extra food, for the claim that it is a moral act to be true it has to be given free of charge to the starving.

If the people urging this development do not intend to give anything away free of charge, if in fact their intention is to make farmers and governments pay through their respective noses for it, we can see that the moral claim is false, it is a smoke screen. We see now why it was that that claim always seemed a little off key, always seemed a bit thin. The claim of morality, which happens to be conveniently allied to profit, always is a lie, a big fat convenient commercial lie.

On a Utilitarian basis the profits made by a few might be considered to be offset by the extra hungry mouths fed by the new invention. However most of us would hardly want to claim such a computation as the basis of all morality. For the hungry, if they really see any extra food as a result of it, then it's better than a kick in the teeth I suppose, but it isn't morality because it is the opposite, it is Bullying-manipulation.

This or that business venture may well do some 'good' in the world, but it is only moral if it is done free of charge, which means the cost to the receiver should be sufficient only to cover the production costs of the inventor. Moral acts are those services that are given freely, done free of charge for one group member by another – not services offered at a price. And especially not at a high price.

Imagine trying to claim that ripping off a poverty stricken farmer, is a moral act. It is the opposite – it is theft. And theft, as we now know, is immoral because it is the bullying-manipulation by one of another.

Where does all this leave us with an issue such as Prohibition in the USA or modern alcohol prohibition in many Islamic countries? In the case of the USA it gave gangsters the chance to step in and supply something a large number of people wanted. This is akin to the argument today that says various illegal drugs should be make legal to clean up a criminal enterprise, because the 'war on drugs cannot be won'.

For the moment the strengths of this argument do not concern us. What does concern us is that such prohibition is Paternalism, and so a question of social skilfulness, not morality. It is an extension of the concept of self-governance because it bans harmless controlled and mature alcohol consumption along with the immoral irresponsible kind that results in bullying acts of aggression.

What also concerns us here is to note that the Prohibition Police, whether they are policing alcohol consumption or the mode of a woman's dress, can easily become Bullies themselves, and worse bullies than the aggressive alcohol fuelled louts they ostensibly protect the rest of the group from. They become the Secret Police who, by using the Power they are given, become Bullies such that the cure turns out to be worse than the disease. Thus in the huge modern groups called countries they display the hand of the biggest bully of all, the bully of bullies, the State, when those who have assumed Power as the Government bear down with all the great weight at their disposal upon the rest of the group.

Here is one of the fundamental differences between those who wish to base society's legislative and policing system on what it says in a holy book and those who wish to base it on the originating underlying basis of human morality. Those who believe in the holy book are unwilling to accept that 'the cure is worse than the disease', they would rather take the risk of a brutal and bullying out of control Prohibition Police than any perceived transgression of 'the book'.

So there are dangers in Paternalism, but we liberals should not be so idealistic as to treat it as the great *bete noire*. Even the most open of Open Societies needs a restraining hand on the helm at times, mainly due to some of our rather immature behaviour patterns – particularly concerning drink, drugs, lifestyles thereof, and their otherwise hard to control effect upon others. Having said that we must be careful...

SERIAL MONOGAMY

For example could there be anything immoral in having a series of consecutive sexual partners, as long as each previous relationship has been honestly and sympathetically ended before the next one begins?

We may advise someone that it is wiser, or more skilful (by which we mean that in our opinion it will make them happier), to aim at fewer good quality relationships, rather than rushing on to the next all the while notching up their score. However as long as no one has been used, manipulated or deliberately hurt, then although personally we may think a continuous succession of sexual partners is overdoing it, is not a 'healthy sign', (ie is unskilful), nonetheless there has been no immoral behaviour, since no one has been bullied.

And ... no bully, no crime – apart from sex-in-public.

We seem to have come back to sex. We left ourselves in a confused state, having invented pornography. Up until then the Sex-in-public prohibition must have been pretty simple, you just didn't do it, and a half or a quarter of a million years ago there were no depictions of it to argue about. And not for a long time after that either.

10. Obscenity

We humans spectacularly fail to agree to what extent the sex-in-public prohibition also includes simulated sex and explicit pictures, the sight of which excites us. We will probably never agree, because some of us are more prudish and some of us more sexually adventurous than others, but before we can argue in any meaningful way we need to be clear what we are arguing about.

We therefore need to take a look at the word obscenity, at how it is used and how it is misused. What do we mean when we say that something is obscene and therefore in 'bad taste'? First we must clear up a confusing side issue – aesthetic taste.

When an artist exhibits as a serious work her unmade semen stained bed, many people find this to be 'in poor taste', and splutter with rage over it. And in so doing they have mixed up aesthetic or artistic taste with obscenity.

They have mixed up two things.

One is their opinion that the exhibition of an unmade bed of any kind is poor art, lazy art, aesthetically unprepossessing and therefore worthless art. Two is their repugnance at the mild obscenity of the public display of the aftermath of another couples' sex life.

They mean it is obscene, but since obscene seems too strong a word for a case such as an empty bed, they downgrade it into 'in poor taste', and in so doing confuse things. It would be far more accurate to accuse the exhibition of Tracy's bed of being lazy and aesthetically poor art, and to label the semen stains alone as being mildly obscene. Clearly we are not seeing the couple in public action, so we can go no further than 'mild obscenity'. This is interesting and is of course why we're talking about it.

Aesthetics is the study of beauty, the study of the concept of beauty, taste and all things well proportioned and pleasing to the eye, it is a rather esoteric philosophical subject. It covers also that which is pleasing to the nose and the other senses such as touching, tasting, listening and it has a long and venerable history. A history reaching back to Plato and beyond, a 2,500 year old history, longer than quite a few religions.

It is a rather ephemeral subject compared to morality.

Yet it has a part to play in clarifying the limit called obscenity that society places on free speech, because one often hears the criticism: "that should not be permitted, because it is in bad taste".

There is a problem of terminology hidden here.

Clearly obscenity is related to the sight of a couple in contravention of the sex-in-public prohibition, maybe in a quiet corner of a public park or on a beach. But what is beauty? What is bad and good artistic taste? Plato, amongst others, started this, like so much else, and also like so much else, Darwin finished it, but many people at first missed the endpoint.

Philosophers of all kinds were long in the habit of praising and raising the Beautiful up on high, as being synonymous with what they called the Good or even God. The good to look at, the good to eat, the good feeling when you have achieved or built something, the good feeling just before, during and after sex, but especially a beautiful painting, building or sculpture.

In so doing, amongst other things, they were very often confusing 'the Good' born of the concept Pleasure, with 'the Right', born of the concept Morality. A beautiful painting, sculpture, dress or building is pleasing, an aesthetic good, a Pleasure to the eye of the beholder. It is closer to the world of fashion than it is to the world of Morality. And though it seems incredible to us that any great philosopher could mix these up, they did so for hundreds of years, in their pursuit of an ideal they called 'the Good'.

Little wonder then that us lesser mortals also get mixed up.

In 'The Descent of Man and Selection in Relation to Sex', Darwin states:

"Let us suppose the members of a tribe in which some form of marriage is practised, to spread over an unoccupied continent; they would soon split up into distinct hordes, which would be separated from each other by various barriers, (mountain ranges, rivers, deserts, etc) ... and still more effectually by ... war.

The hordes would be subject to slightly different conditions and habits of life, and would sooner or later come to differ in some small degree. As soon as this occurred each isolated tribe would form for itself a slightly different standard of beauty; and then unconscious selection would come into action through the more powerful and leading savages preferring certain women to others." (Darwin, [1871] 1981)

In the battle to attract sexual partners, many creatures select upon the basis of the brightest colour, the biggest chest, longer neck, wider wing, tail, eyes, lips, buttocks, in short any feature considered amongst that species as attractive, (just a little more exaggerated than others around it). These attractions also include particular sounds, as well as smells and tastes, we lick, we listen, we smell, we look for that which attracts us, that which pleases us, that which is a Pleasure, and therefore 'accords with our taste'.

In the majority of species it is the males who strike the pose to show how healthy and strong they are, and the females who do the choosing –

by acceptance of the suitor. A young buck jumps high in the air every so often as he runs from the lion. "See how fast and glorious I am, so fast so fine that I do not even need to run in total panic. I can actually waste time jumping as I run, choose me I'm beautiful, choose me, choose me I'm strong, choose me I'm healthy choose me."

Our eyes, our ears, and in some cases our noses become utilised, not just as instruments for survival and searching for food, but also as a means of choosing between the perceived beauty of one mate compared to another, between slightly different versions of the same thing. Our eyes become able to discern the concept beauty, as an adjunct to choosing the best, by which is meant the healthiest, the strongest, the finest, the most beautiful.

In this process evolution has done what it always does, it has used something already available to us for an additional purpose. Our eyes are already able to tell us which things in our world look good/healthy, clean water, a fresh kill, a field of trees with tasty nuts. And which look bad/unhealthy, dirty stagnant water, putrefied fly blown flesh, barren scaly plants of low nutritional value or brightly coloured and poisonous berries.

Now it is refined further, by being used to choose the best, most robust and healthy partners on the grounds of physical beauty, and those who choose correctly producing more healthy and surviving offspring, who in turn choose again in their turn on the same basis. Again, again and again, generation after generation.

And so aesthetic taste is the preference for that which we consider beautiful, that which we find appealing to one or other of our senses.

Thus millions of years later, humans with their much increased brain power develop a very wide and refined range of preferences, which their philosophers come to call aesthetics, and they ponder it for centuries. Well we can cease to ponder, the subject of aesthetics developed from the choices, the sexual choices those before us made over millions of years of evolutionary time.

Hence in art, we exaggerate for effect and by so doing we attract, or sometimes repel. If the particular feature is not so well considered, we incur the judgement in others, 'that is poor or bad taste'. Artistic taste – nothing to do with the issue of obscenity. Our refined human aesthetics is a measure of how attractive we find something.

Thus our artistic talk is to some extent a smokescreen as we show off our plumage whilst admiring the plumage of others. We show off our personal attractiveness via our artistic tastes, like a Bowerbird, we parade the beauty of our pretty productions. Aesthetics produces many lovely things which enhance the Pleasure of our lives, but there is no longer a great mystery about what it is, and whence it is derived, as there was in

Plato's day.

It is firstly a sensual survival technique which is then worked on over time by sexual selection, it is an evolutionary mechanism not, as Plato thought, our imperfect imitation of a perfect harmony wherein the Gods do dwell.

So when we say, that picture is ugly I don't like it, we are utilising our aesthetic judgement. That unmade bed is ugly is neither here nor there, it is a matter of artistic taste. One calls the other an empty-headed philistine and on we both go to the next exhibit or the next gallery.

Those semen stains are indecent, because they are on public exhibition, that display is mildly obscene, is something else, is a different topic altogether. We are saying then that those stains are indecent because they exhibit (a part of) someone's private sex life in public. Those that say that are saying that it contravenes the human sex-in-private pre-disposition.

Most of us wince at the stagnant evidence of another couples' sex life, we find it yucky, it is private and we don't want to know, we don't want such information thrust in our face. We think it is in bad taste for anyone to do so, and the moment we say that we are confusing it with bad taste in art, the ugly, the ill proportioned that gives us no pleasure when we look upon it.

When we really mean that it is obscene, but that seems too strong a word for a few stains. This alleged 'obscenity' is only a very mild case, far less obscene than seeing Tracy and her friend on the bed having sex in public, in the middle of an Art Gallery. But we must pause a moment here because the self-righteous amongst the liberal wing can get very hot under the collar about this.

We are not saying that anything Tracy and her lover do on that bed is obscene, what they do is a wonderful normal human act, blah, blah, blah, etc, etc, blah, blah, blah. What we say when we call the displayed bed mildly obscene is – obscene because it displays a private act in public. The doing of it is the most natural thing in the world, but the displaying of it amongst humans is not.

Although in the case in question, I don't suppose the majority of us would be so offended as to vote to make the public display of Tracy's semen stained bed illegal by dint of obscenity. Therefore we must be teetering on a boundary, and philosophically speaking, boundaries are interesting places on which to teeter.

It throws some light for example on that statement people make from time to time, sometimes by 'liberals' and sometimes by pornographers. You know the one. It goes like this... How come Society allows violence to be portrayed on television and in the cinema but becomes all coy and uptight about the natural and beautiful act of sex?

Well here's the answer, explicit public displays of sexual intercourse are considered obscene because they are public, however privately delightful. The wrong is the public display, not the act itself.

Thus when I see a couple on the street, or maybe at a railway station saying goodbye, and involved in a long passionate lingering kiss, I look at them and then quickly look away again, as if I'm in the wrong. Wrong for me to look and yet also wrong for them to be too intimate in public. Am I a prude to turn and look away? Or am I a voyeur to look? We feel trapped and accuse ourselves of being voyeurs and prudes at the same time.

And this has nothing whatsoever to do with violence in films, because such violence is always a B/A-b moral question. Hence why scriptwriters twist the plot around so that our movie heroes can use the excuse of vengeance when they behave violently. The 'he deserved it' syndrome, the bad guy got what was coming to him.

Phrases which always mean, 'this person is a bully' he has always been a 'wrong un'. He is now receiving nothing other than an eye for an eye, or a tooth for a tooth, because that which our hero is now dishing out is actually less or no more than whatever the bad (Wrong) guy has done to others. He is receiving his just deserts, this vengeance is not bullying, it is reciprocity, it is justice.

WHAT OBSCENITY IS NOT

One hears people say that it is obscene how minor potentates flaunt their wealth while their fellow citizens starve and die in poverty all around them. Or in times of war that 'it is obscene for reporters to criticise our soldiers while they are out there dying for us'. These are confusing uses of the word obscene, it should ideally be reserved for instances of public sexual intercourse. Is it any wonder we get ourselves in a tangle?

The word obscene is used, over used and misused, because the speaker wishes to express utter disgust with the actions being criticised. Is used to give emphasis. Obscene is, unfortunately for accuracy, a wonderful word for adding punch, adding vigour and emphasis to our disgust.

For the sake of accuracy it should ideally not be used in other contexts than either, an act of sex undertaken in public or a public sexual display sufficiently explicit such that it is indistinguishable from the sex act itself. Since obscenity is such a central issue to all human societies it is too important a word to mess around with.

Displaying wealth when surrounded by starvation and poverty is a moral wrong, the rich are still, despite their wealth, members of a social team, and they have taken more than their fair share. Their greed is immoral and

57

disgusting, but provided they don't also have sex in public, then their behaviour should not be called obscene.

In the second example, the reporter may well be telling an honest story about atrocities committed by our soldiers, if he is then well done for him and the person who is trying to shut him up is a liar. If the reporter himself is lying, then he is guilty of libel. A moral issue because to lie about someone is an act of Bullying-manipulation and so is Disloyalty towards a member of the group, and thus is nothing to do with our other use of the word obscene – publicly displayed sex between two humans.

We'll never change our confusing double use of the word obscene. So henceforth we need to be aware of the constant background inaccuracy caused by our using one word to describe two different things. And also be aware that it is certain aspects of public sexual display (displays that stop just short of full public sexual intercourse), rather than couples indulging in the sex act all over the place in public, that are argued over and disputed.

11. Pornography and Censorship

The laws regarding pornography vary in different countries, some being always strictly against any form of it, and some against hard porn but quite relaxed about what is often described as soft porn. Thus some are against everything, some against some and some against almost nothing. Blurred and subjective as the line is we can see that all this amounts to the difference between cases considered to be violations of the sex-in-public prohibition versus cases considered to be harmless titillation.

Since pornography is simulated sex, not actual sex-in-the-flesh it is always a confusing step away from the origins of the sex-in-public prohibition that forms a part of the Contract common to every human group from every human culture. Even so pornography that is so explicit that a society judges it to amount to an infringement of the sex-in-public prohibition is what we legislate against. We are also concerned, this time B/A-b morally, with cases where the pornographer has bullied his subjects into taking part.

Notice how easily this second issue, a clear B/A-b moral issue where the movers and shakers of the sex industry take advantage of women from poor backgrounds, comes tacked onto the primary question of titillation versus contravention. The result is the usual result, confusion, as some of us twitter on about how pornography cannot be immoral because it is a 'victimless crime'.

Meanwhile back to the main subject. In what direction does pornography that breeches the sex-in-public prohibition lead us?

To censorship, where else? Which is an aspect of alleged Paternalism that *avant-garde* liberals hate with a passion, because they think it is dictatorial, against free speech, and prudish (against the sweet beautiful Pleasure of Sex). We easily mix up political censorship, which certainly is bullying by dictatorial governments or their agents and is therefore a moral wrong, with censorship for explicit sexual content.

We should be more careful to differentiate between these two, because sex censorship is not necessarily prudish, does not militate against early sex education for children and is certainly not about branding sex as dirty in some old-fashioned way. It is about responding to the curious anomaly of our human sex lives with its sex-in-public prohibition on the one hand, and our natural enjoyment of a bit of titillation on the other.

In a world in which humans have a unique predisposition for sexual privacy, we should not be as afraid of sex-censorship as we tend to be.

Provided that we establish it upon the rock solid basis of our biology, and not upon opinionated twaddle.

To be afraid of the principle of sex censorship is to mix up this issue with the moral issue of freedom of speech and the dictatorial political censorship that tries to subvert such freedom; by bullying us into silent acquiescence when confronted by the full Power of the State, and in many countries the upper caste who control said Power.

The problem is that one person's obscenity is another person's prudish overreaction, hence these are issues over which we debate and argue, trying to draw a line between being overly restrictive or being too *laissez-faire*. Censorship for sexual content is not as narrow-minded as we have come to believe, as long as we free the censor from the claptrap of the religious right and the self-righteousness of the liberal left.

Most societies, despite the protests of the *avant-garde*, need some form of sex-censorship. We don't trust politicians to run the country without being subject to a series of checks and balances, we don't trust the police to be always scrupulously well-behaved without other checks and balances, we don't trust greedy speculators not to bend the financial laws of the Stock Exchange if they're not overseen. Why would we trust film directors, playwrights, authors, and artists to behave 'responsibly', rather than commercially, without some checks and balances pertinent to them?

Those who claim there should be no sex-censorship seem to believe that local government officers, directors of companies and ... actually the list is endless, can't be trusted without a means of redress, but artists can. It's as if they assume that there is no pressure for critical and financial success, by hook or by crook, on a Director, Producer, Author, Artist or Theatre Owner.

'Pushing at the artistic boundaries' can often be the writer's, painter's, photographer's or film maker's handy euphemism for trying to get away with more than anyone else has done so far, either to increase their public exposure and/or to thereby turn a nice financial profit.

Many of us enjoy a bit of titillation, and perhaps we feel that a little salacious stimulation of our personal sex lives is a harmless pleasure? And seen from this angle it is – a private matter – hence the liberal left's preference for relaxed laws. However, harking back to the animal equivalent, unless one is willing to be watched oneself during the act of sex (by one's closest family, mother, father, children), then one should perhaps not be watching others?

We can see the levels of disagreement, not only between different societies, but also between different times in the same society. Some things we do agree on though, all child pornography is a moral wrong because it is an act of Disloyalty, it is an act of bullying-exploitation of children in need of protection. There we go again, how thin is the line here between the sex-in-public prohibition and the foul immoral bullying-manipulative act of betraying the trust of a child.

Responses to pornography are different in different places because these matters lie teetering along the border of the Contract. Sex censorship is a vexed and difficult issue, we are wary of any undue Power over our freedom of expression. The censor can easily become another example of the preening, self-regarding, overbearing and bullying Prohibition Police. But do we want the airwaves and bookshelves flooded with hard core pornography?

Of course not and rules are made against such activities. Rules derived not from religious revelation, or this or that holy book or cultural tradition (God I hate that word 'cultural', it's so vague and so beloved of those who want to subvert morality), but from the common human predilection we all share, for private rather than public sex.

12. Dress Code

One part of our everyday lives that follows on from the question what is pornographic and what is not, is how we dress in public. Notice at the outset that we are reckoned to have first started wearing clothes about 150,000 years ago, (Kittler, 2003). So in this respect clothes are not dissimilar to pornography (first drawings 5,000 years ago), in that they have appeared in our history long after the sex-in-public prohibition.

Since the connection between the wearing of clothes and the sex-in-public prohibition is somewhat tenuous, it is not surprising that the opinions of various societies appear to vary greatly regarding male and female nudity. Some sophisticated and some primitive societies insist on various rules regarding 'covering up' whereas others, both primitive and 'civilised' are far more relaxed about complete nudity. So the first thing we can note is that there is no unanimity as there is with the sex-in-public prohibition itself, which is applied in all human societies everywhere.

With that in mind let's review the important subject of our public dress code, especially the much argued over female public dress code. We will be concentrating on the female dress code because that is what societies mainly argue about. They do this because the way human sexuality is constructed it is the females who tend to flaunt their attractions in front of the males, who are turned on more by physical attributes than the females are.

1. Certain sights are sexually exciting to males and females, but more so to males because they are stimulated more by appearances than females seem to be. Specifically by simulated sex in films, pictures, plays, books and erotica of all kinds.

2. Sometimes such erotica consists of semi-naked males or females on their own but in explicit poses. Scantily clad men or women play a part in this, but again this tends to 'work better' ie be more effective in arousing men.

3. Despite the effect being less on women they are nonetheless fully aware of the effect scantily clad females have on men. They are aware it is arousing and sexually alluring.

4. Therefore the vast majority of women understand that the way they dress has a considerable effect on most of the males they come into contact with, socially, at work or just walking around out on the street.

5. But women also dress to please themselves, they enjoy dressing up and going out with their friends, on a 'girls night out'. And so we come to the core of the issue, the more attractive they look the better they feel about themselves (as do we all), but at the same time the more likely they are to attract the (wanted and unwanted) attention of males they come into proximity with.

6. We are all, adult males and females, pretty much aware of this dilemma. We often choose to ignore it and dress to please ourselves, but we are aware still that the dilemma is there. On the one hand there is feeling good about ourselves, on the other is the impression we make on others. There's nothing complicated or hidden from view that needs a philosopher or sex researcher to figure out, but that doesn't mean it never causes a problem.

7. For example if a camp gay man was to dress in an obviously feminine way and go for a night out around the centre of a town that has no gay scene, one might say that his choice of clothing was unwise, and in fact that gorgeous as he looked he was being either very brave or very foolish.

8. We would say it because of the danger of attracting the 'wrong kind of attention'. We would say it too if an expensively dressed man, with diamond rings and Rolex watch, were to walk through a poverty stricken ghetto. We would say they were being foolish and that to do so was 'asking for trouble'.

9. In the above examples, neither the gay man nor the wealthy man are behaving immorally. They have done something foolish, but their behaviour is not a moral issue, it is a matter of self-governance or skilfulness if you prefer Buddhist terminology. (There are of course wider moral issues about 'gay bashing' and about poverty stricken ghettos, but that is not what we're talking about.)

10. If each of these men had not strayed away from their usual haunts and habitats we would not consider them to be 'asking for trouble'. And so it would seem that sometimes and in some places it is fine to dress any way one pleases, but in other times and places it can be foolish to do so.

11. Similarly when we turn to sexually enticing female clothing then, the judgement a woman makes is a matter of skilfulness, a matter of self-governance and nothing to do with B/A-b morality. Hence the external part of her dress choice, by which is meant her effect upon others, can

only relate to the sex-in-public prohibition (no matter that the link is a little tenuous) and not to morality.

12. None of us, male and female, boys and girls always behave all the time in a sensible and responsible manner do we? Especially on a drink fuelled night out – we'll come to drunks at the end of this chapter and again in Chapter 18. It's fun to 'let our hair down' and be a bit daft at times isn't it? Including, why shouldn't we dress to please ourselves and to hell with what others say or think.

13. Let's stop right there for a moment and reflect that as ever there is a danger in the use of ill thought out linguistic shorthand, in this case the oft-used phrase 'she was asking for it'. We need to be clear that 'asking for trouble' is not the same as 'asking to be raped'. No one is ever asking to be raped, because rape is one of the foulest acts of ultra-bullying that one human can inflict upon another.

14. Some men will persist and persist in trying to 'chat up' a woman that attracts their attention, no matter how many times they are rebuffed. This is not necessarily a prelude to rape, but it may well be the prelude to a less than pleasant evening.

15. Any woman dressed in a sexually arousing way is entitled to do so, both for her own Pleasure and the Pleasure of others, but she is being foolish, even irresponsible if she is not also aware of her personal security. The more explicitly you are dressed the more attention you are likely to receive, and the more potential there is for 'trouble'.

16. This is not morality it is common sense. The more sexually explicitly one dresses the more attention you will receive. Surely that is a fact that none of us need argue about?

Our arguments hinge around a number of things, firstly the degree of responsibility women have in the way they dress, because their dress code exacerbates the situation described above. Next some people say women should be able to dress to please only themselves, but is this realistic with all those horny men around? Then others weigh in with emotive words such as 'sluts' or 'tarts', after which the water gets very muddy.

All we are interested in for now though is that this is a combination of self-governance and a tenuous offshoot of the sex-in-public prohibition, not morality. We will return to the subject again shortly. Meanwhile let's note that this is a happy hunting ground for those who advocate a Prohibition Police, to make these decisions for those terrible 'sluts', for those wonderful sexy 'loose women', playing what can sometimes be a dangerous (but oh so enjoyably titillating) game.

Incidentally what should we call these marvellous flirts since we clearly cannot call them immoral? Well, a bit irresponsible I suppose.

THE VEIL

For an alternative approach ... one can see the logic of Mohammed's original idea... Reducing the frequency of women accidentally, and accidentally on purpose, wafting their pretty little tails in the faces of the group's males, will also reduce the arguments, internal feuds and sexual tensions within the group. Surely this is no worse an idea than our own society awash with soft and not so soft porn, images used to sell everything from toilet cleaner to next week's TV programmes?

Mohammed's requirement, as far as an infidel like myself understands it, included a shawl covering the hair but leaving the face uncovered and visible. This is important because to also cover the face is to disrespect those around you, your fellow group members, and so the full faced veil is immoral.

Yes that's right, far from being something especially chaste and moral, the full faced veil, where only an eye slit is left or with gauze covering even the eye slit, is actually the opposite, it is (gently) immoral. This is why, as set out below, it should be banned whether the woman herself wishes to wear it or her husband forces her to – either way it is immoral, because it is disrespectful to the rest of us.

There is the proposition by western liberals that men forcing women to dress in a certain way is men misusing their Power over women and that this is bullying and so is morally wrong – which it is, but that is a second matter, a second layer of immorality. I want to concentrate on the primary moral issue – the philosophical core of the full hiding of the face, even when a woman does so of her own free will, that usually doesn't get a mention.

To hide your face from other people is generally considered impolite in all human societies. Sometimes people do it by leaving their sunglasses on while they speak to you, others hide behind beards, but that's not as bad, because it doesn't hide them as much. It is even done when people hide behind the tinted glass of a car. When you drive a car you are in charge of a potentially lethal weapon, with which you interface with others. You can tint the glass in every room in your house if you wish, it is your private space, and is a threat to no one.

We like to, no we feel we must, see who we are dealing with, all attempts to disguise this, like youngsters hiding inside hooded coats, leads to a lack of trust. And it is upon Trust that human morality and indeed all human relationships are built, as a result of Ancient Group Loyalty.

We see in order to feel comfortable – in order to Trust. Our instinct is that those who hide themselves have something to hide, and thus we cannot trust them.

It has been this way since the formation of the first human groups, we must see our fellows. Trust is about openness, we must see so that we can trust, or at least have a basis for trust, after which we get to know people further. We continue to assess and re-assess, but based upon a revision and re-revision of our first impressions.

Hence those who hide, in whatever way, induce in us some nervousness, a withdrawal, a withholding of trust until we know them better – and if we never know them better then we never trust them. Impoliteness is a low level form of Disloyalty, the spurning of another, and it is so slight that we never legislate against it, we frown upon it, and try to discourage it in those around us and in our children, well we used to anyway.

Therefore in any country that is not 100% Moslem, those who hide their face beneath a full face veil are being impolite. The rest of the human race find it strange, we cannot help ourselves, because it is in direct contravention of our usual emphasis on openness and transparency equalling trust. All humans have developed this way for the last half million years, we trust those we can see, those we see are open with us. It's just that Moslems have got used to this masking amongst themselves, as a special religious exception.

This is an aspect of Islam that works badly in non-Moslem countries. It is counter-productive in a multiracial society, because it engenders a lack of trust, when the whole effort of multiculturalism is to build trust between different ethnic and religious groups.

DRUNKS

There is quite a contrast here with problems that occur in society due to the opposite mode of dress. Drunken young men are at risk of violence and even death, but the female equivalent has an extra layer of sexual risk.

Sex is roughly 1000 million years old, whereas morality is only 1 million or so at most. When a woman dresses in an explicit way, whether she means to or not, she is beckoning to 1000 million years of sexual evolution. She is gambling that 1 million years of moral evolution will control the baser parts of the sexual instincts of the men who see her, who talk to her, dance with her, spend time with her.

And remarkably it often does.

But it's always a gamble, and if she is drunk the gamble is bigger. If she is drunk alone it is bigger still. The woman who flaunts her wonderful body as she walks along a crowded Saturday night street has a right to do so (in that she is harming no one), according to the tenets of the Open Society, which is based directly upon the Contract made between our ancestors in those Ancient Groups of long ago. She is sometimes taking a risk though in a world of men with hormones.

She is beckoning to Sex while relying upon Morality to protect her. There are dangers in this, and when sometimes it fails to do so, courts are called upon to judge and people express their opinions, often based upon some variation of 'she was asking for trouble'.

13. Prostitution

To end this section of ancillary sexual matters we should take a brief look at prostitution, since it is a common and longstanding social issue in many societies. Prostitution is a contract, a contract for sex entered into by two people, and as such it is similar to other contracts we enter into, it is a sub-contract of the fundamental group Contract.

It is either a legitimate sub-contract or a skewed relationship forced on one partner by a more powerful partner, in which case it is a bullying relationship and therefore immoral. Every marriage contract includes within it, either implicitly or explicitly, that there will be sexual relations between the two partners. So much so that church marriages are annulled in the event of non-consummation.

Therefore it is not necessarily contracting for sex that is immoral, provided certain criteria are met. Firstly it should be a contract between two people from the same socio-economic group – which in practise it usually isn't. Secondly it should be a private contract – pimping and trafficking are bound to be immoral because pimps are bullies. Pimps are thus an additional layer of bullying-manipulation laid onto the relationship between the prostitute and the paying client.

Provided the above criteria are met then it cannot be immoral when a prostitute of either sex accepts money for sexual services rendered, it is a legitimate contract as long as both of the parties enter into it freely. It occurs to me that humans sometimes marry for money, and thus provide sexual services to an older wealthy spouse. Who is taking advantage of whom here I wonder? Well, despite that we may talk about them behind their backs, no one, as long as both enter into the arrangement freely.

The mini-contract of prostitution may be distasteful to some for a variety of reasons, but it is of the same stuff as every human contract – as long as it is not made under duress. One can ask though, is it ever freely entered into? Is it not always the case that poverty stricken women are in effect forced into the life, and then taken advantage of by wealthier male members of society?

Are these wealthier males really any different from the pimps who enslave and force women into such 'contracts'? When societies are so skewed that wealthy men can in effect coerce women from the underclass into 'contracts' they would not otherwise sign up to, it is a misuse of Power and thus a moral wrong. The moral wrong then is the skewed nature of the contract, not the principle of the sexual contract itself. The bullying-manipulative nature of any skewed 'terms of trade' is referred to again, but this time in an international context between groups, at the end of Chapter 21 and in Appendix 1.

There is thus no B/A-b moral objection to legalising prostitution because if the contract is free and fair it is not a moral wrong. Legalised prostitution would therefore not be immoral since it would have a better chance of reducing the abuses endemic in the illegal and therefore skewed nature of the trade. It would offer a safer environment for the women involved, and thus, in theory, help to make the contract more even and legitimate.

It seems probable that legalising prostitution would increase its usage, just as legalising outlets for alcohol has done, or legalising drug use would probably do. Therefore those who consider this to be a retrograde step are proffering a (possibly correct) Utilitarian argument, in that they consider it would be a mistake for society as a whole.

Every adult human in an adult sexual relationship has entered into a contract that includes sex; it is therefore illogical to frown on those who enter into the same, but much shorter lengths, of similar contracts.

Once again we are able to go back to first principles, get out our tin opener, open the tin and have a clearer look without the semi-hysteria that often clouds these subjects. Well then, with that thought it must be time to address the fascinating layer of complication called religion, divine command, or religious revelation. Actually we should not use the term religion, even though this is a complication that emanates from religion, because there are many more aspects to religion than claims of moral certainty. All we are specifically interested in here are the claims to moral wisdom of religion, the claim of divine commands sent to us allegedly, via the medium of religious revelation.

Do they have any validity, some validity or no validity whatsoever? If they have only some then how can we best express their limits? These revelations remember are often claimed (by zealots, not by all religious persons) to be precise and specific instructions written down in various books within different cultures during the last 3000 years or so.

I use the term 'complication' because this is not just an extra item that is thrown into the confusing dumping ground called morality, it is one of a series of over arching complications that occur as, during the passage of time, our small original human groups become giant societies.

14. The Law

Let's set ourselves down amongst an early human, or even a pre-human community of some description, and speculate regarding how the Basic Morality, the principle of B/A-b and the Disloyalty that lies behind it, might have started on the path towards becoming enshrined as the Law.

As we can see today amongst human hunter-gatherers, and our fellow primates, these ancient communities will have consisted of a number of families banded together under a leader, a male leader, the strongest the most resourceful, the Alpha Male. Not much different to their animal neighbours at this stage, but in order for such foragers to have ended up where they are now, at some time things must have begun to change.

Anthropologists call their leader the Big Man, to distinguish hunter-gatherer leaders from the Alpha Males of other species, for reasons we'll discuss later. Alongside this Big Man are the lesser leaders of each family, and from time to time the Big Man will probably have found himself approached by individuals who wish to air grievances against other members of the group.

He will perhaps have asked for reports, as judges still do today, on the behaviour of the individuals involved, on the record of both the one who says he has been bullied as well as what group gossip says about the one accused of bullying. It seems feasible that he will have asked his Council of elders, the Council of household heads, made up of other leading males and females with their ears to the ground, to report back to him. By this route, or something similar, human rights first appear within the Ancient Groups; a complaint of not fair, made against an alleged misuse of Power by one of the stronger ones within the Group, followed by a hearing, a judgement, and a penalty or resolution of some kind.

And next?

THE LAW
The Big Man and the Council find it simpler and more convenient if they make some general rules, guidelines for behaviour, but also to guide those petitioning the Council, complainers and complainants, plaintiffs and defendants, the bullied and those-accused-of-bullying, the loyal and those alleged-to-be-disloyal. They find this can nip many cases in the bud, because not only do these rules ease administration, but they also describe and prescribe the Rights and Wrongs of group life.

Thou shalt not kill ... your fellow group member.
Thou shalt not commit adultery ... with the spouse of a fellow group

member.
Thou shalt not steal … from a fellow group member.
Thou shalt not tell lies … about a fellow group member.
Thou shalt not rape … a fellow group member.
Thou shalt not torture … a fellow group member.
Just six commandments in these early days, the others will come later.

This is a great idea, it eases administration of the group. It seems a good thing, and I think it is, but it hardly matters what you or I think, because it is here to stay. Unjust, stupid and cumbersome as they often are, there have to be laws, there has to be the codified morality even though it can never hope to keep pace with the real morality, the dislike of injustice born in each of us. The codified morality is slow to react to those acts between group members that we deem 'not fair', it can never react with the speed of the parent to the scolded-comforted child. But we need the guidelines of the law, we need a framework within which to argue, 'my claim is fair, it is him or her that is being unfair'.

These feelings of Right and Wrong, Loyalty and Disloyalty as we have I hope already learned to call them, are the basis of all human morality, and we're stuck with it. Stuck with it even if one is sometimes forced to wonder whether or not the Power system (in which the strongest is almost always 'Right'), is not far more straightforward in operation than our constantly disputed and argued over confusion of claim and moral counter claim.

We can wonder as much as we like, it doesn't matter, doesn't matter a damn that Nietzche thinks our moral system is for weaklings and softies. Doesn't matter because his much vaunted superhuman is the bully, the *über-bully*, the dictator, the strongest of the strong. Of course we are opposed to your superman you clod, he is the dominating bully of bullies, he is that which morality sets its face against, he is its whole *raison d'etre* you numbskull.

Tough luck Friedrich, your 'superman' was on the run from the first day of the very first *ad hoc* council meeting, the meeting that agreed "you have been treated badly". And he will never reign unchallenged again, because we, the average, the silent majority – the whole damn human race apart from the would-be dictators and their henchmen – we hate to be oppressed. But this is a never ending battle, because inside each and every one of us, are the seeds of the bully, the desire to dominate, the desire to be the best, to have the best, food, clothes, house, money and mate. After all, one of the most certain ways to be free of repression by others, is to dominate those others before they dominate you – behold, the moral response of the fascist, the response of Machiavelli.

Here is the reason that our moral system, even at the outset in its early days, is so entangled compared to the much simpler Power system of many other animals. So often in any dispute it is difficult for even the neutral to decide who it is that is bullying whom, let alone for the protagonists. "He started it, he hit me first. Oh no it was her that did such and such, and that's what I'm protesting about, I'm the one who's being badly done to, I'm the one being wronged not her."

Despite all the difficulties though, and more yet to come, we still all agree about one thing, even when we can't quite decide who hit whom first, we agree that Disloyalty-bullying is always Wrong.

Recall the disputes you have witnessed in which you were neutral, how difficult it was to decide who 'started it'. Then pass on, to those disputes in which you were a protagonist, rather than an umpire; the difficulties sky rocket, now you are prejudiced, hence the law and the need for rules.

Nestle up to that; feel its presence, feel its influence over all your relationships with others. All others, every single one of them, from the most loved to the most disliked. There is a moral question to judge; some situation has arisen.

And how do we judge?

We ask ourselves: Who is Bullying Whom here?

Then, as if that weren't tricky enough, the Council unwittingly adds a further layer of complication.

MORALITY REDEFINED

What is it that the first Council of household heads actually does when it formulates those six commandments? It takes each of several individuals feelings as to what is fair and unfair, and pulls these together into a set of rules. The feelings of each individual about what is right and what is not right have been aggregated to achieve a consensus – thus are laws made.

If the whole thing had been done by referendum, with every group member taking part, pretty much the same laws would have been made, no problems on that score. After all these are hunter-gatherers, no one has any great wealth to protect; they all share the work of the group, and need its protection. So there is not much need yet for John Rawls' 'veil of ignorance' or similar intellectual devices.

No, the problem, the thing that will have gone completely unnoticed, especially to later generations of the group, is that morality has just been redefined. And at the same time the origins of human morality have been hidden from view.

Now morality has become the response of an individual to a set of rules, and this accidental obfuscation hides forever the true face of the moral order. Hides morality's real origin the response of an individual to acts of Disloyalty-bullying.

Even this early on, moral dilemmas, the problem of deciding who is bullying whom, have been suffused with an extra layer of complication. It wasn't easy before this first Council, but it was a straight choice, he just elbowed me out of the way, is he 'trying it on', and if he is shall I let him off with a warning or shall I hit back – hard?

Unknowingly the household heads, in pooling their shared common feelings to bring into being the first description of what constitutes specific acts of Disloyalty within the group, using everyday terms of group life, have produced what is soon taken to be an impartial moral standard. A standard whose existence comes to be seen as somehow separate from relationships between individuals.

The Council is the creator of a secondary morality, the codified morality of the law, but they and their ancestors come to think that they are the guardians of the only morality. The codified morality is the aggregate of our individual moral judgements. As we've seen it tries to judge whether the scolding parent is bullying the child it chastises, or if the child deserves it.

The primary morality is the underlying basis from which the codified morality springs. It is the emotional basis of morality, the basis of why we say this or that is Wrong, or that such and such, is not Right.

But from now on, whenever we mean to remind members of society not to bully other group members, we actually say don't lie, don't steal, don't kill, don't covert thy neighbour's spouse, we talk specifics, and we never again say DON'T BE DISLOYAL, don't bully – until now.

The Council (ideally) metes out justice, without prejudice, to individual bullies within their community, but their accidental elevation to font of wisdom status, is a step towards confusion. Set soon to become double confusion. Morality has gained its first codified foothold, and this foothold is itself the first formal framework of human society. Before this, pre-human society is little different from groups of other social animals, a constant jostling for position, a never ending battle for one-upmanship within the pack.

Now ... for the first time ever, there is a framework, a formal basis of do's and don'ts, and along with the advantages this structure brings, come certain disadvantages too. There are two immediate dangers.

Firstly that the Power given to the Council to make laws may result in it itself becoming a bully and a worse bully than any individual alone could ever be. This is the ongoing battle of who shall govern, the battle of dictatorship versus democracy, nowadays in institutional form. Will the commandments be used for the benefit and protection of all, or will they be twisted by an aristocracy, by a ruling caste, to bully a whole group and later a whole country?

Despite the battles we have had, and the many we still have, to control the bully of bullies, the dictators and their henchmen, this is a relatively obvious danger compared to the subtlety of the second.

Secondly it sets the scene for a takeover, in which the laws and edicts of the Council become the source of all morality.

This happens despite the clumsiness of their generalities; despite what a cumbersome ass the law is, despite the fact that they see only results never motives. This subtle change occurs because we, the individuals from whose brains morality really comes, in large part agree with the rules of the household heads. As generalities they sum up pretty much what we ourselves feel to be moral behaviour. Of course they do, that was their original purpose – a summary.

Now instead these same generalities have become the sole and only definition of Right and Wrong. Little wonder that later on we become puzzled and confused by the increasing subtleties and complexities of human moral questions. This confusion happens because the underlying principle has been lost to view.

Wait though, wait, the worst aspect of this is yet to come.

Complicated as things already are, later still the Council takes one last step, a step that makes the laws far more than any aggregated opinion, a step that makes the laws irrevocable, laws now cast in tablets of stone.

15. Divine Command – Medicine Man

On the Council sits the Medicine Man, soon to become the prophet, the high priest, then later the theologian, and who now adds a metaphysical explanation of where the new laws have 'really' come from. And the laws become God's laws, unalterable, sacrosanct, fixed for all time.

And the penalty for transgression?
The ultimate penalty of course – eternal damnation.
Ye shall have no other Gods before me.
Ye shall not make for yourself a graven image, for I am a jealous God.
Ye shall not take the name of the Lord your God in vain.
Remember the Sabbath day, keep it holy.

These four commandments arise as a result of metaphysical speculation followed by religious ideas and thoughts about that-which-is-beyond the everyday physical world. And therefore inevitably, the 'explanation' of these thoughts, also invokes the visualisation of entities that themselves lie beyond the physical surface of things. Furthermore, though they are quoted here in second place, in fact in the Bible, even in the order of the commandments, these come before the moral instructions.

Yet we can see, via the historical actions and interactions I have been describing, and in the social lives of our primate cousins, chimps, bonobos and even monkeys, alive and living next to us today, how the opposite is true; morality precedes metaphysics. It is Morality that walks first upon the surface of this planet, and Metaphysics-religion that appears later. Thus also Morality appeared on this earth before the metaphysical concept God, not vice versa. *(Yet despite this, the arrival of religion amongst us obscures the origins of Morality.)*

Before God and no more, we are not saying that God only comes into existence along with the human mind, along with the increasing size of the human brain – though granted an atheist might say that. What we are saying is only that no creature before us can conceive of the idea God. And so prior to this cannot have any possible hope of communication with, or recognition of, such a thing. All creatures other than *Home sapiens* have no concept of, or concern about Totality, and they are thus what one might call incommunicado as regards receiving messages from God. Clearly this line of reasoning is irrespective of whether or not there is a God to send such messages.

They see only daily life. They never speculate about what lies beyond. So let's keep in mind that the existence of God is not the question before us. We shall leave that argument to the atheists – to those who believe in that other view of Totality. The Buddha wastes no time in arguing about the existence or otherwise of God, and we shall take our lead from him.

Only the time in history, the point at which no living creature had developed a brain that could be aware of the concept 'God' is at issue here, since until this time no one could be capable of receiving a message from God.

At this time it seems reasonable to say that pre-humans and early humans, in not yet grappling with Metaphysics, have not yet produced the first religion. At a glance this might (again) seem an irreligious thing to say, a statement prejudiced in favour of the atheists. It isn't, because I did not say 'produced God', I said produced their own particular vision, their own distinctive image of God/Totality. And as we can see in the multi-cultural society around us, there are many different ways of doing this.

So in effect the no-group-member-shall-be-Disloyal to the others in the group issue exists, but God 'does not', in so much as due to the size of our brains, we are still at this point in time … incommunicado.

In such circumstances Metaphysics-religion cannot possibly define Morality, since Morality must have arrived amongst pre-humans long before Metaphysics, Morality must in fact be thousands, maybe even a half million years older, than Metaphysics-religion can possibly be.

One must admit though that the actual physical evidence for the timing of the appearance of either Morality or Metaphysics amongst our ancestors is thin, on both counts.

METAPHYSICS APPEARS

There is a general scientific view (contested by some), that the single most potent piece of evidence for the first arrival of Metaphysics-religion is the ritual burial of their dead by humans from about 60,000 to 80,000 years ago onwards.

Assuming that the early evidence of such behaviour might have been missed and also that the idea comes before the action, in other words various ideas of God, Totality and worship thereof circulate for awhile before they coalesce into a formal ritual. Then 100,000 years ago seems a reasonable estimate in round figures for the first glimpse of the phenomenon known to us as Metaphysics-religion.

This suggests that 100,000 years ago Metaphysics starts to appear amongst us, and this is followed by the formal rituals of the first long forgotten religions. Our enlarged brain has begun to speculate about whatever it is that lies hidden beyond the everyday world. There must be something, something behind all this, but what?

And whatever this something is, how does it effect me?

What does my life mean?

Religions can be thought of as the first hypotheses about what might underlie the everyday things that happen (good, bad and neutral) in the world-as-we-see-it. Each individual religion is a meta-system, a theory of what lies beyond, what lies behind the problems we come up against, what causes the difficulties we suffer in our daily struggle to survive and flourish. It is an effort to predict and if possible to avoid some or all of that suffering.

The brain of a chimpanzee is 600 to 750cc (cubic centimetres), whereas the brain of a human is generally about 1450cc, twice as big, and not just different in size, but different in shape as well, different in the emphasis of its development. Along with all the advantages of a bigger specialised brain comes one problem in particular.

The brain that is big enough to conceive of a concept such as Totality is big enough to be frightened and confused by this vast world from the moment it realises that it is only a tiny insignificant part of it. Thus for the atheist this brain, 100,000 years ago, comes up with the concept God, to reassure it. While for the theist, God can contact us directly for the first time once our brain is big enough to receive a message.

LOYALTY

Compare this to the indicators we have for the length of time Loyalty has been around.

Loyalty to the pack must be very old to be present in wolves and in dolphins as well as monkeys, humans and chimpanzees (de Waal, 1982). These species all have groups, the individual members of which seem to have rudimentary relationships to each other, based upon bonds of Loyalty. How long ago must this phenomenon have started, for it to be present in elephants and whales as well as in chimps and monkeys? There is no doubt that Loyalty-to-the-pack is older than Metaphysics-religion, because the various common ancestors shared by these creatures lived hundreds of millions of years ago, not a paltry 100,000 or thereabouts.

SPEECH

Is speech an indicator? Can one moralise successfully without speech?

To moralise one has to point out specific instances of bad behaviour, discuss them, gossip with others and compare notes regarding what shirking they have noticed too. What reticence in the sharing of work, what laziness or selfishness did others see on the last hunt, and how did it compare to previous conduct? What is the Duty-history as it were of the individual currently under scrutiny. One must come to a consensus and then organise the reprimanding of offenders.

The expert's various estimates of how old speech is vary from 150,000 years old to as much as 1 million or maybe as much as 2 million years old. A large range, no specific dates for us there. I suppose in part this is because there is so little evidence to work with, no pristine vocal chords left neatly fossilised for us? Either way though, longer ago than 100,000 years it would seem (Dawkins, 2005).

Speech and time, time to discuss, time surely is also paramount?

FIRE

Did we sit for lengths of time in groups, in group discussions, before we had fire? Time, night after night around the campfire, fire gives time for increased social possibilities, time to talk in private, the privacy of night.

Have I not been wronged?

Brother am I not entitled to redress?

Speak brother speak!

Sister cast your vote!

Human control of fire is something that has left traces, thin layers of ash, and based on this evidence is thought to be between 500,000 to 750,000 years old, or maybe longer according to some (ibid. 2005). It's tenuous of course; we're trying to look back into the darkness of our beginnings, and utilising secondary factors to help us do so. We are looking back, so far back, back before *Homo sapiens,* back to *Homo erectus, Homo heidelbergensis* or *Homo ergaster* our predecessors.

TRADE

As we have discussed, at the start of Chapter 3, it seems unlikely that a creature without a sense of what is fair and what is unfair could possibly trade with others. From stone and bone artefacts found in one area that can only have been produced from materials found in another, sometimes hundreds of miles away, trade is reckoned to be up to 1 million years old (Ridley, 1997). A pattern of exchange develops, regular meetings and maybe discussions, about ... reputations, about who is fair and who is unfair in his dealings, in his or her relationships, with others. Thus trade at a half to a million years old is likely to be much older than Metaphysics-religion.

Is it reasonable to guess that primitive Morality, but something we would recognise if we could see it, is half a million years old? For now, to get us started after such a brief look, let's take Morality as being maybe a half million, about 500,000 years old, certainly at least 250,000 as a working hypothesis.

Suffice to say that no human appears to have been concerned with God prior to 60,000 to 70,000 years ago, and none of the religions we are familiar with today are older than 3,000 to 5,000 years at most. Whereas the history of Morality appears to date back at least 500,000 years, thus Metaphysics-religion did not give birth to Morality.

No, Morality arrived on this earth long before Metaphysics. Morality is likely to be about half a million years older than Metaphysics-religion can possibly be. And so I put it to you that the origin of human Morality is based upon something else entirely, is based upon the simple principle thou shalt not bully. Itself derived from thou shalt not be Disloyal, and it is this, not Metaphysics-religion, that is the bedrock of that which we humans call Morality.

Slowly along with the changes and increases in our brain size and development came Morality, followed later by Metaphysics-religion. The modern sciences of archaeology, anthropology and evolutionary biology suggest that this was the way round it was, not Metaphysics-religion first with Morality following.

Morality – 250,000 to 500,000 years, or maybe longer ago.

Metaphysical-religious concepts – from perhaps as much as 100,000 years ago, followed by the first human religions, long since disappeared, leaving no written records. Then the earliest still extant mass religions with written histories following them:

Hinduism and Judaism – 3 to 5,000 years ago.

Buddhism – 2,600 years ago.

Confucianism – 2,400 years ago.

Christianity – 2,000 years ago.

Islam – 1,400 years ago.

On this basis, amongst other reasons, it seems to me that we are expecting too much of our various religions when we ask them to define Morality, and we should stop this overreaching expectation forthwith. It is surely lunacy to ask a 2,000 year old entity to re-define a 500,000 year old one? Instead we should leave religion to do what it is capable of doing quite well, the job of encouraging us to be more just, encouraging us to be more fair in our dealings with others and more forgiving too.

All of which is why we can say that it is the job of Loyalty/Disloyalty to DEFINE its progeny Morality. The job of religion, one of its functions anyway, is to ENCOURAGE us to behave morally. Morality is a Contract between humans living together in groups, and if you are a believer in God then God encourages us to obey the Contract.

16. Divine Command – Metaphysics

As the human brain continues to increase in size it asks – how does the sun rise and set? Why do the seasons change the way they do? Asks for the first time certain different kinds of questions – where do our family and friends go to when they die? Where will I go? Will I join them? What does my life Mean? This last is the question of our place in Totality. The question that only humans ponder is thus first asked. Some way back we took a turn down a different road – called Morality. Later, as is the way with evolution, our still enlarging brain took another turn off this road – a turn we later come to call Metaphysics, speculation about 'what lies beyond' the physical surface of things.

Metaphysics is the seed of every human religion, the attempt to answer: What does my life mean? What will happen when I die? Are those who were so close to me but have now died gone forever? Or will I see them again? We say to our dying parent, sibling, lover or comrade-in-arms, any one of those friends close to us for many years in our battle through life.

We'll meet again you and I, what times we will have, what a meeting and a catching up there will be. Oh how we'll laugh, oh how we'll pound each other's backs over everything we've shared all those stupidities, and all those fine things we've done together. What coups we pulled off.

What a catching up there will be, of all that's happened since last we were together, oh the fun we'll have, what times await us down the road ahead, we'll be together again you and I, what times await us down the road in paradise."

This seems to me to be the biggest and most important of the various functions of religion, to turn a dark, cold and pitiless universe into a warm comforting and comfortable friend. What a marvellous trick it pulls off, what genius, how lovely, oh let's talk about it some more.

Metaphysics is good.
Every human hope, and every youthful dream, of a life of adventure, exploration, of a life of religious meditation, or of scientific discovery, is part of our own personal metaphysical-religious system. All the ideas in our heads, along with the beliefs our parents and community have imparted to us, plus the ones we've gone out and found for ourselves, all these are metaphysics.

All these are wonderful, marvellous life affirming metaphysics. The religion we choose (or none) to build for ourselves, from the materials to hand, is a personal view of our place, and the place of human life, within Totality. Every idea, before it becomes reality, every theory before it is proved by empirical observation in the real world, each hypothesis as yet unproven by science, all these are Metaphysics.

METAPHYSICS is the sixth of the six great strands of human life.
Metaphysics is good because it is part of our inner inspiration.
Metaphysics is good because it is the way many of us relate to the vast empty Universe beyond ourselves.
Metaphysics is good because it keeps us going when all else fails.
Metaphysics is good because...

Metaphysics is good, but let me tell you of the illusion that the priest, the monk, the brahmin, the mullah, the imam, the shaman carries with him all of his life. He thinks he is part of one single entity, a mass religion, and a religion he shares with others. He is not.

Clearly there are communal religions. Religious frameworks common to members of a particular society, but each one of us has behind this surface communality a private religion, a personal way of communicating with God, with the Totality beyond ourselves.

It is this unseen personal religion that is the basis of belief, and it is this that provides the hidden foundation upon which all communal religions are built. How could it be otherwise? Religions are built upon belief. Or faith is the other word often used, though you won't catch me using that, I dislike its sanctimonious overtones.

Where is this belief? It can exist nowhere other than inside the heads of the adherents of each religion, it is firstly a personal experience, and only secondly a shared experience. When you think about it, where else could it be? Where else could belief exist? Except inside individual heads?

You don't agree with me?

Show me the person with whom you agree about everything.

Show me the religious or social organisation of any kind that has not split and split, and split again, and again and again, into schism after schism, sect after sect.

Show me a mass religion, and I will show you a mass of rituals, rites, mores and laws by which human beings live, laws they use to produce certain modes of concerted action, but none of those million upon millions of individual beings actually believe in the exact same way.

Raise up an issue, and you will see disagreement, debate and dispute, I will show you individual after individual, not cattle or sheep, ants or bees, but human individuality. Are you the same as the person next to you? Do all your thoughts and opinions exactly coincide? Do you agree with every word that your favourite priest, poet, pundit, pope, politician, guru, rabbi, writer or imam says?

Of course not.

Ideas and hypotheses, we humans live by them, we cannot BE without them, we cannot be sane, we cannot be happy individuals.

We need Metaphysics just as much as we need justice and Morality.

Just as much as we need to 'do the Right thing'.

How did the world's religions get the idea that we can't pick and choose the parts we believe in and the parts we don't. Why would we put all our eggs in one basket? At their behest? When in fact there are some good things in one religion but different good things in another?

Every single one of them should be referred to the Monopolies Commission.

Metaphysics is the 'moment' of asking-about-meaning, the moment that comes just before Metaphysics-religion and the many varieties and different religions that follow. These are the many religions that vary with our differing circumstances, influences, cultures and backgrounds, before which comes the 'moment' when all religions are the same.

Ra is the Sun God, but rainfall is the Male God fertilising the earth from which things grow, the Mother God. When do we feel good, in harmony, when are our bellies full and happy times, surely it is when we live lives that are in harmony with those-who-decree-all-this – the Gods. This then is our purpose this then is the meaning of our lives.

To hold the Gods in reverence, to worship them in harmony, they give us all we have, they give in times of plenty or they take away in times of famine. This must be the Right way to live; to offend against this is surely Wrong?

Just as whoever is stealing from the seed store does Wrong – wrong.

By stealing what the Gods have given, he offends the code; he breaks the pact, worships the devil – he does moral wrong.

At the moment of the birth of questions about meaning (questions about what underlies the reality we see around us) at this moment, the moment of the birth of Metaphysics-religion upon the surface of this little planet, instantaneously ... Morality becomes subsumed within it. The roots of Morality are lost, they vanish from sight, and in a flash the child becomes the parent.

The predecessor is henceforth unseen, hidden for thousands of years of unrecorded human history. Hidden by the successor masquerading as the predecessor.

I know, I know, this sounds like religion bashing again, but as I hope you can see I am not one of those who has it in for religion, I believe in the importance of religion to many of us, maybe more of us than we realise. All I am asking of the ultra-religious, and of the mass religionists too, is that they should be a little less arrogant. Your religion, whatever it is, 1400 years old, 2000 or 3000 years, cannot reasonably be expected to define the 500,000 year old phenomenon we humans call Morality.

Why is it that religions in their different ways all talk about Morality, and do so in broadly similar terms? Because Morality pre-dates them all, and if this is the case it is a healthy, sensible and wise task to separate out Morality from religion, so that it becomes a common meeting place for us all.

Let's be careful with words, they are important, definitions are important. Metaphysics is in part a sort of question and answer routine that comes immediately before the birth of a religion, or for that matter before a new scientific hypothesis, and goes on as micro-metaphysics inside each of us for all our lives. Each person's Metaphysics is like a shelving system inside one human head, a system that is used to order our mental scheme of things, our vision of what the world outside means.

Atheism is Metaphysics, because it is a belief system.

The real atheists are our cousins the chimpanzee, and the other animals, because they have no interest in, cognisance of, or any questions about Totality. Whereas our human so-called atheists are as interested in and as fascinated by Totality as the rest of us.

Agnosticism is Metaphysics – Buddhists are agnostics.

Islam is Metaphysics, Hinduism is, Christianity is, Judaism is, but these are just the famous ones on which the world's great Religions are built.

Unfortunately, nonsense like the 'Domino Principle' is Metaphysics too.

Remember that one?

A real beauty...

'If just one South or Central American country goes Communist then all the countries of Central and South America will follow, falling over like a stack of lined up dominoes'.

That was a crackpot Metaphysics of the CIA amongst others.

It was a belief system.

A part of the larger right wing US Metaphysics that said, 'no matter how oppressive the bullying dictatorship is, as long as it professes a hatred of Marxism, another Metaphysics, we'll support it'.

Since the Metaphysical goal x is vital for the good of the state, then y has to be carried out no matter how painful it is, to ensure the good result called x. Where x is Nazi racial purity then y is the extermination of the Jews. Or where x is the eradication of communism throughout the world, then y is the large-scale murder by right wing militias of poverty-stricken peasants who are trying to claim their human rights via communism.

The Domino Principle was a belief so strong that it produced a 'foreign policy' based upon Metaphysics, and not upon Morality. Which is insane, since it is Morality that lies at the heart of all human social relationships, whereas Metaphysics exists only in the heads of individuals, exists as an inspiration for their lives, as individuals.

Let's keep it there, where it does so much good, let's not turn it loose to rule countries, societies, tribes, or even little families. It's not fit to rule Mum, Dad and a couple of kids, it's not fit to be let out on its own.

It's great inside our heads.

We humans live by Metaphysics. By our beliefs, our hopes, dreams and theories that make us willing to sally forth, to try and try again, again, and again, in the face of incredible odds. Belief, which includes the placebo effect, that makes us able to battle on with indefatigable fortitude, with never say die spirit, remaining positive when no reason to stay positive remains. Somehow staying positive even when we're in the grip of an illness as brutal as cancer.

Hope – Metaphysics is the great guardian of hope, without which our lives become pale husks, transparent, weak, depressing nothings. Without which we cease to strive, without which many of us give up.

Metaphysics-religion: wonderful, life enhancing, inspirational, optimistic, positive life affirming Metaphysics – the thief, the usurper of Morality.

17. Blasphemy and Belief

Thus the greatest service religion does for us is to strengthen and assist our innate ability to 'believe', and with belief on our side we seem to be able to move mountains. No matter how meagre our talents, no matter how lacking in courage or energy we can find extra courage, extra energy just by believing, by sharing in the gift of belief.

Hopeless at everything?

Don't give it a second thought, belief will pull you through. Simply find something to believe in, and kiss the thought of failure goodbye. Only one thing though, whenever your beliefs clash with reality or morality, it is beliefs that have to give way.

Say someone criticises our opinions and an argument ensues, during which evidence is brought forth by both sides and points are made and disputed. We may become angry with the sheer stupidity of the other person, but each of us has the Right to express our opinion – this is free speech.

LIBEL AND SLANDER ARE IMMORAL

If the disagreement degenerates into personal insults and accusations that are false and that are unsubstantiated by facts, we are in the land of libel and slander. And these are legitimate and important limits on freedom of speech. Slander (spoken) and libel (written) occur when one member of the group publicly besmirches the character of a fellow member and is unable to produce evidence, including any witnesses, to prove that the something said is true.

We know and understand what slander and libel are, we see enough cases ending up in court and then being covered in the newspapers. It's clear enough that telling public lies about someone has to be a limit on freedom of speech. Such lies result in a slur on our reputation amongst our group, they are therefore an example of Disloyalty because other group members are manipulated into unjustifiably viewing us in a bad light.

As with the rest of morality, the concept has long since passed over from within-groups to apply also between individuals in different groups, but not to the dead. You can't slander the dead, even though it must often be very painful for their close relatives to listen to dubious claims written or spoken about the recently dead, as 'revisionist historians' have a habit of doing.

It is an interesting question to ask why, if such historians are not able to justify their criticisms with facts, should certain categories of close relative, children, parents, siblings and spouses of the deceased not have the right to sue?

Is this still not libel or slander?

Lies which cause suffering to other group members?

Maybe just parents and spouse would be best, and leave it at that? We don't want people's kids, who weren't around at the time of whatever it is their parent is now accused of, defending the family honour and dragging the thing on for another generation.

One can see of course that death is a neat legal full stop. But forgetting legal conveniences and speaking philosophically?

Hold onto that for a moment as we take a look at an allied issue.

BLASPHEMY

Blasphemy is defined as being disrespectful towards God or towards holy and sacred things. Therefore blasphemy cannot be immoral. Blasphemy as it is defined above in law is not immoral because it is not an act of either Disloyalty to, or the bullying/bullying-manipulation of, a fellow group member.

Yet one wonders can it be Right to allow Jesus, Mohammed, Confucius or the Buddha to be gratuitously insulted? Even though they are dead? Note please JC, Buddha or Mohammed, not God, and not holy and sacred things. Can it be Right that pygmies not fit to wash their feet are allowed to get away with insulting without evidence these special people, these Saints who founded great world religions?

After all even though they are now dead, in a sense they are always with us. I ask myself can it be Right to Libel-a-Prophet or Slander-a-Saint? And is it not this that has an element of immorality about it, and yes isn't this why we sometimes feel sympathy for the protests of fervent mass religionists, even when we don't share their fervour?

Don't we all despise slander?

Isn't it the Slander-of-a-Saint rather than the strange outmoded concept of blasphemy that disgusts us? To the secular Open Society the concept of blasphemy is ridiculous, utterly ludicrous because blasphemy is a command driven 'wrong', it is based upon blind obedience, and the Open Society doesn't do blind obedience.

That is what it is set up specifically to combat, the blind obedience demanded by all sorts, shapes and sizes of special cases, special rulers, kings queens, emperors and empresses, tin pot dictators, semi-gods and demi-gods. The Open Society is designed to combat and question all those who claim obedience, claim blind obedience because they 'know best'.

It doesn't do blind obedience because not doing it is precisely how a balance of power is maintained in society, that is how tyrants are controlled. Not doing blind obedience is democracy, not doing blind obedience is freedom, not doing blind obedience is morality.

Morality standing upright on its own two legs.

Morality shouting out, loud and proud, for its Rights.

Shouting for the Right not to be bullied by the Alpha Male, even when he comes shrouded in clerical garb.

In the secular Open Society all accusations of blasphemy are always going to be met with laughter. Not insulting laughter, but genuinely bemused uncomprehending laughter, because those who shout blasphemy have missed the whole point. Blasphemy is about insulting authority, but the primary definition of the Open Society is that it doesn't accept 'authority'.

Just as thousands upon thousands of years ago the first human groups declined to accept the up to then unquestioned authority of the Alpha Male. And as we shall see soon in Part 3, they demoted him to the status of Big Man.

I don't accept 'Authority', do you?

It is the policeman, politician, priest, lawyer or lowly army corporal given too much Power. And in their hands and in the hands of oh so many like them 'authority' becomes the mother and father of all bullies.

Not me, no thanks, I'm free of that and I'm staying that way.

I'm free because my ancestors, and yours, fought for our freedom, and I won't be giving it up. I won't be insulting my own dead by pissing away that which they sacrificed themselves for, that which some of them died for, no not me, not today, not any day.

The concept of blasphemy has become meaningless ever since society became secular (based upon Disloyalty and B/A-b morality), and also became composed of many religions rather than one. But we can see how there is still a case to answer – the case of the Slander-of-a-Saint.

THE SLANDER-OF-A-SAINT

Certain books, films or plays ridicule and poke fun at religion, but in doing so make a valid point of criticism, and that's fine, keep it up. Others are just a series of gratuitous insults, Jesus in a huge demeaning nappy for no apparent reason other than shock value – not so fine.

Jesus portrayed as a homosexual based upon no offered evidence, or said to have fathered an illegitimate child with Mary Magdalene, in the latter case with evidence that would be laughed out of either a court or a science lab – even less fine.

If someone walks down the street with a banner proclaiming that Mohammed was a toy boy. Or that Jesus had a bastard child with Mary Magdalene, or Moses and the Buddha were paedophiles, Guru Nanak a pederast, and Confucius a thief and a liar, they have insulted a human being once living but now dead. And the close adherents of that Saint accuse them of blasphemy, which is utterly meaningless to most of us, but what if instead they were to be accused of slander or libel?

We have to be careful, we are trying to balance freedom of speech against the use of gratuitous insults used controversially to boost the circulation or sales of some second rate production by a third rate artist or impresario.

It is a well known fact that the dead don't sue.

A fact dear to those selfish small minded little minnows whose only aim is to create a furore, a brief sensation in order to get bums on seats, or gain the kudos of a little public notoriety. Even though I understand the legal difficulties and dangers, should we not protect the names of those special few who founded the world's major religions and have millions of adherents still today, who in a way are always with us?

It's tricky, I admit, but I'm pretty sure we should. The law should be revised and they should stand accused of the Slander-of-a-Saint. At least this would be legally clear and meaningful.

Certain of the dead only: Moses, the Buddha, Jesus, Mohammed, Guru Nanak and Confucius. Those special cases who founded world religions, not the founder of every tin pot sect and schism, and not those religions whose origins are so clouded in mystery that they have no unique founder. These have to be real people, not vague Hindu figures or mystical entities like Lao-Tzu the founder of Taoism.

To be philosophically consistent and to be moral, we ought to introduce such a law, and kick the meaningless concept of blasphemy into touch.

18. Left and Right

A young boy of 15 comes out from the big city slums one night with a couple of older men, to break into a house out beyond the edge of town. A wealthy country house, where he gets himself shot and killed by the householder.

Some of us side with the owner against the boy, who wouldn't have been shot if he hadn't gone stealing. And some of us side with the 15 year old lad who never got a chance in life, shot by a privileged fat cat. Shot by a member of the upper caste, with his big house, his cars, his wealth, his dogs and his guns.

The forgiving-left wing side with the boy and the rough-justice-right take the side of the homeowner, but all of us, left wing right wing and those in between, make our decision based upon whom we see as the bully and whom we see as the bullied. It is then that the left and right call those of us in the middle indecisive. They maybe call us pusillanimous vacillating cream puffs, and we return the compliment by calling them bigots.

Morality and also matters that are not morality, but are issues so close to it that concerned people with strong opinions often claim the title of morality for their point of view, generate the oft used terms left and right wing. Sometimes these views are prejudices, but sometimes they are legitimate moral views based upon a genuine weighing in the balance of who is the bully in a given situation.

For instance if the 15 year old has been bullied by his two older accomplices into helping them break in, and the victim is a greedy slum landlord, then those of us in the middle will be inclined to go with the left on this one. Thus those who instead continue to persist with the right wing line seem likely to be bigots.

On the other hand if the lad is a vicious little thug with a string of violent offences to his name, and the houseowner and others in the area are virtually under siege from inner city criminal gangs, we vacillating cream puffs will favour the right wing. These are over-simplifications, and we will pay more lengthy and appropriate attention to this aspect of morality in Part 4, for now though they serve as an introduction to remind ourselves that left and right wing views are not always prejudices. Instead they can be a useful distinction when in various situations we try to figure out who is really bullying whom.

Getting back to that 15 year old, we tend to judge less harshly those we consider have been bullied themselves when they treat us roughly. We are more inclined to forgive those we think have 'never had a chance in life' due to their social circumstances.

So henceforth in our discussions forgiving-left will mean inclined to forgive many times, even though this is not a universal left wing political trait. Whereas rough-justice-right will mean inclined towards fairly quick retribution, an eye for an eye. These labels will do for now to describe those who lean one way and those who lean the other when judging who is bullying whom, within large societies.

In reality there are bigots on both sides, extremists who don't try to judge at all, they just espouse left or right wing dogma as the only solution for whatever situation is under discussion and judgement. These are extremists, and we can continue to use the terms left and right for them, adding the term bigot or extremist when their unthinking diatribes seem to demand it.

Politically of course the left are in favour of rule by the many, whereas the right favour rule by the few, rule by 'the best'. This is sometimes the especially intelligent few, or in Plato's Republic the wise, or elsewhere it has been the bravest and strongest, Nietzsche's superman embodied by Napoleon – always the most talented in some way. In the Capitalist era, their talent is likely to be the best at making money, but most often and in all eras the few who rule have a tendency to be, or to also be, the Army.

It is now well known that in huge modern societies rule by the many in the form of Marxism and Communism, even though these purport to be on behalf of the many, in practise becomes rule by the few. The elite of the Party takes over, so political labels only go so far. Nonetheless it is still fair to say that the left are for the many and the sharing of group wealth, no matter how big the group has become, whereas the right are for the few they consider to be outstanding in some way. These are the Alpha Male and Female and their cohorts.

The left wing think that any form of elite, no matter what talent it is based upon, are or soon become selfish and greedy. One might say that they consider any such elite as a betrayal of the group ethos, all are equal but some are more equal than others. One might say they consider that the formation of any such elite is an act of Disloyalty to the rest of the group, an act that results in the bullying of the rest of us.

The right wing on the other hand think that the cream, not the scum, rises to the top and that those who work hard deserve to 'get ahead', by which they mean in part financially. They don't see why lazy feckless nonentities should be allowed to be leeches on the backs of the hard working go-getters of the group. One might say that they consider this to be a betrayal of the group ethos by inadequate wastrels who fail to contribute properly, or even attempt to contribute at all to the group, who fail to perform their duty to the group. One might say that they consider such behaviour to be Disloyal to the group, that in effect these useless freeloaders are manipulating and bullying the rest of us.

These two opposing viewpoints are both morally valid, because they are opinions regarding who in the group is Disloyally manipulating other group members. And since these opinions are also based upon evidence of human behaviour, in effect of how large societies work, or don't work, these opinions are not bigoted prejudices.

On this analysis left and right represent viewpoints that set themselves against either the risk of dominant bullying Alpha Males and their lieutenants on the one hand, or of bullying-manipulative freeloaders on the other.

As a result of the above the right have a tendency, only a tendency, to be less forgiving and primarily concerned with people getting 'their just deserts'. Whereas the left tend to be more forgiving, blaming people's failings on the stratification of society that dump some of the group in an underclass, into a lower caste, from birth. Or at least this is true as an overview, which is what we are looking to establish here, though it varies in detail between individuals.

And we are all found somewhere along this spectrum are we not? Except perhaps that those of us who occupy the middle ground are sometimes more left and other times more right wing, as opposed to the rabid right or the loony left who are always at the extremes on pretty much everything. Thus we humans are sometimes of the forgiving-left, but other times side with the rough-justice-right. And this is a moral spectrum is it not? Based upon who we think is Disloyal, who we think is bullying whom and thus who we think is most Disloyal and therefore most despicable within the group?

Have you noticed how every social entity has its right and its left wings, its conservatives and its radicals? How every government, company, religion, social club, how every group of humans has its hawks and its doves? We humans feel very strongly about 'who deserves what' and who doesn't deserve what others want to give them, so strongly that these feelings cut across all our gatherings. A group such as the Church of England for example has members who are pro-gay people and gay clergy and others who are anti-gays or anti-gay clergy, its left wing and its right wing opinions.

In the Anglican church we can see in this struggle that there are right wing and left wing views even inside religious bodies. In the cases of gay rights and the appointment of women bishops we can use the term right wing bigots, because there is no B/A-b basis or logic to these right wing opinions, which are therefore prejudices. We will see as we proceed in later chapters that this is not always the case with all right wing views, some of them have B/A-b logic on their side, and in these cases it is the left who are the bigoted extremists.

This in itself is another little illustration that morality is something separate from religion. Within Islam, Judaism or Hinduism there are liberals and conservatives too, modernists and traditionalists, left wingers and right wingers under other names. Morality is about something other than your religion.

The rough-justice-right often favour 'a short sharp shock' as a means of punishment and reorientation, whereas the forgiving-left tend towards 'the talking cure' as a mechanism to run alongside or sometimes replace incarceration and thus rehabilitation. With some people one approach may be best and with other offenders the other, which is where those of us not committed to either extreme hover.

These well used labels then are also moral tendencies, in which the left tends to be liberal/modernist and the right conservative or traditionalists. Left and right are vague terms, but they will be of some use in what still lies ahead. For example...

VIOLENT DRUNKS
Many Western European societies are now in a situation where drunken young people take possession of town centres and streets on weekend nights and quite often at other times. It is clear that this drunken behaviour is at the least a nuisance and is often unpleasant and intimidating. Aggression or intimidation is by definition bullying behaviour. And according to the principles of the Open Society it is therefore immoral behaviour.

Why do Western societies allow drunken people to wander about the streets being aggressive and abusive to other members of society? Why do they/we seem almost to think that they have a Right to do this? Is this a mistaken belief in giving people their freedom? Or is it the fear of being labelled illiberal, or a killjoy?

It might be the latter, the left wing liberals amongst us tend to be afraid of being so labelled.

One has the Right to have a drink in a public place and even to get drunk, as long as you then go home without intimidating anyone. As soon as you start to give grief to others you have violated the single principle on which the Open Society is based, because such drunken behaviour is in violation of B/A-b morality.

It is bullying behaviour. It is equally clear that being arrested and facing minor fines has no discernible effect upon their behaviour. Some Islamic countries go to the opposite extreme, and public displays of drunkenness can result in public lashings. It is clear enough that this is a right wing approach, irrespective of whether it is derived from the Koran or anywhere else, because the response of a lashing seems to many of us to be out of proportion to the offence of being drunk in public.

In effect Islamic societies, which prohibit public drunken behaviour, are in agreement with the Open Society and with B/A-b morality when the drunks are being aggressive towards others. We can also see that this is an example of a legitimate right wing view, since it is based on an opinion of who is bullying whom.

At present the left wing view representing libertarianism has the floor in the West. But when one sees the spoiled, pathetic and petulant way a proportion of young drunks behave, including towards the police, giving some of them a 'short sharp shock' seems like a reasonable enough idea. Especially since the Open Society has become lax in applying its own rules, and has thus allowed the current situation to arise. Maybe we didn't think people would behave so badly?

The legitimate rough-justice-right wing view on this particular issue is that the Open Society should live by its principles and not do as it does at present, pay woolly minded lip service to its own values. We could not class this as bigotry, because it is a reasoned response, to a violation of B/A-b morality, a violation of the Basic Morality that is the central principle behind every human society on this earth.

No wonder extreme left and right wingers spend so much of their lives angry and frustrated. In their different ways they are trying to apply emotional responses bred into us half a million years ago, when we lived in small groups of 50 to 100 at most, to today's mega-societies. The left wants to re-produce the ostensible egalitarianism of those small groups of people with no possessions and no land ownership.

The right also wants to hark back, in their case to the Alpha Male and make him the boss over us again, wherein he takes whatever he can get – food and sexual spoils back then. They want to turn the clock back to the time of the dominant male we can still see in other animal groups, back to the time before he was demoted amongst humans to Big Man. In the next chapter but one we will see how that demotion happened, it could be argued that this demotion was the most important event in human history. Certainly it was the time in our history that the fascism of the Alpha Male was first labelled as such, questioned and found wanting, and what could be more important than that?

Because up until then he was partly above morality, until then, might was still almost always Right. After that, might, even though frequently still applied, was never automatically Right.

Part 3

The Contract through Time

19. Torture and all that

Where then should we start back into the Contract? Before we go back in time to look at 'the turning of the Alpha Male', let's plunge in at the deep end – torture. Let's ask ourselves can a principle as simple as Disloyalty extended as bullying and then all the way to torture really lie hidden at the heart of morality?

If it does, then one thing would be true. Torture, not murder, would be the ultimate act of immorality, because if Disloyalty-bullying is the source of morality then the more extreme the bullying the worse the crime.

Do you feel arrogant?

Do you feel proud?

Step into the torture chamber, the secret home, the very core of evil, and learn humility. Learn how small, frail and weak you really are, little human, see evil face to face, eye to eye, and scream, scream, scream, and hear the silence.

The silence of no one listening, except your torturer.

To kill a human is an immoral act, a bullying act, to torture and kill is worse; to torture endlessly, for years and years is worse than murder. The reason we regard torture alone as less bad than murder is because we assume that somehow, somewhere along the line, the torture stops, whereas you stay murdered forever.

But what if the torture were to last the whole of your life?

What if, you were destined to remain a prisoner for years, and were to be tortured every day, and finally killed, and that this was a certainty, that there was no hope of any reprieve, no respite, no glimmer of a chance of escape, no pardon, and definitely no mercy?

Surely it is the hope that one day this will stop, that helps sustain imprisoned victims of torture? But if you remove this, and guarantee instead endless-torture, then torture can be seen to be worse than murder.

A fate worse than death.

A hell on earth.

Then torture is seen for what it really is.

Endless-torture is the ultimate immorality, is the defining end point of all that is immoral. Endless-torture is the ultimate misuse of Power, the ultimate bully and the ultimate victim. It is evil defined and personified.

If endless-torture, torture ending in death without hope of reprieve, torture-unto-death, is the ultimate form of Disloyalty-bullying, it would appear that our condemnation of murder is based upon it being the next to worst form of bullying.

We abhor the crime of child abuse; we detest the policeman torturing his victim, because these, like the dictators who bully whole countries, are the ultimate bullies. These are instances of those who are supposed to protect the people in their care, turning from protectors into bullies, the ultimate betrayal, the ultimate Disloyalty.

The ultimate crime, and thus the ultimate immorality.

To be bullied by your protector, in secret, alone in a dark room, to be tortured-unto-death is surely a fate worse than death itself, worse than a quick death.

That is the ultimate evil, the full stop at the end of those things we humans designate as morally wrong.

Is there anything worse in this world than endless torture?

Anything worse than torture-unto-death?

I don't think so.

Reflect on this, we will return to it again, but meanwhile reflect on this as I do human, you who are so much like me reflect on this.

SUICIDE AND EUTHANASIA

If endless-torture, not death, is the fundamental end point of our moral world, then it would seem that euthanasia cannot be morally wrong. Death is only Wrong when it robs someone of the most precious thing they have, life itself.

Bullies them by stealing from them something they want to keep.

Conversely, when someone pleads with us to take something, it is not stealing, it is the fulfilment of a trust, it is the act of a Loyal friend – it is a privilege.

Therefore to assist someone with a terminal illness (so bad that they wish to give up their life) to do so, cannot be either a Disloyal act or a bullying act.

It therefore cannot be an immoral act.

SPERM

No one can bully or oppress a sperm because it is not a sentient being – it feels no pain. Therefore catching semen in a trap of rubber is not a moral question.

How can one be cruel to a sperm?

It is not an independent living creature capable of suffering, and any act devoid of a bully or a bullied, is a non-moral act.

ABORTION

One limit of bullying lies somewhere between a 23 to 24 week old foetus, capable (with hospital care) of independent life, and that same life as a sperm and egg, at or just before the moment of fertilisation. And we argue over this difficult decision.

Some say that all-human-life-is-sacred, but the truth is that all human life must die. The truth is that what we believe is 'sacred' is the right to live without being bullied, and when the time comes to die without being bullied too.

Some say abortion is Wrong because all human life is sacred, but they are mistaken to call this morality because this is a metaphysical-religious opinion.

If they were to say that abortion is Wrong because it is an act of bullying of a human foetus, the bullying of a potentially fully-fledged human life, they would have a point, they would then be making a moral not a metaphysical-religious argument. Arbitrary as it seems, in practise we draw this boundary to differentiate between a blob of tissue so insignificant that we cannot bring ourselves to realistically apply the bullying principle to it, and a being almost human that we have difficulty not applying the principle to.

For the moment the issue is not where we draw the line, we'll come to that later, but that we draw it based upon the true source of moral behaviour in the human race, and not upon a metaphysical chimera, a religious dogma, an error.

HOMOSEXUALITY

Two persons of the same sex, a couple in love, go into a private space somewhere together to have sex, as we all do. Two consenting adults, neither of whom is under duress of any kind, emotional or physical.

Who is being bullied?

Who is the oppressor and who the oppressed?

Let me think, stand back let me see, let me judge.

No one.

No one?

Neither of them?

Then we will withdraw the old law and make a new one, a more just law.

Shoving your penis into the anus of another male, who condones, co-operates and (so I'm led to believe) actually enjoys the act, cannot be immoral. It is only immoral if one party is coerced, pestered or bullied into taking part in an act he would not involve himself in voluntarily.

It may not be how you or I would choose to pass the time. But, apart from them having sex in public, in direct violation of the sex-in-public prohibition, no bully – no crime.

And that's why we made it legal all those years ago.

No matter how odd their behaviour seems to us, the majority, since no one is being bullied we cannot designate their behaviour as immoral. We therefore cannot and should not rule it illegal, between consenting adults, in private. The sex act is a private matter – for all of us.

INFIDELITY
By the definition of bullying-manipulation, infidelity is clearly immoral, because it is the manipulation of another – it is betrayal, the breaking of a trust. And it is upon the concept of Trust that the whole of the Ancient Group co-operative is built, so those who betray a trust behave immorally.

The great force irrevocably allied to survival is the great force of Sex – the third of the six great threads of human life. And as we look across the animal world it seems extremely unlikely that we are creatures created to be totally monogamous. If we were so created, would we really have all the temptations to have sex with so many others we meet, wouldn't we on bonding, truly bond for life as certain birds do, with those having the urge to wander being as statistically rare as those undergoing sex change operations?

Infidelity, is a place where morality meets a selfish urge, but not any old selfish urge, born solely of our own personal avaricious nature and therefore to some extent controllable, it is the urge of urges, the one imprinted in our genes. To describe it as selfish is not really sufficient; it is the urge that underlies the concept "urge".

Then it is an exception to the rule? No it is not, and that's what makes it especially interesting, because we see that even in a secular society we disapprove of infidelity, because it is the betrayal of a trust. It is an act of Disloyalty.

It is bullying-manipulation by misinformation, by the use of a lie.

So even here, where morality faces the urge of urges, the urge for which the word urge was invented, even here faced with the most natural urge in the world, Morality wins. By which I mean that, despite all the temptations and even when we give in to them, the vast majority of us believe that infidelity is morally wrong. As opposed to serial monogamy, to which we have no moral objection. To do otherwise is to be Disloyal to your spouse, to the one person you have sworn to be especially Loyal to.

A million year old influence on our behaviour countermanding a 1000 million year old influence. Yes even here Bully/Anti-bully wins, going head to head with the urge behind all life. Thou shalt not be a Disloyal manipulative-bully is so deeply embedded in us that it even transcends thou shalt scatter thy seed.

Quod erat demonstrandum

20. Democracy appears

How then did we start down this road? A road that has led us to feelings that condemn even the subtlest examples of bullying. How did we start to conduct the administration of society according to the principles of B/A-b? We've seen how in outline already, but as we come back to the Contract again, we will look now at some of the twists and turns of the road that morality has travelled. For example, who is it in the whole history of the human and pre-human race that first claims the Right not to be bullied?

Who knows for sure?

We can only guess – in an educated way. It must happen many times of course, many many times, in many different groups. Over and over again until it becomes established as a specifically pre-human trait.

We do know though who the biggest bully must have been, and still is potentially, because we see him operating all around us. He is the Alpha Male, the leader of the pack, just as we see amongst our primate cousins and in many other animal groups around us to this day. Ha, what am I saying, just as we see in numerous human groups to this day, being the biggest bully is how the position of Alpha, top dog, is gained and then kept, against all comers.

There must have been squabbles in all the pre-human hominid groups, just as there are now in chimp and monkey groups, but the biggest and most serious squabbles are challenges for leadership. Often these are nothing other than one bully pitting himself against another bully. But amongst primates: leaders of chimp and monkey groups don't only rely on throwing their own weight about, they also form alliances with some of the other leading males and females.

Would-be challengers must themselves have backers, must have allies, or at least potential allies, males at least willing to change sides if they see the way the wind is blowing. No one can rule alone, including alpha male chimps (Boehm, 1999).

In primate groups the Alpha Male has his favourites, his inner circle of lieutenants, his ruling Council as it were. We will never see, but against this background who might we reasonably suspect of being the first to build on and extend this beginning? Who is most likely to claim, (and claim most vociferously, a half or quarter of a million years ago, in the long lost groups of our ancestors), the Right not to be bullied? Claim in effect, the Right of free speech, in return for duties performed?

It has to be someone who is not cowed, someone not dominated, or at least not fully dominated. Someone strong enough to have a voice, and yet not quite strong enough to be the dominant Alpha Male.

To be strong enough back then he was probably male.

A male almost-leader, one of the henchmen of the Alpha Male. And he is watching and waiting, for his chance, for his chance to take over from the current incumbent.

What is the Council of these Ancient Groups?

A band of the toughest males, next strongest after the leader, a band of henchmen. They are the heads of pre-human 'households' consisting of younger males, women and children, gathered together in family groups to form a larger group. The Council members are the leader's loyal lieutenants, his storm troopers in times of disputes with neighbouring groups, his right hand men – his (almost) equals.

And in times of peace...

Amongst human hunter-gatherers extant today there is no Alpha Male, there is no all powerful Chief, instead there is what anthropologists call a Big Man, first amongst (almost) equals. The position of Alpha Male, common in other pack animals, has become instead a temporary appointment, abolished as soon as the crisis of a looming war with a neighbouring group is over, or a time of famine ceases. Signalled as being over by the simple expedient of any (or all) of the senior males ignoring orders and commands given by the leader (ibid. 1999).

Ignoring also any and all statements that sound as though they could be interpreted, or misinterpreted by either party, as being construed as an order, rather than a request. In hunter-gatherer societies every senior male does his own thing and will not be subordinated by or to any other male, except in times of war, or on a hunt, or some other temporary and specific mission.

This is not an imaginary society, not one of Jean-Jacques Rousseau's dreams. This is a description of extant forager societies that have been studied in the last 100 years. It therefore seems highly likely that it is the Alpha Male's loyal lieutenants who first claim the Right not to be bullied. Who in effect thereby claim the Right of free speech, and while doing so alter forever the status of their leader – change him from Alpha Male into Big Man, with curtailed powers.

My proposition is that this is an important event in the long history of humanity, an undocumented event, but one that the B/A-b hypothesis predicts. Predicts in a simple hunter-gatherer society maybe half a million years ago, and it is it, not the Greeks, that formed the first democratic society. And in its day, this limited first hunter-gatherer 'democracy', ruled every human on this earth.

This temporary and limited leader compromise is not achieved by some ideal harmony or time of sweet simple innocence as Rousseau envisaged, it is achieved instead by a balance of Power. Which, as we know with our own modern version, is the only reliable and believable restriction on unbridled Power.

When the – accepted on sufferance due to practical necessity for the moment Big Man – steps arrogantly one half pace beyond his jurisdiction, he is slapped down so quickly that it makes the later invention (by Knowledge) of supersonic flight seem slower than a crawling snail. He is simply ignored, humiliated, and most crushing of all, laughed at, by any and every high ranking male whose fierce independence he attempts to usurp in this high handed manner. Humiliated by having the temerity, the stupidity, to issue an order beyond his remit.

Laughed at – this is the start of freedom of speech, the first limit upon those who were once unquestioned dictators. Laughed at, how simple, how immediate, and how effective. The first limit on the unbridled Power of the former Alpha Male is the scorn and derision of his almost-equals. Hence perhaps why we are so expert at recognising the slightest nuance of arrogant behaviour in others.

This then is the start of the moral age, when B/A-b morality takes its hold on governance. Thus comes the first uniquely human society, a time, the first time that a leader's Power is limited. No longer the sexually domineering Alpha Male of earlier primate groups (and of other pack animals too), there are now social limitations placed upon him. It is the first time others dare to speak freely in his presence, more than this, claim the Right to speak freely any time they wish, without fear. The Alpha has been demoted, demoted to the Big Man, and we can see him, or someone very like him, alive and well, in the forager societies in existence today.

On a hunt if he makes a good kill, his senior males belittle it – the prouder he proclaims his worth, the greater is the tumult of piss taking. Nothing more subtle is used than mercilessly taking the mickey out of any male arrogant enough, big headed enough, to put himself forward as any kind of permanent superior to the other leading males.

It's maybe how and why making fun of someone first originated, a non-violent way of taking them down a peg or two, and it is how it is done to this day amongst the nomads of the Kalahari desert. Actually it is how it is done to this day in every organised human enterprise, group and club, business or bureaucracy isn't it?

It is the self-same entity that we credit the Greeks with inventing around 500BCE and ourselves in Western Europe with re-inventing over 2000 years later. It is the first democracy.

Well it turns out that the Greeks were re-inventing it actually, and that it had been in existence for maybe as long as 500,000 years before them. The Greeks were re-inventing democracy for use in an agrarian society, while we, with modern democracy, have re-invented it again for our own even bigger and more complicated industrial society.

Thus do we have democracy, the form of government decreed by B/A-b morality, the only form of government that follows logically from its original premise. Be loyal to this joint, largely egalitarian, enterprise of ours, do not bully even if, especially if, thou art the strongest of the group.

Even if thou art the richest merchant, the sharpest trader, the most successful farmer, best hunter, toughest warrior, highest ranking priest, smartest lawyer, whoever you are you are also a member of the Group.

Thou shalt be loyal to the Group is the whole of the law.

Despite all the rhetoric, despite all the complicated and erudite books about politics, there are in fact only two forms of government; there is democratic government, and there is totalitarian government.

It's hardly likely that you don't know the difference, but just in case.

In a democracy when you don't like the government, you get rid of it.

In a dictatorship when you don't like the government, it gets rid of you.

It's really very simple.

THE GUARDIANS

Those who in the packs of the primates, were the able lieutenants of the dominating leader, helping him maintain control and thereby earning for themselves a larger share of the feeding and sexual spoils, these now have become something else. Have become the first Guardians of the first democracies, democracies without written constitutions, with nothing more than the Anti-bully instincts of the leading males to rein in the former bullying Alpha Male.

The balance of Power these males provide is the first limitation placed on dictatorship. These men, for they must have been men, men watching, jealous of another's Power. Men with clubs, no bows and arrows yet, we're too far back for that, men with stone clubs, these men are the first guardians of democracy, (Sober and Wilson, 1998).

Of course.

Of course!

Jealous men with stone clubs are the first foothold of democracy. In times of war or other crises they still act as the Big Man's lieutenants and are willing to die for or with him. But in times of peace they act also as his jailer. They hold him in check, limit and proscribe his dominance, make him constantly aware – there is a line – don't cross it. In all the books you will find the Greeks given credit for the founding of democracy. That is an error, when we look back we see that democracy must have originated within simple hunter-gatherer societies.

Eureka – of course it did!

These watchful jealous men are the first Judiciary, the first Parliament, they are the first foothold of morality in governmental form. No, this is to insult them, Parliament, *habeas corpus* and modern legal systems are but pale imitations of these men, are mere shadows of their brilliant and instantaneous effectiveness in holding Power to account.

A laugh of contempt, and a walking-away-to-sit-down-and-ignore.

A laugh in the face of the dictator who would issue an order beyond his remit, if only it were that easy these days.

The humiliation, the utter humiliation, and all done in front of other 'Council men', who are watching, watching, waiting, waiting.

The Greeks or Western Europe the inventors of democracy? Don't make me laugh, no way – what hubris.

Democracy was invented in Africa, maybe a quarter, maybe even half a million years ago.

21. Large Groups

Wait though. If this is true, why do we have to keep re-inventing democracy? Why do many countries, and modern societies, reject democracy? Surely if the new Bully/Anti-bully society helps to form and/or embed the Basic Morality even deeper into the members of each group, we should not have to struggle so much?

THE SECOND COMING OF KNOWLEDGE
About 30,000 years ago, Knowledge commenced on what eventually proved to be a great change in the way humans lived, it started the process of learning how to take the seeds of certain grasses, plant them, harvest them, and subsequently improve them from harvest to harvest. Also around the same time, in many of the same fertile river valleys of China, the Euphrates, the Tigris and maybe the Nile, Knowledge figured out how to domesticate animals. We could call this event the Second Coming of Knowledge, the first being lost in the mists of time, when our behaviour first separated us from other primates.

As a result the human world changed, and changed forever. From being wandering nomads it became possible for us to stay in one place, static, for the whole of our lives, bringing the food to us rather than us following it. And this tolled the death knell of the once totally dominant hunter-gatherer form of society, the final throes of whose demise continues to this very day on the edges of the driest deserts, frozen tundra and inside the deepest jungles.

By about 10,000 years ago, largely unseen, reminiscent in this respect of the all consuming challenge of Metaphysics-religion 70 to 90,000 years earlier, there came a new challenge to Morality, this time from Power. Power resurgent and enjoying its own Second Coming, (though it never really went away), on the back of this great upsurge in Knowledge. Being stationary allows the build up of food stocks, the hoarding of grain reserves and animal products. We thus started to settle down into large tribal societies numbering thousands of people, as opposed to small 50 or 100 strong groups of foragers. And along with this comes ownership of a larger spread of farmland than your neighbour, by dint of either hard work or better farming abilities, or both plus a streak of ruthlessness. Thus is wealth built up, wealth a concept unknown in hunter-gatherer society.

Wealth makes Big Men into separated leaders again, they become Tribal Chiefs who own more, then most, and eventually all, of the land within their domain. Thus does land ownership come into being and with this new concept the Alpha Male returns, after maybe as long as half a million years in remission he's back, this time as a King, and now with

Power beyond his wildest dreams.

TRIBAL CHIEFS

From a hunter-gatherer society that has no concept of land ownership, there develop Chiefs and Kings who tax their neighbours, neighbours who have now become their subjects. Tax them to offset the expense of their households, the expense of administering their leadership duties you understand. Their many responsibilities, their retinues, their standing armies, required to protect their people, and to protect their land.

In the new agrarian society, brought into being by inventions due to knowledge, the Alpha Male reasserts himself in a flash, as those who are both successful farmers and also successful traders build up stores of goods, stores of wealth. And wealth is Power. And so the new Alpha's neighbours become his subjects, his underlings, peasants, farmers, and herdsmen. While the Chief, and the lieutenants who swear loyalty to support him, become a special warrior class, a caste soon to become the Army, who vaunt themselves above those others, their former neighbours, those without 'aristocratic blood'.

Back with wealth with which to bribe. Back with so much that he can afford to be generous to the Council men, can afford to give them, his fellow aristocrats, lands, wealth, women as far beyond their dreams as has been his own lucky windfall. There is no need for them to watch and wait anymore, they can have a nice big chunk now. Still not quite enough for some of them maybe, because we still see *Magna Carta* style rebellions and plots against Kings, but we also see that it is goodbye to checks and balances, hello aristocracy, the rule of certain wealthy families and their hangers on. The Alpha Male is back, back as King, back as Dictator.

THE SECOND COMING OF POWER

And not just back, but back with a vengeance, back with knobs on, back *fortissimo* – oh boy he's back, he's back all right, back like he's never been away, back like he's never been seen before. Back with weapons, wealth, land and property, new forms of Power, he even has subordinates. Subordinates to do his dirty work for him – the torturing for example. There's always some torturing required – it has to be done, to keep things organised and controlled, to keep people 'on side' a regrettable practical necessity, *pour encourager les autres*.

Of course the Dictators never really went away. You can see their seed in every school playground, in every family, where brutal father, nagging mother or spoilt brat rules the roost. In bosses bullying their employees, in the committee bullying the individual, in bullying businesses not paying their taxes or their debts, while those they owe the money to go bankrupt. In every bribed public official, in every policeman who misuses the trust he holds, in every secret policeman, in every torturer, every rapist and murderer. All the way up to cruel dictators starving, terrorising and imprisoning those they are supposed to be protecting.

The Dictator and his Army become a Group within the original, much expanded Ancient Group, they become a ruling class, a caste separated from the rest of us by their wealth, by their inter marriage of wealth with wealth, by their avoidance of breeding with commoners.

Until to following generations, the origins of democracy are lost, lost along with the origins of morality. And now the double insult, the irony of all ironies, these people who steal the moral concept democracy from the rest of us, convince both us and themselves that kingship, monarchy, aristocracy, dictatorship, call it what you will, is the right and only way to administer human society. They steal our birthright from us and convince us, and themselves – which is why they're so convincing – that we never had it in the first place!

More yet, worse yet, they even steal our Metaphysics from us too, they use religion to bolster their claim of the Divine Right of Kings. They steal our religion from us, steal our crutch and comforter, our inspiration when all we have is it and nothing else. They steal it from us and feed it back to us as a ghastly state sponsored mass religion – to bolster their claim to Power, to bolster their Power over us.

And thus ever since we have been engaged upon wrestling back our Right (not to be bullied) from Power – from the Alpha Male with all his modern trappings. And this is where we find ourselves, having now established even bigger and more complex industrial on top of agrarian societies. Some of us still struggle to establish working democracies in the face of naked Power, and even those of us who have managed this still grapple with the sheer size and stratification of modern society.

The Agrarian Revolution was followed by the Industrial Revolution and as a result societies became even larger, came to be numbered in millions upon millions, and in the cases of India and China just under and well over a thousand million respectively, a billion each. As human population increased exponentially so too did the complications of morality. If you are Indian or Chinese how can you be loyal to a billion other people the vast majority of whom you don't know and will never meet?

If you are American how can you be loyal to 270 million?

If you are Russian how can you be loyal to 150 million?

If you are British how can you be loyal to 60 million?

And so forth, for every country on earth…

Hence our many sub-groups command our first loyalty nowadays, with varying degrees of loyalty rippling outwards like circles on a pond from this inner core, in the same way that those front line soldiers we talked about are loyal firstly to their comrades in arms. These sub-groups may be religious sects, or sub-groups loyal to a football team, or the sub-group of the rich, the poor, the upper class, the middle class, the working class, the north, the south, the Welsh, the English, the Scottish, the Irish, the country folk, the urban dwellers, the immigrants, the unemployed, and last but most definitely not least, the establishment. The list of sub-groups is very long when there are nearly sixty million of you, God knows what it must be like if there is a billion purporting to be one united group.

With this state of affairs as our background, we can see how difficult it is in any group of millions of people to treat everyone in that group fairly. It was, and still is hard enough to give everyone exactly what they deserve in any small enterprise of 100 people, let alone an enterprise of 100 million and more.

The huge societies we have created confuse and hide the core of human morality more than ever. They result in a further moral complication, the loss of immediacy – wherein persons from a higher stratum of society judge, and often find wanting, those from a lower. Are the people who live in this country really a single Group of 60 million, or are they actually many fragmented sub-groups? Can we really expect a moral system that evolved amongst groups of 60 or so individuals to be easy to apply to groups of 60 million?

Such societies can never match the direct simplicity of the inventors of democracy – the Council men armed with stone clubs, who laughed in the face of the Dictator. Nothing we have come up with, separating the Executive from the Legislature, separating both from the Judiciary and the Police, every single modern democratic artifice just doesn't measure up, each is a clumsy device for controlling the urge for Power, a device for laughing in the face of the Dictator.

He-who-laughs-in-the-face-of-the-dictator is the first democrat, is the first Guardian of this new order. He has the courage to laugh directly in the face of Power and defy it because he knows that when he correctly smells a whiff of arrogant presumption, and challenges it, his fellow 'Councillors' will back him, with their stone clubs.

Notice that in his role of watching-the-Big-Man he doesn't defy Power as previous challengers to the Alpha Male have done, solely so that he can then be Boss himself instead. Oh he does it out of arrogance, out of pride; this male egoist who-will-not-be-dominated does it out of jealousy. But this is neither here nor there, because nonetheless in effect he is Anti-bully glaring back – glaring long and hard at the Bully. He thus defies the bully on behalf of others, on behalf of the whole group.

These democracies we are so proud of are but poor substitutes for the Council men, with their scornful laughter and their antennae always turning, always primed to spot arrogance, primed to spot those who are trying it on. Primed to spot any bid for Power, any bid for power-beyond-a-limited-remit, and primed to slap it down in an instant.

We must keep things in perspective though, this golden dawn of that which we now call democracy, will not have been so golden for the women, young males and children of the group. It is unlikely that the jealous males watching the Big Man so assiduously will have themselves been anything other than little dictators when they returned to the bosom of their extended families. Who knows? It would be ridiculous to think one could look back in detail with only the behaviour of modern foragers as our limited and maybe inaccurate guide.

TODAY
In a world in which human morality has developed as described here is it really so surprising that many people accuse the USA in particular and the West in general of hypocrisy, of a double standard of democracy at home and tyranny abroad? On the contrary in the moral world as described in this hypothesis it would be extremely odd if they didn't behave like that, they are a group of 270 million, taking care to look after the perceived interests of that group. The same way all humans have for 150,000 years at least, ever since we've been human, and probably a lot longer.

They, like the rest of us, hate to see bullying, hate to see the upper caste of a neighbouring group bullying, torturing, depriving the human Right-not-to-be-bullied from lower caste members of that group. But when it comes to a clash between their own prosperity and survival, the survival of Our Group versus the prosperity and survival of a neighbouring group, they are a little less concerned about the group next door, and about who is bullying whom. Hypocrisy, well yes and no, or rather only within the limits of that term described in Chapter 2. The West does genuinely want to help reduce the bullying and torture prevalent in dictatorships worldwide, but not at the price of their own survival. We can only be honest with others and admit that we care about our Group more than we care about yours. It's the way we're made, and the way you're made too.

We are hypocritical, because we (like the rest of the human race) were born that way, born with the double pull, the double standard of selfish-selflessness tugging away in two opposing directions inside us. Yes OK, we admit it, we're hypocritical, but not as hypocritical as a lot, if not most of our accusers, those out there with chips on their shoulders the size of the twin towers.

The real hypocrisy in all this is that, in order to appease their conscience and the consciences of the rest of us, (that is we who vote them in), our governments lie about these slanted terms of trade, and pretend they (and we) want and do no such thing. Now that is hypocrisy, but against even this background we still get genuinely angry at the sight of dictators ripping off their countrymen in the group next door.

We would far rather trade (ideally to our advantage) with democracies that treat their people fairly than with bullying dictatorships. Our anger and dislike of dictators is genuine, but not so great that we find it easy to sacrifice what we have, and that includes scarce jobs in our armaments industries, to help members of another group far away of whom we know very little.

To review then, history and the present shows us that groups of any large size soon become stratified into various sub-groups, the first of which are castes or classes of citizens.

By this stratification does arrogance and presumption marry arrogance and presumption, and in turn breeds more arrogance and presumption. Bred both via the genetic passing on of such inherited traits and in addition via education and the attitudes of all those who surround the newly bred next generation of arrogance and presumption. Thus do upper castes lord it over lower castes and classes, all the way down, amongst others, to the untouchable caste of India. We are all part of a single group, we are all in it together, but some are more in it than others.

And worst of all, those in clover at the top of the caste system come to believe they deserve to live in clover, because of how hard they've worked, and that those at the bottom deserve their fate also, because of their lack of effort. Which brings us back to those differences of opinion, between the right wing and the left. And brings us also to the way that we in this group judge the conduct of you in a neighbour group, both conduct within your group and conduct in the relationship between your group and ours.

22. Groups judge other Groups

In addition to the complication of massive caste ridden societies we must take note that it is not just the individuals inside groups who judge each other. Individuals (and their governments) also judge the corporate actions of the whole of neighbouring groups, including and especially when they make war on other neighbouring groups.

How do they do this? Well provided they are neutral – and are not, for one reason or another, biased or allies of one of the neighbouring groups, due to being of the same racial type, or the same religion, or a close trading partner, or other skewed political reason – then they judge by bully/anti-bully. How else could a neutral judge? They do so using the same emotional reaction first described in Chapter 3, because no matter how corporate the response, it is the minds of individuals that actually do the judging. Where else could judging be done?

THREE TRIBES
Let's say there are three tribes. Tribe 1 was ousted from its land by Tribe 2 many, many generations ago, they were scattered and forced to live in small enclaves among Tribe 2, including a very small enclave remaining in their native land. Sometime later Tribe 2 was ousted by Tribe 3, who then took over these same lands, and was actually less harsh to the remnants of Tribe 1 than Tribe 2 had been.

Suppose that all these three tribes are actually different religions as well as different racially, but that they all stem from the same original religion, one, two, three in that order. Over centuries Tribe 2 continue to be cruel to Tribe 1 this finally culminates in mass mechanised murder on a sickening scale never quite seen before in all the many massacres of human history.

By this time Tribe 2 are very much in the ascendancy, even to the extent of dominating Tribe 3 in the old lands of Tribe 1. After the mechanised murders, many members of Tribe 2 feel so guilty about what other members of its tribe have done that they decide they must do something for Tribe 1 as some kind of apology.

Tribe 2 help to take a chunk of land that used to belong to Tribe 1, but which now belongs to Tribe 3, and 'give' it to Tribe 1. Clearly this is an unusual kind of apology, because the land they 'give' doesn't belong to them, it is actually Tribe 3 land, but it is the land Tribe 1 wants because it was their ancient homeland from before Tribe 2 evicted them many generations ago.

This example presents us with a strange idea, putting practicalities to one side, in terms of moral philosophy I mean. To give as compensation to the people of Tribe 1 who have suffered the torture and extermination of millions of their fellows at the hands of Tribe 2, a big chunk of land belonging to Tribe 3, who had nothing to do with the millions of murders. Strange because two Wrongs don't have any chance of making a Right unless the second wrong is visited upon the perpetrators of the first wrong, otherwise all that results is feelings of injustice (amongst Tribe 3) and further conflict.

We all know which international situation this is a crude description of, and the point here is that those of us who are neutral can and do judge and form our moral opinions and condemnations based upon who we see as bullying whom.

This part of what is in actuality a complicated problem-between-groups really is that simple, our emotional response to the Contract treats even international issues dating back 2000 years as being that simple. Tribe 1 was given a chunk of land from amongst the land belonging to Tribe 3, and so Tribe 3 surrounds them. On this basis some people have sympathy for Tribe 1 because they see the surrounding Tribe 3 countries as the bullies, whereas those who sympathise with the dispossessed members of Tribe 3 see the returning Tribe 1 and its Tribe 2 allies as the bullies. We neutrals use the term aggressor, as with so many of our judgements we don't actually use the term bullying let alone Disloyalty, we reserve bullying for children in the playground or tyrannical bosses in the work place. But when we point our finger accusingly and blame one party for their aggression, this is the B/A-b moral judgement we make.

If it were not so would the Israelis and Palestinians, and their various allies, really spend so much time and effort justifying their latest act of violence to the 'neutrals' of world opinion by pointing out it was actually in response to aggression by the other party? The latest murder is always claimed as reciprocity, claimed to be proportionate (and therefore not an act of bullying), proportionate to an act of unprovoked and unwarranted murder by the other side.

Or closer to home, just across the water in Northern Ireland, it's the same story. In discussions over an independent Ireland the Protestants were afraid of being overwhelmed (bullied) by the Catholics and so were willing to fight against it. So, in the name of peace, they were given their own little country, in which they immediately launched themselves upon the task of disenfranchising (bullying) the minority Catholics left behind in it. Over and over again, the bully and the bullied.

The tricky bit of course is gathering sufficient impartial evidence to fairly judge who it is that is actually bullying whom. That said there is nothing complicated or difficult to understand about the relevance of the B/A-b mechanism in these cases. There is certainly no need to confuse the issues by dragging everyone's (slightly different) religion through the mud.

Those religions are there to sustain and help the people on each side to get by in times of trouble as best they can, but they have no bearing upon defining the moral issues. The definition of which solely concern who it is that is bullying whom. This is how we judge nations, the same way we judge individuals, the way we differentiate Right from Wrong. Heavens above, neutrals even support the underdog in football matches. Or is that just me?

Forget the complications of religion, the claim and counter claim, the West the East, the material the spiritual, the greedy the dispossessed, the democracy the dictatorships, all confusing smokescreens. Often deliberate smokescreens. *The only difference between 'the West' and Islam is that we have shed more of our Christian Divine Commands than the Moslems have – yet.* Neutrals sit in judgement upon whichever party they see as the aggressor, the term defines itself. How else could neutrals possibly judge except by bully/anti-bully?

To judge by any other standard … well I'm lost for words, what other standard could there possibly be? Something in the Talmud, the Bible, the Koran, the differing and overlapping religious books of these tribes? International relations are between-group relations and we can't help ourselves except judge them using the same human emotional response as we judge other moral questions we are faced with. We ask ourselves who is the bully in the situation presented to us, and who is the bullied.

The moral element within the religious books of each of the parties in this dispute can only ever be derivative and never definitive, because the moral principle of B/A-b has been around for at least 250,000 years and probably much longer, whereas the religious books of Tribes 1, 2 and 3 have been around for only 3,000, 2,000 and 1,400 years respectively. Their presumption, self-regard and absurd pomposity would be funny if it weren't so serious. They are important books in other ways, but they can never define morality.

As Bully/anti-bully has shown us, claims by any Tribe that "God has given this land to us" are philosophically meaningless and morally laughable (but extremely bigoted and dangerous). They are Metaphysical not Moral claims – clearly one tribe's God does not agree with the other tribe's God on this occasion? Even though they are the exact same entity. Different versions of the same God – actually different versions of the same book.

And somehow these holy books are meant to sort this out? Are meant to be the cornerstone on which we build a common human morality? Give me a break. It is the founding bedrock of Disloyalty and the principle of

Bully/Anti-bully derived from it, it is the Basic Morality, not anyone's holy book, that is the backbone of all human morality. And when silly braggart historians talk of the 'triumph of the West' it is the revival of this Basic Morality via the concept of the Open Society that is the triumph, not how many tanks, missiles, automobiles or pampered luxuries we have per head of population.

If we allow ourselves to be side tracked by holy books, useful as they are for things other than defining morality, we'll end up like my old boss (I'm Buddhist C of E remember), the former Archbishop of Canterbury. So confused he thought it would be a good idea to import Sharia Law into a nominally Christian country that has progressively come to base its laws upon the commonality of human rights – aka the one human right not to be bullied by others in your group. We've made progress towards forming our laws on the true basis of morality, and he (and others) want to turn the clock back.

It is never the function of morality to serve religion.

Morality is the older partner.

On the contrary, it is the function of religion to serve morality.

23. Kant and Utilitarianism

Thus for the moment we will turn to what largely amounts to secular derivations of morality. The philosophies that vie for the honour of defining morality, now that we can no longer rely upon religion to do so without confusion, bias, fantasy and inaccuracy, are Utilitarianism and Kant's Categorical Imperative.

As mentioned in Chapter 2, the principle behind the formation of the Ancient Groups is something different to the principle that controls the inner tensions within the Group. So let's discuss the formation principle first.

UTILITARIANISM
Our banding together into groups occurred so that the team so formed would increase and improve our chances of survival, in the same way that chimps, wolves and many others also do. In other words for the greatest happiness of the greatest number – a principle we are familiar with as Utilitarianism. Since 'the greatest happiness' is a Pleasure versus Pain assessment, then this part of Utilitarianism is not much of a contender for the vaunted title of Morality, because Pleasure or Pain is an assessment common to every life form including plants and earthworms. They, like us move towards or flourish in pleasurable environments and move away or fail to flourish in painful ones.

The second part though, our consideration of OTHERS via 'the greatest number' sounds much closer to being a moral assessment, because to consider the pleasures and pains of others is to be selfless. Therefore the Utilitarian mechanism behind the formation of the group is something we could describe as being half-moral. Only half, but that 'half' can be very important sometimes when arriving at group decisions, as mentioned in Chapter 9 when the group ponder moving camp early.

Or for example when an out of control lorry is directed by the driver at an old man on one side of the road, rather than a young mother and her two small children who are actually crossing the road. The driver is choosing between the lesser of two evils on the 'greatest pleasure and least pain of the greatest number'. And inasmuch as this is thinking of the Pleasure as opposed to Pain of others, it has a moral element.

Thus Utilitarianism is half-moral, or part moral, and so lies on the other side of the boundary between the internal control mechanism of the group, and the reason for the formation of the group in the first place.

We have seen that The Contract is 'drawn up' between the members of groups bound together for this overriding Utilitarian purpose, but inside the group each of these individuals must compromise by sometimes reducing their own self-based desires in favour of the happiness of other group members. It is thus not difficult to see how Utilitarianism, an expression of this overriding purpose, can then sometimes be re-imported, in certain situations back into the internal workings of the group itself, and can prove helpful in making some important decisions.

This Utilitarian principle describes the group's purpose, but to achieve it, as we have seen, there has to also be some means of encouraging the individuals concerned to work together. They have to act as a team, have to limit tensions and disputes between their personal individual egos, and as we have also seen and discussed at length, reach a compromise with the desires and the egos of others in the group. And thus the case under discussion is that this controller-of-tensions is morality, and is something different and separate from Utilitarianism.

KANT

The great philosophical supporter of the Contract is Immanuel Kant, who via the approach he calls the Categorical Imperative essentially proposes two rules, or maxims. These, if adhered to, are the iron rules, the basis of how the inner tensions of the group are held in check – or so he reckons.

Maxim One – God has laid down a law (expressed by Jesus and other religious teachers as: do unto others as you would be done to). And by Kant as: do not will an act that you cannot will being universally allowed to everyone. For example, do not steal unless you are willing to agree that everyone should be allowed to steal.

Note here that although Kant is seriously religious, he does not simply do what the holy book says, because it doesn't say anything DEFINITIVE enough, or coherent enough, to satisfy him. We can see he is seriously religious because he insists that God watches us in order to dispense final justice, since clearly no one else can see into the hearts of others, no one else can see our motives and intentions.

The most obvious problem with the first Maxim is also the most famous. When a knife wielding angry neighbour comes to our door and asks have we seen his wife lately, Kant says we must be truthful and say yes. If we lie to him by saying no, even though she is hiding in our house, we have broken Kant's rule, and if lying is allowed to us, then it is allowed to everybody. We excuse ourselves, because we consider the lie we have told is told to save a life.

We have told a 'white lie'.

What is this white lie?

What is a lie? It is an untruth told to Bully-manipulate someone, hence the need for and our use of the term 'white lie' to differentiate between

117

this and a lie told for the opposite reason, a lie told to help someone. Kant, possessed of an incredible towering mind, seems to have fallen for the oldest trick in the book, the confusing misuse of a word. He uses 'to tell a lie' as if it were definitive of all lies, whereas in fact the definitive term is 'to tell a Disloyal bullying-manipulative lie'.

In the knife-wielding example Kant insists that the householder is in the moral wrong when he tells this lie to the knife-wielder, thus Kant appears to think that there is no such thing as a white lie.

What about theft? Surely his Maxim is correct on that one?

Well almost.

But if it is then why do we condone and praise the actions of Robin Hood, who steals from the rich (Norman aristocracy) to give to the poor (Saxon peasants). It is an important underlying principle that we prohibit theft within the group (to avoid the group disintegrating) on the grounds that if one is allowed to steal all should be allowed. But if someone does steal food and later the victim 'steals back' something of equal value to the food stolen from him, then the second theft is generally considered to be a justified response, *quid pro quo.*

So the underlying principle is not actually don't steal, but is don't be-disloyal-by-stealing, or in later times don't bully-by-stealing. Don't bully-by-lying, don't bully by ... and so forth. Thus the acknowledgement of the underlying Disloyalty and the principle of Bully/Anti-bully that flows from it improves upon what is otherwise a piece of Kantian academic theory. An intellectual theory so far removed from real life as to be an inaccurate representation of our lives, and thus to render it of only limited value.

Kant's rule, that no one should steal for example, is correct only when starting from a blank sheet, a rule for the group as a whole, but not applicable in practice when someone has stolen and another steals that same stolen item back, this is reciprocity, a proportionate response. Thus Kant's rules are excellent principles, for the framing of national and international laws, but fall short of establishing the central principle behind what we call morality.

Kant's Categorical Imperative is an accurate expression of the central principle of morality only at the 'starting point' within each individual Ancient Group when no one has stolen from or otherwise injured anyone else. They are the rules inside each of those first groups, at 'day one' as it were, because to break any of them is to break the code of loyalty and bully others of the group.

Hence why Kant's Maxims are valuable as the fundamental principles underlying our legal systems, but we should not expect them to cover every moral nuance, because they are true only when there is a blank sheet, and there never is one in the real world. He can't even handle the scolded-comforted child, his first maxim would say 'don't smack unless all are allowed to smack', whereas really the rule we apply to the parent is don't bully-by-smacking'.

Maxim Two – act in such a way as to treat people as ends and not as means. That seems logical since as we have said we have formed the group for the benefit of all. Thus don't sacrifice the life and well being of any member of the group, (without his or her permission) in order to further the ends in some direction of the group as a whole.

With their permission is different, there have been many fine human beings who have volunteered to sacrifice themselves for the sake of the group as a whole. The soldier who stays behind to cover his comrades retreat by holding up the progress of the enemy, or Horatio and his two comrades, defending the bridge into Rome.

Surely then this maxim has no feet of clay as the first one does? It is rock solid that anyone who performs the heroic act of sacrificing themselves for the safety of the whole group must do so voluntarily. If someone is coerced or forced into such a sacrifice against their will, then not only is it not heroic on their part, it is also the rest of us using them as a means to an end.

Yes, but what if the person in question, the person you are accused of 'using as a means' is not from your group? Or, what if he is someone from your group, but has always been a lazy, ungrateful, backsliding, backbiting, freeloader. What if, with this track record, with this atrocious Duty-history as we might call it, he has now, for reasons of petty jealousy or for money paid to him by some other group, turned traitor and planted a dirty bomb hidden somewhere in the midst of our community?

24. Dirty Bomb

In order to illustrate the differences between Kant's Second Maxim and Utilitarianism, a Professor of Philosophy, with a television camera in tow, put the following case to people 'on the street'. 'Suppose that someone plants a dirty bomb in the middle of London, which will be capable of killing many and irradiating a large area, but is caught after he has planted it and before it is timed to go off.' *Professor Michael Sandel of Harvard, Justice, a series of lectures in 2012 on BBC 4.*

The question was an exercise to facilitate a discussion of the responses received in the light of Utilitarianism and Kant's Categorical Imperative. When people on the street were asked 'is it morally right to torture him into revealing where the bomb is' a majority of them said 'yes it would be Right'.

Kant's disciples say that owing to the moral truth of the second maxim one cannot torture someone, because this is to use him as a means. Thus they claim that the minority opinion is correct that it is morally wrong to torture the bomb planter. Proponents of Utilitarianism on the other hand say the majority opinion is correct, and that people are judging on the basis of 'the greatest happiness/good of the greatest number'.

I'm not so sure about that though, because one could also say that the majority answer yes to the question as it is put because they consider that to torture this individual is a proportionate response, is merely reciprocity compared to the imminent slow death of hundreds. The majority response is thus in accordance with the contractual basis of morality, and has nothing whatsoever to do with Utilitarianism. It is a moral response, not a half-moral one.

When a thief steals your handbag it is not inappropriate for you and your friend to chase after him, catch him and dish out a little physical chastisement to encourage him to hand your bag back. This giving him a thick ear is clearly not forgiveness, but neither is it inappropriate, if you are only as rough with him as he was at the theft.

Whereas if you and your friend were to corner him and savagely beat him to within an inch of his life in an alley, disfiguring and crippling him for life, you would have become bullies and thus in the Wrong. It's simple stuff that we're all familiar with, the concept of sufficient or reasonable force, reciprocity – do as you would be done to.

Utilitarianism claims the judgement of the majority is Utilitarian because Immanuel Kant's Categorical Imperative states 'act in such a way as to treat people as ends and never as means'. This is fine as a legal (human rights) principle, but in the circumstance of the dirty bomb as described 'the greatest good of the greatest number' is one explanation only to the response of the public. The other equally valid interpretation is that to advocate the torture of one individual to obtain life saving information is a non-bullying reciprocal response.

So when people 'in the street' respond that they consider it 'not inappropriate' to torture the bomber to extract information from him, they are not necessarily taking a Utilitarian position. Instead they may just as easily be taking the B/A-b contractual position. Thus the conclusion that the majority opinion recorded in this brief and unscientific experiment supports Utilitarianism is invalid.

To be fair to the Professor he was no doubt only concerned with starting his students thinking. The proposition and question he put, either deliberately or accidentally, lacked various parameters. We will now add in some of our own in order to take the discussion forward. It needs to be taken forward because if Kant's Second Maxim is conditional on proportionality, then it too is vulnerable along with his First Maxim.

1. Firstly notice the way the question is phrased, it is framed such that we are seeking immediate and specific information to save hundreds of people from the slow painful death which will result from the detonation of a radioactive bomb. We are not being asked to condone torture as a generality, or to agree to torture as a means of extracting vague non-specific information in any conflict at any time.

Thus those canvassed probably still consider it is inappropriate to torture someone to obtain such vague and ill defined information because this is overkill, unlike the specific and proportionate scenario posed above to those 'in the street'.

2. Secondly we are given no information as to whether the bomber is from 'our group' or is a member of another group. Is this person an enemy combatant or one of us turned traitor?

This brings us to the main part of our discussion of the Second Maxim.

GROUP MEMBERSHIP

It seems to me that if Kant is accurately describing the moral part of the Contract between us then he should say: treat 'fellow Group members' as ends and not means, rather than saying treat 'people' as ends and not means. Thus in the current example when a member of an enemy group is captured after planting the bomb we have first to address the issue of 'reciprocal rights'.

Where does our Right not to be treated as a means, but instead as an end come from? It is difficult to see how it can come from anywhere other than our membership of a group and in particular from us doing our Duty towards the said group and its other members. Doing ones Duty is the fulfilment of ones part of the Contract, the moral part of the Contract that binds each group together.

Those in the neighbouring group who have done their duty whilst in that group have earned reciprocal rights by being a loyal hard working member of another group. This brings us back to Chapter 3 and all those years ago when Loyalty to the group made the first jump across the boundaries between groups. Our right to be treated in accordance with the Second Maxim is dependent upon us having done our duty by our group, our duty to be a Loyal, sometimes self-sacrificing and always hard working member of that group.

Those who are lazy backsliding members of our own group are not fulfilling their duty, and so they have not earned the right to be treated always as ends and never as means. Similarly if someone has not been a loyal hardworking member of a neighbouring group, they will not have earned their rights in that group and so will have no reciprocal rights that can be transferred over when we consider their case. The word 'rights', though convenient in many ways, is an oversimplification, which though fair enough for everyday practical usage can lead us into philosophical error. We have no rights across international boundaries, we have only reciprocal rights across those boundaries. But 'Reciprocal Human Rights' is a clumsy phrase, and so even if we realised that that is what we were saying we would probably still not use it.

This has been true ever since the time when we came to recognise that our trading partner in a neighbouring group could sometimes be in the moral right and our own brother be in the moral wrong, from then on reciprocal rights existed.

Kant's second maxim fails also because it assumes that all persons are equally deserving of their rights, even though every single one of us, in whatever series of groups and teams we work and play in are constantly aware that some pull their weight more than others. Kant is very big on Duty, but doesn't take into consideration people's Duty-history as we can call their record of behaviour.

These days, due to the size of the groups we live in, we have little chance of knowing whom amongst our fellow group members are doing their duty by us and the rest of the group. We have even less chance of knowing which of those who are not our fellow group members have done their duty in the massive group next door to us. Kant assumes that each person to whom his maxim applies has done their duty, because, due to the size and complexity of the groups we now call countries, he and we have no way of checking.

It would get very messy and impossible to administrate the law if we were to request of each party at the opening of every trial that they first provide evidence and witnesses to confirm they had earned their rights by doing their Duty. So instead we assume that they have earned those rights, and we further assume that if they have not been earned amongst this group, where a case has come up for trial, then reciprocal rights have been earned instead in a neighbouring group. But if we are pursuing this philosophically, rather than for the practicalities and conveniences of administrating the law, then we must always ask, what is his or her Duty-history.

The worrying conclusion to this is that it is therefore morally incorrect to grant equal rights to everyone.

Sorry about that.

What we grant to everyone are common rights, or more accurately common minimal rights, often in the face of governments who prefer that we have no rights. The problem with Kant is that his First Maxim is confounded because he appears to think there is no such thing as a white lie, or an entity such as a freedom fighter like Robin Hood, when there clearly are such things in this world. And morally legitimate things they are to boot. Whereas his second trips up because he thinks that our moral rules are 'universal' when in fact they are group orientated. To have had no ancient human groups is to have had no moral rules. There is no such moral entity as a 'citizen of the world'; we all belong to a group. And all our rights (our Right-not-to-be-bullied) come to us via our membership of that group.

Clearly in large modern mega-groups there will be many in the lower caste who are never given a chance in life by the group. Obviously this must be taken into consideration any time we assess their Duty-history, which may be either when they appeal to the State for financial help, or when we face the decision of whether to torture them or not, to reveal the location of the dirty bomb.

Kant trips up because he seems not to see that to treat people fairly we must know their Duty-history. How much we trust someone is based in part upon his or her Duty-history. Without knowing this we can never be fair, we can never be just, without knowing their history we allow villains to take advantage of the system. A right winger would say we actually mistreat other members of society, by being too fair to offenders, we bend over so far backwards to 'be fair' that we end up being too fair. And let's note that this is a legitimate right wing view, it is an anger not born of some prejudice, against homosexuals, immigrants or whatever, but born of a genuine reaction to the cumbersome unjust nature of our huge societies.

Kant's Second Maxim is written as if one's Duty-history is irrelevant, but in the case of the traitor from our group who has turned against us, after a life of freeloading, due to some petty sexual jealousy or as a result of being bribed by our enemies across the river, it clearly is very relevant. He has not turned against us because he has been treated badly; he has turned because he is a selfish little shit. If he had been treated badly in some way by the rest of us, then fair enough he is 'within his rights' to no longer be Loyal to us, and we have no right to torture him because we are the ones who have wronged him.

So here we are back in the present, and as far as I can see B/A-b is a more accurate picture of what morality is and how it operates amongst us than either Kant or Utilitarianism. Kant's effort is a valiant attempt to solve an intellectual puzzle, but the trouble is that morality is far more than an intellectual exercise. However the real reason for his failure, the main reason for the inadequacies of Kant's Categorical Imperative, is that his theory was worked out before we understood the details of the evolution of our species.

As a result his solution is not applicable to the real world, because it is not a true model of human behaviour. It works though as a legal principle and should, and will, no doubt continue to be used as such, for the writing and administration of the codified morality. Because, as I think we all pretty much understand, if you do not write international human rights statutes that say 'torture is always Wrong' then every brutal tin pot dictatorship in the world will claim the cases where they use torture are all special exceptions.

These exceptions will be portrayed as either fierce enemy aliens about to visit Armageddon on the dictator's happy and contented people, or a case of one of his own happy people having a less than satisfactory Duty-history. What am I saying, this won't just be dictatorships, the USA has been doing this to perceived Islamic terrorists ever since 9/11. Well then we still need Kant, to write laws that are in the main part true, there are in fact very few cases like the dirty bomb about to go off in the next few hours, and we happen to catch the perpetrator an hour or two after he's hidden the device. Yes we need Kant, he's a good lad, but his proposition is not an accurate representation of reality. The fact is that, purely on the grounds of reciprocity, and therefore morality, there are some revolting humans who deserved to be tortured, what about Adolf Hitler for starters?

In order to have rules of war, such as the Geneva Convention, that disallow torture of any kind no matter what the circumstances, we must

124

act as if Kant's second maxim is true no matter how bad have been the actions of those we are tempted to torture. Even though in reality the Contract written into our human emotions is not so written.

One has to write down national and international laws and so 'Kant's laws' are excellent as a summary of the principles behind such laws. But we are in discussion here for another purpose, to delineate the commonly shared moral principle behind the legal principles we use to make our laws.

Let's not get mixed up between philosophical truths about the world and the laws we are forced to make due to the clanking pedantic nature of the codified morality we call the law.

Which brings us to the twin subjects of human rights and forgiveness.

Part 4

Human Rights and Forgiveness

25. Animals and Humans

Let's digress a moment onto the subject of animals, because to do so highlights the fact that all rights are actually sub-rights of our one over arching all consuming Right, the Right not-to-be-bullied. We originally earn these rights by doing our Duty to be Loyal to others in the Group, by not bullying them, but animals are not members of these Ancient Groups...

Gradually some time after we learned to domesticate animals, and more recently invented weapons that helped us to dominate the ones we can't domesticate, we put ourselves in a position whereby we can take pity on them. No longer do we run in fear from any creature on this earth, and as a side effect of this dominance we begin to have mercy upon our former competitors, as well as towards those we have domesticated.

Just as the concept 'don't be Disloyal' can only be expressed as 'don't bully' between groups and within huge groups, so too this same 'don't bully' comes to be applied to animals. Our sympathy is extended, and we come to feel a similar emotional reaction when we witness the bullying of animals also. For most of us it is not the exact same emotion though, and this seems likely to be because obviously no animal can ever fulfil the Duties expected of a fully paid up member of a human group. Whereas humans from other groups can, and often do, become members of other groups, for example when they emigrate from one country to another and then subsequently take up full citizenship in their adopted country.

Sometimes those who champion the cause of animal rights ask why we grant full human rights to children, but don't grant the same rights to animals. Or there is an argument that runs that since certain classes of humans have reduced mental capacities to a state below that of many animals, why are they then granted the same rights as all other humans. We are asked if these human vegetables have rights, then why aren't other equally or more responsive species not also granted those same rights?

Well it is true that children don't have a Duty-history, but instead they have a Duty-future, in other words they are granted rights because we assume that they will be dutiful members of the group when they grow up. As for human vegetables, they are what we might call Duty-crippled, and once again we assume that if they were not so afflicted they too would be dutiful.

When we find a chimp or other animal that can fulfil all the obligations of a full member of the human team then we might have to give all chimps the benefit of the doubt too. Until then we should concentrate on not being racist, or groupist as we should more properly call this attitude.

Since we have, I hope, established that endless-torture is the ultimate immorality, then we can though surely agree that, despite their not ever being able to be members of the human team, we nonetheless shouldn't torture them.

I see a turkey, bred and bred to increase its size, so that it can barely walk, let alone have sex or fly, I see it kept in a dark endless warehouse, which it occupies together with thousands upon thousands of other similarly stunted and manipulated birds.

I see bullying.

I see endless-torture, it goes on for the whole of these creatures lives.

I see endless-torture, torture-unto-death.

I see the human definition of the ultimate immoral behaviour.

To inflict such misery is immoral.

Thus those who apply to us on behalf of animals are correct, when they say that it is immoral to torture an animal, for example by its conditions of confinement or by cruel methods of slaughter. But to take this further and say that we should give equal consideration to animal life as to human life, has the big hole in it, the big hole of 'Duties they cannot perform'. As a result they can have only proto-rights, for example to a life free of torture, in particular human-inflicted-torture, and the proto-right to as quick and as painless a death as possible when the time comes.

SPECIESISM

There is talk these days of Speciesism, some philosophers say that we shouldn't assign lesser rights to animals on the basis of their membership of different species to our own. In the light of human Morality having developed amongst us as 'Groupism' this is clearly nonsense. In fact Speciesism is exactly why morality evolved amongst us in the first place. As we have established Morality is first and foremost a bond of loyalty between a group of humans. This 'Groupism' is designed to exclude other human groups, let alone the groups of all other species in the long battles we have had to survive.

One could say animals 'should consider themselves lucky' that we hate bullying (within our human group) so much that we actually transmit this same emotional reaction, not just across to other humans from other groups, but also to animals as well. We are even angry when we see the biggest chick push the runt out of the nest to die, or when we see a cat toy with a mouse we think it is cruel. Oh boy do we hate bullying, no wonder we never tire of arguing over Morality, it takes nothing to 'get us going'.

When in preceding chapters we have discussed relationships between human groups, we have been in effect discussing how Groupism later becomes extended, with considerable (and ongoing) difficulties, to other groups. The first reason for this extension is due to the fear of constant wars between neighbouring groups. These other groups have the Power to wipe us out, and we need to compromise with them and include them in the application of our moral rules. (This is a not dissimilar compromise to the balance of Power that first reduced the Alpha Male to the Big Man.) We are forced to come to an accommodation with other groups to avoid endless wars, but we still, to this day, think of our own national interest first and put the interests of other groups (now called countries) second after that.

The second reason we extend the same rights to other human groups is because we recognise in them the same responses that we ourselves are capable of: trust, comradeship, loyalty, generosity, selflessness and selfishness, or in other words a sense of Duty, and one that each member is able to communicate and agree by the use of words. Due to the background of these shared attributes we find it illogical to fail to extend the same moral parameters to those similar beings in other groups as we do to ourselves – hence reciprocal rights.

Neither of these two important parameters apply to members of other species, even though we now have the Power to destroy many of those species. We still have an abhorrence though of bullying them, or even of seeing they themselves involved in 'bullying', as we consider it, be it the cat or the killer whale playing with their victims. Hence the importance of the concepts of 'reciprocal human rights', and 'animal proto-rights', to remind us again how easily our use of shorthand terms, such as 'animal rights' fools and confuses us.

SPORT

Hunting, Fishing and Shooting for sport rather than for food are all bound to be acts of bullying, because as soon as you use the word 'sport' you introduce the concept of 'enjoyment'. These sports are immoral because bullies take pleasure in the exercise of unopposed Power.

Sport is without doubt about Pleasure – and is 'for the fun of it'.

Nothing Wrong with Pleasure, nothing Wrong with fun, but in this context it is what makes the act into a bullying act, and therefore immoral – it's difficult to see how it can be anything else. One hears protests by those who like to hunt with hounds, that banning hunting infringes their human rights. But all rights are granted as a protection from bullying – one cannot have a right to bully (even animals).

That would be a complete negation of the concept of rights.

There can be no 'Right to bully', the phrase is a contradiction in terms. It is the bully who destroys the rights of others by bullying in the first place. All human rights are granted in the face of bullying.

All human rights are Anti-bully.

Human rights can never be pro-bully, as those who enjoy this activity in effect claim.

Rights are granted in opposition to bullying.

Rights are not granted to bullies.

Bullies take what they want by force, in the teeth, in the face of the rights of the rest of us. (Or the proto-right in this particular example.)

All rights are Anti-bully, Anti-bully, Anti-bully.

Hunting for sport (rather than food) is bullying and therefore immoral, but I'm picking on hunting with hounds here only to illustrate that all rights are anti-bully and that this is in fact the one and only Right there is. Such sports as hunting are not as Wrong as the torture-unto-death for every single second of their lives of battery hens and pigs reared and confined in factory conditions, because hunting grants, well in theory anyway, a reasonably quick death to a wild and free animal, rather than a whole life of stunted, tortured deformity.

HUMAN RIGHTS

So despite the many human rights we talk about, I put it to you that there is only one Right, the Right-not-to-be-bullied by others, and especially by the State the potential bully of all bullies. The Universal Declaration of Human Rights was written down after the second World War as a response to the Holocaust, to record the many ways, some subtle and some not so subtle, that the clique in Power in a country can be Disloyal to and thereby torment and bully their fellow citizens. Despite there being 30 summarising principles what they boil down to is that the individual members of a group have the 'right not to be bullied by their own government'.

These 30 principles are nothing other than a summary of all our within-Group rights, by which I mean our right not to be killed, raped, stolen from, blackmailed and otherwise bullied by other individuals within our Group, and in particular by the group-within-a-group that is in Power. We are forced to write these rights down in seemingly endless legislative detail because 'the group' has become so big that the concept of 'rights' and a list of those rights are needed due to sheer size and complexity.

Written human rights are an effort to avoid upper castes from bullying those lower down the pecking order. Or equally commonly, as countries establish boundaries that contain within them various smaller ethnic and religious minorities, are an effort to stop those minorities from being bullied – racism. A prejudice, since it judges by skin colour rather than by trustworthiness, judges by ethnic origin rather than by someone's Duty-history.

Notice that this trampling underfoot of lower castes or classes has no international element, human rights legislation, though recently written, is actually ancient and originated as nothing other than the Right not to be bullied by one's own government. The international element is required to put pressure on, and try to hold to account, governments of countries who are mercilessly bullying their own citizens, often with impunity.

We have had human rights ever since a 'Council man' first laughed at and ignored an order, and those other Council men stood watching, watching, waiting, waiting, quietly hefting their stone clubs. They were the first challenge to Power, the first balance of Power. They have always been and still are to this day, the basis of all our laws, though often twisted out of all recognition by the Tribal Chiefs, and the Kings and Queens who followed them, the aristocracy, our Lords and masters by divine decree.

All those so called 'countries' that contain within their boundaries great injustices and disparities of opportunities and wealth are sham groups, countries in name only, since a true country is a group of humans living and sharing together for the benefit of all. Why should those who are denied their fair share obey the rules of a society that ill-uses them? The rules of a society are only moral and justifiable if they reflect the central principle from which Morality springs, namely we are all in this together. If 'we are all in it together' is a blatant lie because some are in it a lot more than others, then the moral duty of the underclass is not to tow the line, on the contrary their moral duty is to rebel – to say no.

26. Universal Declaration

So let's look at the thirty principles and review the proposition that they are all rules intended to guard against acts of Disloyalty, acts of bullying by the ruling clique against other members of their own Group. Let's check out whether any one of them sounds as though it is something other than this.

1. All human beings are born free and equal in dignity and rights, *because each of us is a member of our Group (nowadays called countries) and as such deserves equal minimal treatment to, and the right-not-to-be-bullied by, any other member – no matter how powerful.*

2. Everyone is entitled to all the rights and freedoms set forth in this Declaration, without distinction of any kind, *because they cover the one inalienable right not to be bullied common to us all, whatever group we live in.*

3. Everyone has the right to life, liberty and security of person, *because these are the fundamentals of not being bullied by those who lead our Group.*

4. No one shall be held in SLAVERY or SERVITUDE, *since these are the antithesis of non-bullying relationships within any community.*

5. No one shall be subjected to torture or to cruel, inhuman or degrading treatment or punishment, *because torture and in particular torture-unto-death is the worst form of bullying that one human can inflict upon a fellow group member.*

6. Everyone has the right to recognition everywhere as a person before the law, *since without this recognition they can be victimised by other members of the Group.*

7. All are equal before the law and are entitled without any discrimination to equal protection of the law, *because without this safeguard some of the Group can be singled out and bullied in contravention of their supposed equal status.*

8. Everyone has the right to an effective remedy by the competent national tribunals for acts violating the fundamental rights granted him by the

constitution or by law, *because otherwise those in Power can bully with impunity.*

9. No one shall be subjected to arbitrary arrest, detention or exile, *since these are all ways in which those in Power bully those whose opinions it dislikes.*

10. Everyone is entitled in full equality to a fair and public hearing by an independent and impartial tribunal, *since such bodies, independent of the State, represent a balance of Power against bullying by the State.*

11. Everyone charged with a penal offence has the right to be presumed innocent until proved guilty, *so that if the Government attempts to bully certain individuals by using false charges, it shall be forced to present credible evidence.*

12. No one shall be subjected to arbitrary interference with his privacy, family, home or correspondence, nor to attacks upon his honour and reputation, *that is arbitrarily – in other words unless such interference can be clearly shown to be to protect other members of the Group from his or her bullying behaviour.*

Interference with privacy refers to the secret police arbitrarily listening in on members of the community so as to intimidate (bully) them. It does not mean that the police who investigate criminal matters (the bullying by certain individuals of other members of the group), cannot obtain permission for a wire tap if they produce sufficient evidence to a Judge. A judge in this case means a member of an independent judiciary capable of being a check on the Power of the Police and the State, and the danger that they may bully some individuals if no such balance of Power exists.

13. Everyone has the right to freedom of movement, *because to restrict such freedom is an act of bullying designed to confine some members of the community without reasonable cause.*

14. Everyone has the right to seek and to enjoy in other countries asylum from persecution, *otherwise there is nowhere for those who are being bullied by the worst bully of all, the State, to run to. We have now seen that to be philosophically correct we should say **reciprocal right** to seek...*

15. Everyone has the right to a nationality, *because to deprive them of such is to rescind their membership of the Group. This is to rescind the*

respect due to them as having a bona fide Duty-history amongst the Group, which is the very basis of their one inalienable Right-not-to-be-bullied by other members of the group.

16. Men and women … have the right to marry and to found a family, *since to deny a member of the Group the right to sex and procreation is to deny them the most basic driving force of life itself, and thus is to bully-manipulate them.*

17. Everyone has the right to own property, *because to deny them a roof over their head is to bully them into poverty and deprivation.*

'The right to own property' is intended to avoid sections of a community from being bullied by being dispossessed and poverty stricken. It is not intended as the right to own vast swathes of property so extensive that the owning of so much is out of all proportion to the person's contribution to that group. Since clearly such an imbalance of wealth is disrespectful and Disloyal to those in the same community who have next to nothing, such ownership is therefore immoral. Which is why we dislike to see it, and not for the reason the wealthy like to give – our jealousy.

18. Everyone has the right to FREEDOM of THOUGHT, CONSCIENCE and RELIGION, *because these are aspects of our interior lives and thus it is an act of bullying to interfere with that which does not itself interfere with others.*

19. Everyone has the right to freedom of opinion and expression, *since these are the products of the interior lives referred to above and affect no one else in the group, provided they are not used to incite the bullying of other group members.*

20. Everyone has the right to the freedom of peaceful assembly and association, *since to curtail such freedom is to bully them by placing restrictions on them while other members of the group are unrestricted.*

21. Everyone has the right to take part in the government of his country, *because to deny them this is to bully them into being forever part of the powerless underclass.*

22. Everyone, as a member of society, has the right to social security and is entitled to realisation … of … economic, social and cultural rights, *since human rights are intended to stand against the various social, political*

136

and economic ways we can be bully-manipulated into society's lower caste.

23. Everyone has the right to work … everyone has the right to form and join trade unions, *because without work and a trade union they can be exploited (bullied) by those in charge of the means of such work.*

24. Everyone has the right to rest and leisure, *since to have no leisure is be treated as a slave (bullied) by the higher caste who control the means of production.*

25. Everyone has the right to a standard of living adequate for … health and well being, *because to be denied such is for them to be condemned and thus bullied into a life of permanent poverty.*

26. Everyone has the right to education.
If certain members of society don't receive an education or similar rights, they remain permanently in the underclass, the lowest caste of society, condemned to clean up after the rest of us. To forever undertake the dirtiest, foulest, meanest and most back breaking jobs, when they have work at all that is. How subtle are the ways of the bullies, especially in large modern mega-societies.

27. Everyone has the right freely to participate in the cultural life of the community, *because to marginalise some members of the community is to bully-manipulate them into long term subservience.*

28. Everyone is entitled to a social and international order in which the rights and freedoms set forth in this Declaration can be fully realised, *means that the one underlying principle thou shalt not bully is true for every group and every single human in every group upon this earth. The international element is the granting of **reciprocal rights** between groups and thus as a result the taking in of asylum seekers.*

29. Everyone has DUTIES to the community.
*   In return for the human rights of free speech, thought, conscience and religion, the right not to be tortured, and not to be kept in slavery or servitude, in summary the Right-not-to-be-bullied, one has DUTIES to the Group one lives amongst. In fact this is how your one Right is earned, by being Loyal, by playing fair with the others in your Group.*

30. Nothing in this Declaration may be interpreted as implying ... any right to engage in any activity ... aimed at the destruction of any of the rights and freedoms set forth.

DUTY

The concept of Duty plays a major part in defining Morality and we must look at this more closely now. Without the concept Duty there is no moral order, it's that important. Duty is the opposite of Disloyalty. It is our Duty to be an honest, loyal and hard working member of the group, to put in a fair day's work for a fair day's pay, as long as the group is being fair to us.

When someone persists in taking a petty case all the way to the Court of Human Rights, by appealing and appealing, and won't take no for an answer, essentially to get their own way, why does it seem so revolting? And why does it undermine our faith in the Court and its processes? Which in turn results in right wing contempt for the Court and thus sometimes for the concept of human rights itself.

Is it not because our rights come to us from the group, only as a result of the active part played by each of us, the contribution each of us makes to the group? Our group grants us our rights as long as we fulfil our Duties, or more accurately our single duty to be Loyal to the others in our group. Whereas the Court of Human Rights automatically assumes the appellant in question has done his or her duty, because it has no way of checking their Duty-history to ascertain otherwise.

Thus some of us are revolted by the sight of someone taking their pathetic little case as far as they are allowed, when we suspect that they are not the kind of person we would be able to rely on to do their duty. And it is this 'as far as they are allowed' that can undermine the court, that can render us contemptuous of its well intentioned but never ending granting-of-rights to those who (we feel) are probably, by the look of them and their mealy mouthed attitude, failing to do their duty to the other group members they interface with..

The Right-not-to-be-bullied doesn't grow on trees. To speak in correct philosophical terms, everyone doesn't have rights, there are no rights floating around in the air. They must be earned by pulling your weight, by being fair to others. When certain claimants of their precious rights ignore this we despise them, and thus the Court too, when we think they are all about claiming all they can, and not one single jot about fulfilling their obligations, their one obligation – Loyalty to the Group.

We grant the same rights to all to be fair, we have to in practice, it's an administrative necessity because of the size of our massive societies. We mustn't forget though that we do this on an assumption. We do it on the theoretical basis that all have done, are doing, and will continue to do their Duty, even though in massive modern societies we can't check up on them the way we could in the small groups of our beginnings.

Granting equal rights to everyone is an injustice to those who do more than their share of the work and responsibilities of group membership, because these people actually deserve more than the freeloaders. We use the term 'equal rights' because our main concern is to establish 'common minimum rights' in order to fight against governments who constantly attempt to subvert and infringe upon the Right of their citizens to live free of being bulled by the State. 'Common minimum rights' would be a better term, they are the lowest common denominator of rights, but some group members deserve more. We should keep this in mind, but not worry about it too much, because those who deserve more are in fact not the type to waste our time and their lives making constant claims for such.

This is why when we see, what looks to us to be, certain petty minded selfish types whinging about their rights, some amongst us lose respect for a Court that not only fails to check up on Duties performed, but also seems to be too stupid to realise it should.

Thus we can see that right wing contempt for the Court has validity, because it is due to a genuine moral problem, and is not based merely on prejudice or bigotry. Complicated as things have become in our huge societies, to be Loyal and non-bullying in our actions to those around us is still the fundamental basis of the whole of human morality. It is enshrined in Article 29 of the Declaration, yet of all the articles this is the one that the Court never thinks to enforce.

27. Human Rights

There are many confusions we cause ourselves because we use the shorthand term such and such is 'a human right' when what we mean morally is such and such is 'one-aspect-of-the-human-right-not-to-be-bullied by a Disloyal and powerful member of our group'.

Any case we take up for consideration is simply one aspect or specific case of the sole and only human moral right there is or can ever be. One such is the concern some people have over their 'right to privacy', so let's look at the limits of this concept.

Where did we get the absurd idea from that there is a 'human right' to privacy? This claim and the term itself is a dangerous oversimplification, there is no right to privacy – the expression is another bit of shorthand that leads us into error.

What there is, is the right to not have your privacy invaded by anyone who may use what their invasion tells them about you to bully or bully-manipulate you. In other words the reason for privacy is to prevent the bullying of individuals by anyone, but in particular by the State or by agents of the State. And so not at all for the reason many individuals, especially certain public figures, desire to maintain their privacy – to prevent us knowing about the lies they tell us.

Of which we have every right to know.

In fact more than 'every right to know' it is an absolute fundamental staple of human groups that we do know such things – it is the central principle of human morality and thus of the Open Society. Do 'as you would be done to', and do it in plain sight of all so that justice can be done and 'be seen to be done'. That we should know when others are backsliding, when others are reneging on the Contract is vital, is the very backbone of human morality and society. There is no human right to privacy, we must stop this short-hand nonsense in its tracks.

On the contrary there is a human right to know when people are trying to hide their immoral (bullying-manipulative) behaviour, by projecting one public persona but living otherwise in private. Information in our original smaller groups will have been just the opposite – all our actions were transparent, except for sex between ourselves and our spouse.

Thus when for example certain public figures are photographed by newspapers involving themselves in lurid orgies, it is not the nature of the orgy that defines whether or not such stories are 'in the public interest'. No, what is relevant is whether or not they are projecting an image of respectability, which in fact is a lie to the rest of the group. The question is therefore not what they did, how they were dressed, or who whipped whom, but are they manipulating us by living a lie. Including are they married and does their partner know about their little peccadillo, because otherwise this is an act of infidelity to one member of the group, along with a manipulative lie to the rest of us. A lie that is often told because their well paid living depends in whole or in part upon them having a different public persona.

Imagine some public figure caught in such a lie to their spouse trying to claim the moral high ground! Most of us couldn't care less about the pathetic and boring details of the banal orgy they were involved in, what we care about is that they are liars. They have broken part of the Contract and so might well be breaking or willing to break other parts – and we always want to know who are the ones to be trusted and who are the liars we need to watch out for.

If the newspaper has done something illegal to obtain this information, then they are also breaking the Contract, and therefore also in the moral wrong – checks and balances as ever, from those hunter-gatherers with their stone clubs onwards. Or if you are single footloose and fancy free, and have told no lie to another or other members of the Group, then your sex life is no business of ours and the paper is again in the moral wrong, by exposing something that is private. Except if you proclaim yourself a virgin, celibate or the epitome of upright respectability for some reason to do with your public life and you are not, then again you are lying to us, you are by definition manipulating us. And rather than you having the right to privacy, we have the right via the newspaper to expose your manipulative lies.

All 'human rights' are items enshrined in legislation in an attempt to protect individuals from being bullied by their own government, by the secret police, or by the death squads allied to their government. If we unthinkingly transmit them into an argument between some public figure caught with his or her pants down, we are bound to run into difficulties. Once you write human rights down they are no different to laws and legal systems everywhere, they are written codes, they are not and never can be a living adequate response to the scolded-comforted child. They can never keep up with our lively, quick as a flash anger at each single moral wrong, at the twists and turns of every case of bullying we see.

When puzzled we should always ask – who is being bullied or bully-manipulated here? Ask yourselves that every time as you search for moral rights and wrongs, over and over again the same now as for all the time there has been since the Ancient Groups, and for all the time yet to come, until humans vanish from this earth forever.

The human right to privacy is actually the right to 'keep as much personal information as possible private if it is being used by the state or organs of the state to bully you in some way', but that's not quite as snappy and succinct as 'the right to privacy'. And that laziness is a mistake because if someone well known has a certain reputation in the media and sells their films or other products using this reputation, then the rest of us are entitled to know if it comes to light that this reputation is false.

We are entitled to know when someone is lying to us – aren't we?

We are entitled to know when one of our enormous group is behaving hypocritically, telling us one thing, spinning us a yarn, and acting in their 'private' life a different way. They are 'having us on' and we feel angry when they fool us and vindicated and vindictive after we find out we have been had.

Yes these are often cases of sexual infidelity, but they are not private if they concern a public figure who projects a lily-white public image. And our vindictiveness is not a prudish reaction to their sex lives, it is a reaction to being lied to. If some Casanova and serial womaniser admits to and even projects this image in public and also adheres to it in private then *c'est la vie*, we have no business poking our nose into his sex life. Our anger is directed at the lie, at the manipulative act of Disloyalty. An item is 'in the public interest' if it exposes a lie told to the rest of us.

We must be careful to not mix up such cases with those cases where the press for no good reason, other than newspaper sales, pursue people relentlessly and intrusively, photographing them because they've put on weight, or have lost weight, or are wearing a skimpy bikini. When they do this they are the bullies who are invading someone's privacy without just cause and so they are the ones contravening that person's right not to be bullied. That differentiation is a lot easier said than done I hear you say? Yes it is, there you go, that's democracy for you, or rather that is trying to administer a complex modern society of 60 million people using a moral code imprinted in us when we lived in groups of 60 individuals or less.

DNA AND CCTV

The same shorthand errors are bandied about in discussions regarding camera surveillance of our streets by the police, or the retention of DNA samples from people the police have arrested. The destruction of such samples, or the suggestion that camera surveillance should be reduced, in the name of human rights is mistaken nonsense. What those, including the European Court of Human Rights, who make such statements are doing is getting mixed up by using the same old shorthand terminology we have been discussing.

CCTV may sometimes be misused by Big Brother, in the same way that the police can misuse many pieces of information. But it is such misuse that is the violation of rights, not the fact of the existence of the cameras. In the main such cameras benefit us by giving the police a chance to either see the early signs of trouble and intervene or at least have evidence of (often violent) wrongdoing, which would otherwise be denied without such evidence.

The same applies to holding a bank of DNA samples, if you've done nothing criminal then your rights won't be affected. And if they are in some way then it is the misuse that we must be alert to, just as we try to be alert to any such abuse by the authorities. To get rid of the samples is to use a steamroller to crack a nut; one might as well say 'there are many cases of police corruption so we must get rid of the police'. DNA samples bring rapists and murderers to justice – do we want the police to have a chance of doing their job or not?

To remove the cameras and the samples one must first prove that through their abuse they have led to more abuses than the cases they have solved. But for you and I all this is circumstantial tittle-tattle compared to the underlying fundamental philosophical reason behind the need for CCTV surveillance cameras and DNA samples to be maintained.

You know it; you know the argument by now.

Our societies have got bigger, bigger and bigger until they number millions upon millions of individuals, instead of a hundred or so. As a single individual we cannot possibly know, let alone keep an eye on all the other members of the group to spot bullies and lazy manipulative freeloaders who are trying to take advantage of the rest of us.

We need DNA samples and CCTV cameras to compensate for the impractical difficulties of surveillance due to the size of modern societies. We need these devices to 'reduce the size of society', back towards the group level. We need them to help us to get back as close as we can, provided they are not misused by the state and its agents, to those groups of our beginnings, those groups inside which morality first grew in us. Those groups where we knew everyone in the group and could gossip each night about who was pulling their weight, and praise them, and who was behaving reprehensibly, and how big a kick up the backside they deserved.

Far from there being too many surveillance cameras there are actually too few, we need more, along with oversight, by the modern equivalent of those men with their stone clubs, to ensure no misuse by the organs of the State. Far from destroying DNA samples we should be taking samples from everyone at birth, again as long as we have and maintain a system with the usual balances of Power, to watch out for police misbehaviour. These devices can help us emulate as best we are able, the comparative simplicity of Morality at the time and place of its birth in those Ancient Groups now gone forever. For thou shalt not be Disloyal, thou shalt not bully is still the whole of the law.

28. Unnatural

Certain activities, often of a sexual nature, are sometimes described as unnatural, with the inference that these are therefore immoral. But acts that are 'unnatural' are just that, not natural – end of. The correlation between unnatural and immoral is made in the mind of whoever makes the statement, usually about something they object to. Now that we have touched upon our relationship with animals we can address the concept of unnatural, since one of the most common of these is some form of bestiality.

The other weakness of the term 'unnatural' is the argument that any activity undertaken by someone cannot be unnatural because someone is doing it. If someone is doing it how can it be unnatural? Homosexuality for example, if say 2.5% of the population are homosexuals, as research suggests, (Kinsey, 1948) then there are 1.5 million homosexuals in Britain alone. If 1.5 million people are doing something, then it seems a rather weak argument to suggest the activity is unnatural. Scientific research has now recorded homosexual behaviour in more than 100 species of animals, (Balcombe, 2011). This weakens yet further the use of the term unnatural, including in the case of homosexuality, (de Waal, 1997).

Another interesting aspect of this is that we only condemn unnatural activities that we pre-judge already as being morally wrong, celibacy for example. Why is that not condemned? To be celibate is to have a rather 'unnatural' sex life, but in this case it is not one that is generally deemed reprehensible, so is not designated as 'unnatural and therefore immoral'.

CELIBACY
Celibacy is a personal choice and so is a matter of self-governance for each of us as autonomous beings. It is often part of the attempt by monks, priests and others to be less selfish by denying the strongest of 'selfish' desires. An effort to rise above one kind of desire and so 'conquer' our selfishness, but it is not an easy path for most of us when young and vigorous, even Gandhi only moved towards it in later life.

We could condemn celibacy, there are some grounds, but we don't. We could condemn it because there is a danger that if men who take up the priesthood for example cannot control their sex urge, first they begin to think they are weaker than they should be (when really they are just normal), and next an immoral act does occur. They break out, cause hurt to someone, perhaps someone young and vulnerable, and now what started as a high minded (but not essential) goal, if one is strong enough, backfires. Backfires, and instead of delivering a greater level of selflessness, instead delivers an act of immorality.

The idea behind celibacy is that those who can control their desires become more selfless, become less focussed on the pleasures of the flesh and thus move instead towards 'higher things'. But even if it really can be controlled, rather than suppressed – or worse, paid lip service to and the vows broken in dark guilty corners – it is still the control of a secondary phenomenon.

The real Moral purpose is to triumph over selfishness, the seedbed of Disloyalty-bullying, not triumph over the sex urge. All sex is Moral that is non-bullying sex. So why bother struggling to control this most natural of urges? Besides we all know that we can, should and do think also of our partner while having sex, it is not just about one's own Pleasure, so why not settle for having sex in an unselfish way?

There is a Moral versus Metaphysical-religious mix up here. Entering into celibacy voluntarily, can be an act that demonstrates a determination to live a spiritual life, a life devoted to the higher more spiritual side of human nature, plus care for others, control of ego, and so forth. But these are personal choices, for those inclined that way, for those who find such a life brings them liberation from the thrall of desire, they are not for everyone.

All this is fine for spiritually inclined individuals, however there is nothing intrinsically moral in being celibate. What celibacy demonstrates when practised sincerely, and not as a burden to attain the kudos of the priesthood, is a genuine above average effort to beat or at least to reduce desire, to reduce 'I want'.

And since it is selflessness that is such a large factor in people being trustworthy, some religious traditions quietly and mistakenly place the cart before the horse. They thus come to believe that celibacy itself is intrinsically moral, but it is not, it is selflessness that results in a person behaving morally. And so it is selflessness that lies behind Morality, not celibacy. Celibacy is often an irrelevance and can be a burden in these important moral matters.

BESTIALITY

Bestiality is defined as sexual intercourse or oral sex between a human and another species, that is sexual activity between two separate species. The first thing to say about it is that observations (Bagemhil, 1999) have shown that it occurs between other animal species as well as our own. Therefore it is an act undertaken for Pleasure, in the same way that all sex is Pleasure driven.

Bestiality then is a sexual deviation, not unlike those who wish to be dominated during sex, and other oddball sexual fetishes that most of us find difficult to understand, but some of us seem to enjoy. Not being a fetish person I can't actually name another. Men wanting to be treated as naughty boys by a school mistress figure or other dressing up sex games perhaps? There is probably a long list, but I've led a sheltered life, and as long as none of these acts involve the bullying of one partner, which means that domination roles must be pre-agreed play acting, then they cannot be immoral. Thus sexual deviations that do not involve the bullying infliction of physical or mental pain by one party on another are not immoral.

So according to B/A-b then, bestiality is only immoral if the human inflicts pain and suffering on the animal, perhaps by tying it up in a painful position and forcing entry. Bestiality is odd and pathetic, but it is a question of self-governance, not morality. Provided there is no infliction of pain upon the animal involved then it cannot be bullying and so is not immoral.

For most of us the thought of penetrating an animal is mind boggling, but some sexual contact is maybe more understandable. I had a teenage acquaintance who trained his pet dog to perform oral sex on him, and in return he masturbated the dog. That is easier to understand especially when kids are young, experimenting with sex and finding members of the opposite sex hard to approach.

In this case the animal experienced pleasure and no pain and so we cannot declare the act immoral. Kind or unkind – does it involve cruelty to the animal is where the borderline stands. Since masturbation (Sommer and Vasey, 2010), inter species sex and homosexual behaviour have been observed in a variety of animals, this further confirms that these behaviours are not even 'unnatural'.

Can we say that to have sexual relations with an animal without its consent is a case of bullying? No, we do not ask animals for their consent before we trap, then (quickly) kill and eat them. To require consent to sex would thus be absurd. Bestiality, in particular full sexual intercourse, is in fact a sexual deviation that is so unusual and peculiar, that it is a source of shame for those who are caught at it, but is otherwise not worth spending too much time on.

The only reason we are discussing it is to dispense with and separate ourselves off from another category of confusion – those things that we designate unnatural. Since sexual deviations are not public displays they are not a violation of the sex-in-public prohibition, as would be someone having sex with their pet dog in a public park. Bestiality is a private act, unskilful and pathetic, but private – provided it does not inflict suffering.

From the above we can conclude that behaviour classified as unnatural is not automatically immoral. Because … no bully no crime.

29. Not Playing God…

If endless-torture is the extreme limit of the Disloyalty principle, and thus is the full stop that helps to define it, where is its gentle hidden start point?

One place is the smallest unprovoked impoliteness or snubbing of another, because such spiteful insults are the subtlest form of Disloyalty in the Group. Sometimes of course we use such slights as a means of letting others know we are displeased with them, and if they have ill used us or hurt us in some way, they are then a justified response to bullying. But when unprovoked, being impolite is Disloyalty, the first insult that is often the start of more and worse to follow. Politeness affords us the respect we deserve, the respect we have earned as a hard working and equal sharing member of the group. And those who withhold it from us without just cause are themselves failing in their Duty towards a *bona fide* fellow group member.

SAVIOUR SIBLINGS AND MANIPULATION
Take the case of a couple with a very sick child. They want to have another child, so as to produce a baby who would be a supply of the necessary bone marrow to help save the first sick child. But they can only do so by *in vitro* fertilisation, so as to precisely manipulate the fertilised egg.

Manipulative behaviour towards someone to suit our own ends is immoral, even when nothing is stolen, nor any blood spilt. To produce a child for the purpose of saving another, understandable as the parents' actions and feelings are, is nonetheless a manipulation of the proposed baby, and those who manipulate others are (gentle) bullies. This must surely be the opposite extreme from torture-unto-death.

When we say, 'I feel used' it is said as if this feeling is a 'bad' thing, as if those who use others are doing a bad (Wrong) thing, and this is because to use others is an act at the gentler end of the Disloyalty-bullying scale. And even though in this case the users are caring parents who will no doubt love and support their new child for the whole of their lives, the moral issue is the manipulation of another.

Maybe the new baby will grow up to love big brother, or maybe these siblings won't get on at all, but either way, this new person, now a human with the same rights as every other member of the group has been used. Not just used, has been born already manipulated, no matter how much also loved, so as to specifically be used, indeed for the primary purpose of being used, albeit to save another. Which is why this act of designer birth is immoral.

Of course it is all done in a good cause, the cause of saving a life – the parents do not want to lose their first born, they are being caring about an ill child. Hence the difficulty faced by our medical ethics committees, but the act itself is unethical, because it is bullying-manipulation, it is the most gentle, the most subtle, the least brutal bullying any of us are ever likely to encounter, but it is a subtle form of bullying nonetheless.

It may be that 'the manipulated', when he or she grows up, will be the big hearted type who will think the whole business of their birth is wonderful and marvellous. Or, if they are a different type, peevish and small-minded, they may be permanently resentful of the circumstances of their birth. I was born for the sake of another, not for the love of having me for myself – or some such. Either way, the act itself is immoral.

We are speculating how the manipulated will feel when he or she has grown up, but we can never know this beforehand. We know what a good cause this is, and in practice surely most people so manipulated will find it pretty easy to forgive, after all it is forgive or do not exist.

It is immoral – but only just.

It is technically immoral.

They do something technically Wrong to get a good result, to save a life. In this kind of case it seems very harsh to condemn them as behaving immorally.

This brings a little clarity, but no simple solution, chiefly because the problem is so refined and so far removed from Morality's origins. Clearly this is not the kind of problem that the principle of Disloyalty ever encountered in the Ancient Groups, which is the reason for our difficulty, both here and with some of our other moral dilemmas.

DESIGNER BABIES

What if the test tube design of the baby is done so as to produce a child that is athletic, good looking and intelligent, an all round supreme human being? The parents in this case want a child that will be a joy to itself and themselves.

The moral question is again, has this new human being born fresh upon this earth already at the moment of its birth been bullied by manipulation?

If it has, then this is an immoral act.

Has this child been bully-manipulated?

It seems to me that it has.

Decisions were taken to give it certain characteristics, traits perhaps that the parents admire or wish they had. While other traits that they do not like in themselves are weeded out. They mean well, but who is to say that they have made good decisions, who's to say that this creature they create will be as happy as they think?

Notice that there is no need to invoke the tempting but ridiculous phrase 'playing God', a morally meaningless term designed by those who use it to invoke an accusation of supreme arrogance towards those it is used against, and thus they hope win whatever argument they are in the middle of. We can now be far more precise than this; it is sufficient to say morally wrong because it 'bully-manipulates a living human by genetic manipulation prior to the birth of that human'.

DESIGNER BABIES AND SAVIOUR SIBLINGS

Any procedure to produce a fertilised egg with certain characteristics and without others is a manipulation. The resulting human being has been manipulated, and its manipulators are there, readily to hand to be held accountable – two in particular, the chief manipulators, its loving parents.

When the one manipulated is a saviour sibling, an argument can be made that he or she has been instrumental in saving a human life, the life of their sibling. Therefore this most gentle of manipulative acts is not an act of bullying (aggressive interference), but is instead a (proportionate) response to the imminent death of the other child.

On the other hand what if the attested purpose of the manipulated birth is to "balance my family" (one male child and one female child – God help us what a concept)? Then this is clearly not a response to a crisis and so is not sufficient to weigh against an immoral act.

Thus the concept 'designer baby' is immoral, but even though saviour siblings are also manipulative we are loath to condemn the parents as immoral, because we feel their response is proportionate to the situation that they are facing. In the next chapter we shall be delving further into the importance of reciprocity and responses that are proportionate and disproportionate. For now we need only remind ourselves that any response that is proportionate cannot be an act of bullying. Only overkill responses are acts of bullying.

We are thus back at the crossover point noted on the second page of Chapter 24, where we were trying to weigh up whether the response of 'torturing the bomber' was based upon Utilitarianism, or proportionality. In declaring the birth of a manipulated saviour sibling legal are we allowing B/A-b Morality to be overridden by Utilitarian half-morality? Or are we actually declaring the process of manipulation legal by dint of it being a reciprocal and proportionate response to the imminent death of the other sibling? We'll leave that to the Professors, but one thing is certain, our ancestors never faced this in the Ancient Groups, which is why the subject is so tricky.

If in the case of saviour siblings we are calling upon Utilitarianism to help us, it is fine to do so (we need all the help we can get), as long as we don't make the confusing mistake of at the same time calling it Morality, when it is actually half-morality. Either way, whether we use Utilitarianism or rely upon the contractual principle of a proportionate response, behold the subtle opposite to cruel merciless torture. Can you think of any form of bullying more gentle than manipulation before you were even born? There is an irony here in the comparison with abortion.

ABORTION
Since morality is based upon Disloyalty and its derivative the principle of Bully/Anti-bully we must decide the abortion issue upon whether or not a foetus can be bullied. It seems to me that abortion is not immoral, because there is never an independent human life that can be bullied. You cannot bully a sperm, or an egg, or the embryo that forms in the weeks before it is capable of independent human life, for up to that time there is only a woman with tissue for a potential human life inside her.

There is at this time only one person, only one member of the group, one human being who is a member of the group, not two. Any tissue inside her has no rights at all separate from hers.

How could it?

It has no existence.

The only rights that can possibly exist are the rights of this woman to choose what she does with the inside of her own body. To talk in terms of the rights of the 'unborn' is illogical.

Some people consider this to be too harsh a cut-off point. But that is all there is to discuss, it is the moral issue here, the only one – where, or rather when, at what length of time after the sperm reaches the womb should we draw the cut off line for bullying. At that very moment or at sometime after? Can you bully a sperm as it fertilises an egg? How old is the embryo before it can be bullied?

How can a being as yet unborn have rights? It is not a member of the group, because it does not exist. Sadly for the foetus, you have no rights until you are born. Only members of the group have rights, tissue as yet unborn cannot be a member of the team – the Ancient Group that first gave voice to the concept: that's not fair. The team that first said you have been wronged, you have been wronged my fellow Group member.

As soon as you are an independent being, hey presto, you have rights, full membership and the one Right-not-to-be-bullied. While you are a baby and a small child it is assumed that you will be a hard working member of the Group as soon as you are old enough to share some of the burdens of the Group.

Thus the irony, that the baby who is manipulated and used as a saviour sibling comes eventually to have existence, and thus the moment of its birth, technically the moment it is capable of independent life, is the moment at which it attains all its rights. Or as we now know, its one Right not to be bullied by other group members, including its own mother. At that very moment it immediately also has a claim for bullying, or rather for disloyal manipulation against its own parents.

Whereas the aborted foetus, sadly, never has any claim because it never has any rights, because it never has independent existence. It is 'got at' before it is awarded its official 'certificate of group membership', and that is painful and mind boggling to some of us, especially now that we can photograph a foetus. But since there never exists a separate individual human member of the group that is or has been bullied, there can never be a valid moral claim either.

Only humans that have independent existence can have rights that are separate from the rights of the mother. To juxtapose the concept of the embryo's possible future rights, if it survives, and place them at odds with the mother's existing Right-not-to-be-bullied, as a fully functioning team member, is to put the cart before the horse.

As for Metaphysical-religious beliefs that rest for example upon concepts such as a claimed knowledge of 'God's purposes', these are not and can never be Morality. They are beliefs, on a par with for example the beliefs of Jains who wear breathing masks when they go out, in case they breathe in and kill a gnat, because it might possibly contain the soul of their dead grandfather – oops. That idea, the transmigration of human souls, is a belief, a metaphysical-religious belief, a mystical belief, a cultural belief, an ancient belief, a mumbo jumbo belief, an unlikely belief, whatever you prefer, but always a belief, never Morality.

And a belief that you have knowledge of God's purposes is a similar, albeit rather more arrogant, belief. As we have seen Morality is B/A-b, it is either bullying, or bullying-manipulation, based upon Disloyalty to the Group – and metaphysical beliefs just don't come into it.

And the rights of the unborn?

I honestly can't say that phrase, it's so ridiculous it sticks in my throat too much. The unborn have no rights. I understand how painful that is, I do, but how could they? How can that which has no separate and independent existence have rights?

Are the unborn standing with us in our Ancient Groups of long ago? The place where we go, for clarity, to figure out any moral question, no matter how modern, that comes up? No, only living human members of the team have rights, possible future members just don't come into it.

Some find the arbitrary nature of this cut-off point difficult to come to terms with, yet we choose an age for voting, 18 years old at present, the age of 2 years old would seem absurd. We choose an age for criminal responsibility in our courts, below which a child is held to be not fully responsible.

We choose an age for sexual consent, 16 years old, giving a 6 year old girl the 'right' to consent to sex would be sick. A child is not old enough for the right to be applicable, thus also a foetus incapable of independent life ... but we hesitate, of course we do, because the stakes are so high, a life itself.

Incidentally, if I were to claim that we should not object to abortion because there are already too many mouths to feed in Our Group, or in the whole world, then this would be a Utilitarian argument rather than a moral one. So in this case then, the half-moral Utilitarian argument happens to support the moral conclusion. But we should be aware that when there is a clash, rights (B/A-b) trumps goals (Utilitarianism), as Ronald Dworkin has it (Dworkin, 1986).

STEM CELLS

Once we ban the Metaphysical-religious term 'playing God' from our moral language, it clarifies that there can be nothing immoral about undertaking stem cell research – how can you bully a stem cell? A blob so small you can barely see it with the naked eye, a blob that is never going to be a fully-fledged human being, a blob that is never going to be a group member with the Right-not-to-be-bullied.

It might prove stupid and dangerous to poke and mess about with stem cells, in the same way some people think that the science and practice of Genetic Modification (Chapter 9) is potentially disastrous. It may well be foolish scientific arrogance, but it is not immoral.

Don't use either of those phrases around me please, don't insult me, spare me that, the 'unborn' have no rights. And there is no question of 'playing God', the only question is – have you bullied another sentient being or not?

30. Limited Forgiveness

That's enough for the moment about defining acts that are morally wrong, let's look instead at the much vexed subject of how to respond to those who actually do wrong. In essence the operation of a criminal justice system hinges around whether to be soft or tough, whether to forgive or not, and to what extent. Let's have a look at this in the next few chapters, because it throws more light on the origins and boundaries of morality via these, moral-response dilemmas, as they could be called.

Over the course of the last half century, some computer people have come up with a simulation of human behaviour that shows how co-operation developed in those funny, awkward, slow, weak creatures with very small teeth – our ancestors. In its original form elucidated by Flood, Dresher and Tucker it is called The Prisoner's Dilemma, a part of Game Theory, but it could just as well be called The Moral Dilemma. And this is how selflessness, or as we should more accurately say, occasional acts of selflessness, gradually appeared amongst us via the evolutionary process, (Axelrod, 1984).

FORGIVENESS/CO-OPERATION

The choices we have out in the wild are either to bully or to co-operate (rather than forgive). We see it in the wolf pack gathered around the carcass once the hunt has succeeded – should I observe the pecking order, or fight for a higher place within it?

A seemingly simple computer game is set up in which each player has that choice in each round of the game, to bully or to co-operate with every other player they interface with, amongst the various players in the game. Surely to always bully is a winning strategy? Well one time it was, before the primates came to play.

If you bully and your opponent gives way (co-operates), then you have all you want to eat and your opponent, especially when times are hard, gets nothing, so you get 5 points and your opponent gets zero, hooray, you've won! Not so fast, this game is different to any other game you've ever played – it never ends.

It is the endless game, it goes on forever, the game that doesn't even end after you're dead, via your genes, passed on to others like yourself it continues, continues, continues on and on and on and on.

In the next round of the game, in the wild at the next hunt a few days later, your opponent last time is still on the team, he's hungry and he knows your face, he's a primate and he has a good memory for faces. This time he doesn't co-operate. Just as you attempt to bully him he bullies-you-back.

In fact you fight each other almost to exhaustion. Now neither of you eat much, catch much, because of your injuries, because of your mutual opposition. We'll give you 1 point each, you ate a little more than he who lost last time, but at the price of injury, exhaustion, pain and wasted time while others of the pack ate well, or worse, neighbouring packs ate well.

Next time, at the next round of the game, you both decide to go for co-operation, partly because you've now tried out each others strength and realise you're almost equal, and partly because you're still too hungry from the last round to waste time fighting again. Your co-operation is successful, it is a good hunt, you both eat well, you have meat for the pack, and everybody has a good time.

You didn't get as much as when you bullied, and got away with it, but you've still come out ahead. You're well ahead of the time you fought yourselves to a standstill, this time you both get 3 points, which while not as good as 5, is a damn sight better that 1 or zero.

Of course quite often your opponent, or should we say playing partner, looks a bit weaker than you, a bit less sure of himself. So you push him a bit, and try to get 4 points, by hustling him, by crowding him, by putting or keeping him in his place. Whatever expression you fancy, they all mean the same thing – borderline bullying.

Sometimes you get away with it, and sometimes you don't, but the scary thing is that sometimes it's seven, eight, nine, or even more rounds later before you find out you haven't got away with it.

These creatures have long memories, they wait and then suddenly, they bully-from-behind, just when you thought you'd got them where you wanted them. They stab you in the back, or simply hang back at the vital moment on the next hunt, when they're positioned next to you. They do a Serpico on you – the cop in the film of the same name, whose 'comrades' hang back at the vital moment.

Back in Computer World, something interesting happens when you play this game by computer simulation, with real people partnered together, devising permutations of strategies, between the two extremes of always co-operate and always bully. This is the same way that the game has been played through the thousands of years of our evolution, and the results fed back into our genes, as those who play best survive longer and procreate more. The thing of interest is that reciprocity always wins most points overall.

Reciprocity, do as you would be done to, an eye for an eye, that most ancient principle found in the Bible, Koran and other religious books of all shapes, sizes and ages worldwide always stacks up most points.

RECIPROCITY

That is, a friendly strategy of co-operation on the first round, followed by doing on the next round whatever ones partner/opponent did on the last, always stacks up more points than any other behaviour pattern. Except, when the game gets really subtle, when by feeding back this information to all the players and running the whole thing again for another hundred rounds, a strategy of one more forgiveness / co-operation then stacks up even more points. That is instead of tit for tat, tit for two tats, one extra round of forgiveness before you strike back, (Dawkins, 1989).

Tit for two tats, behold the evolutionary mechanism that creates the first judgements, as opposed to an automatic response of a slap, punch, kick or bite – and a 'don't try it on with me'. These are judgements regarding the extent to which the other individual's act of less than full co-operation should be regarded as an act of Disloyalty. Judgements that in time, as we interface repeatedly with others in the group, creates what we come to call Morality. Many members of the group forgive once, others twice or even perhaps three times, but any more than this and forgiveness stops, the offender is branded as Disloyal and therefore as immoral, and in need of chastisement.

LIMITED FORGIVENESS

Limited forgiveness is the building block, is the dawn of the concept 'I must make a judgement' before I react. It is thus the dawn too of the concept 'too harsh', of the idea 'over reaction', of the human feeling 'that is bullying'. Thus it is the means by which Disloyal/Loyal, the B/A-b response was built, which in turn is the means by which the Basic Morality was built. It is therefore the means by which co-operation was built between individual members of the group who are unrelated by blood, built by extending the forgiveness we afford those who are of our blood. Thus competitiveness within the group, though still present, comes to be reduced in intensity.

Witness the gene that says first be friendly, if hit forgive, if hit again, hit back or sometimes forgive just one more time. Witness how it appears and is nurtured by the evolutionary process. As it works its way amongst this species learning to co-operate like no other individual mammal ever has, in a way new upon this earth half a million years ago. The human 'moral gene', the gene for acts of selflessness steps forward, or should we say carves itself a niche, because that other selfish dog is yapping at its heels, the dog that is the selfish Disloyal bully doesn't just fade away.

For wolves and many others, the pecking order, wherein the strongest rules, is sacrosanct, inviolable, the rule of rules. The rule which shapes their social world, the rule which is the basis of their whole social order,

155

the rule which governs every single one of their relationships. Not so with us... It is limited forgiveness, that first decision to hold back a moment, and he or she who responds by taking it, not as weakness, but as a sign of magnanimity, a sign of friendship, that builds a different social order.

Thus the use of the word Morality should stop at limited forgiveness. Tit for two tats is its evolutionary end point, tit for three tats at most. We should maybe stretch it that far, to three, after all what Game Theory does is based upon using the actions of people today, in a modern computer simulation. Perhaps our ancestors were more forgiving than we are now?

If all this is true then what is the unlimited forgiveness recommended by Jesus and the Buddha, or unconditional love as the psychologists call it? Unconditional love is vague terminology so let's straighten that out first, because it should really be called unconditional trust. Trust and Loyalty are the cornerstones of human morality, not 'love', which is a word we use for many other things, too many other things.

TRUST
Here take this food, take this water, come closer to the fire.

Let me help you with that, sit here, there's a storm coming, there's a herd of wild beasts coming, there is a famine coming, sit here by me, let me protect you, for it is my Pleasure so to do.

No don't thank me, don't thank me, it is my Pleasure. It pleases me to help you, and especially to do so without any hope of gain.

My generosity makes me feel good about myself. It thrills and pleases me more than mere words can say to offer this, my stronger helping hand to you, a weaker member of our pack.

Here give me your hand...

It thrills me too to see that look of friendship I see shining in your eyes.

I have seen those looks before.

Oh yes, I know how long they last – sometimes forever.

So don't thank me, I thank you. I thank you for giving me this chance to be the best a human can.

It matters not to me how weak you seem this winter.

One day, years from now, one day when neither of us expect it, you'll guard my back without me asking, maybe even without me knowing that you've done it.

And you...

You will feel best about yourself if you guard and save me without my knowing it – because this proves you do it altruistically, without the hope of gain.

Here give me your hand...

This is just the way we are, we humans.

Well some of us, some of the time anyway.

And this is what we call trust.

It is unconditional trust the psychologists really mean, and it is this that allows us to use the mechanism of unlimited forgiveness. We humans are actually capable of giving to others without asking for immediate or even any return at all. This is just the way we are, sometimes. And those that are not, those that are so selfish as to be Disloyal, those who bully other members of the troop, these we do sometimes forgive, but other times we have to take action against – to make them stop.

And now we have come full circle.

That holding back, by both parties, takes us down a road that leads the group further and further away from the wolf pack mentality, a road that soon… Produces neutrals, who decide, this is Right, that is Wrong. Who decide: yes, you have been treated badly, too roughly, unfairly, unjustly, you have been bullied, when there was no need for such a harsh response, no need to … over react, no need to … bully.

Behold the last piece in our puzzle is the first piece also.

31. Trust

The first time I came across Game Theory it seemed ridiculous that it could throw light on the subject of human morality. Morality isn't a game I thought. It is relevant also to other aspects of human life than Morality, but even so maybe calling the concept 'Game Theory' is an unfortunate choice. So I understand how one's first reaction is to be doubtful, but this computer simulation does model, and therefore represent, generations of human behaviour, and it does it using real live humans, though admittedly in a controlled setting.

It shows us how and why to forgive a specific low number of times is a limit of morality. It is a limit because the fact that reciprocity, or tit for two tats, stacks up more points than any other strategy tells us that this must have been the strategy that developed amongst us as pre-humans. This resulted in the survival and reproductive success of this type of co-operating group. Thus to forgive one or two times is how Morality was formed amongst us, back in the Ancient Groups now hidden from view.

It is thus one of the boundaries of Morality, as we have seen not its only boundary, but a definite demarcation line, an end stop. Many of us find it difficult to forgive when people hurt us, yet others, often under the influence of their religion can find it in them to forgive many times. To forgive much more than this can sometimes result in one being 'walked over' by other group members, and thus to be reduced to a low status within the group. This in turn increases the probability that your breeding opportunities will also be lessened, and so you will be less likely to reproduce more 'forgivers' like yourself.

Tit for two tats may seem rather a sudden end to Morality, but when you look around do people really forgive each other much more than that? Isn't giving people another chance (just one) about as far as our patience frequently stretches? And often rightly so, it's all they deserve maybe? Or maybe not, either way I think we can reasonably stretch the concept of limited forgiveness to tit for three tats, but no more. After that we can no longer legitimately use the term Morality, because we have gone beyond how it was formed in us. We will come to the incredible forbearance that is unlimited forgiveness again in Chapter 33, for now all we need do is be aware that whatever it is, we shouldn't call it Morality.

In addition to philosophy another reason we are looking for a limit to forgiveness is an argument from the world of evolutionary biology, it revolves around whether we can ever be altruistic. No it revolves around how biologists say we cannot ever be altruistic if evolution is correct.

There's a mix up here that biologists have got us into, or maybe we've all got ourselves into, let's take a look at it. All actions within the context of evolution are undertaken via the mechanism of Pleasure. Hunger is unpleasant and it is therefore a Pleasure to eat. Sex is a Pleasure and so we procreate. If we do not eat first others will eat and we will starve to death, if we do not have sex first others will take our potential partner and we will not propagate our lineage.

Therefore all individual creatures are inherently selfish, because all of us pursue our own Pleasure, and the whole of evolution is based on this. (Certain life forms such as ants and bees are exceptions in that they are in effect one organism with many bodies, rather than many individuals working in close co-operation as packs of mammals do.) Fair enough, but biologists use the term 'altruism' to mean acts whereby a sacrifice is made that benefits another's capability and opportunity to breed, while reducing our own. But 'everyday' human altruism is much subtler than that, we apply the word altruism to many other acts than those that effect an individual's opportunities to breed.

Everday altruism is a proximate cause whereas evolutionary altruism is an ultimate cause of altruistic behaviour (Alcock, 2001). We humans have evolved in groups such that we take great Pleasure (sometimes) in helping others, and it is this feeling of personal Pleasure that we seek. Mostly our pleasures are selfish, as are the pleasures of other creatures but look what happens when a creature also gains Pleasure from helping others.

'Here, come sit by me, give me your hand, lay that burden down and let me bind that wound. Let me help you with that.'

By this act I think of myself as generous and unselfish, and others see me as this too, and they trust me for it, but that is by the way. In order for me to believe this myself and thereby claim this special Pleasure, let alone convince others, I must perform acts that are genuinely at a cost to me. The fact that I gain the secret, and in some cases almost unconscious, Pleasure of thinking of myself as a genuinely unselfish person, and am therefore 'really' a hidden egoist, not an altruist, is neither here nor there as regards the way others are treated by me.

Thus even though our help is given because 'everyday altruism' gives us selfish Pleasure, the act is still done at some cost to ourselves, and is a benefit (though not necessarily a reproductive benefit) to the recipient. Because if it costs us nothing in the world external to ourselves, no money, no effort, no time, then we cannot even convince ourselves, let alone anyone else that we are altruistic. And if we cannot convince ourselves then we cannot feel the warm internal special human Pleasure that says to us inside our heads – 'you are a generous, giving, unselfish person, you are fully human, you give to others without expecting something in return. You give to them because it gives you Pleasure'. And if you keep doing it, keep doing it, so that you do it always, instead of only sometimes, then look out, look out because you are becoming, you, you … who knows you may become … a Saint.

You are doing your Duty, or in the case of a Saint more than your Duty, you are behaving morally because you are making a sacrifice on behalf of others, and members of the group see you make it. They see you can be 'counted on' in a crisis, they see you give to others freely, and so, they reciprocate. Thus you frequently get something back in addition to the Pleasure of feeling good about yourself, you receive help from others when you need it – because they see you are unselfish, and therefore worthy of their friendship and their trust.

Out in the real world as long as it is a genuine sacrifice on our part, which confers a benefit on the recipient, then it matters not to that recipient that also there is a secret Pleasure in it for us. I help others free of charge and thus I am fully human, even maybe a great human, is like so many of our pleasures, a private Pleasure.

And this is all there is to the biological confusion over altruism, as with so many philosophical problems, it is due to the misuse of a word. The biologists use altruism only and solely in the context of reproductive success, whereas the rest of us use it far more widely, meaning any time we give freely to others.

Our generosity gives us an inner Pleasure, and so, for all it matters, we probably are, strictly speaking, 'really' always acting selfishly. This then complies with evolutionary expectations: creatures are always seeking after their own Pleasure, which nine times out of ten equates to their own survival.

'One day you'll guard my back without me even knowing it…'

If they think of me as a 'genuine altruist', they will come to no harm by it, because irrespective of my secret Pleasure I am the genuine article in my acts towards others.

Whereas were they to mistakenly think a selfish arrogant egoist was an altruist and place reliance on him, (one who gets far more Pleasure from his own gratification than he does from acts of generosity), that could be a mistake from which they would suffer hurt, even death. They will not be let down by me, despite, no, no wait, they will not be let down by me, because of, my secret Pleasure. They will not be let down by me because to act selfishly would negate the view of myself that I have, would negate the core of my ego, my view of myself as generous.

And we all have egos, even the Buddha. Don't be fooled by that stuff about peeling off the layers of self via meditative practice, the only people without egos are the glorious dead. For sure we should be engaged all our lives upon controlling our egos more, more and more, via Buddhism or whatever, but not destroying our ego's very existence.

Let's get these terms correct, to be without any ego is to be dead, or dead inside, believe me, I've tried it – the concept of being 'ego-less' is just a convenient term that is neater than the term ego-under-control, and so we fall into the trap of using it. An ego-under-control is our true goal, never no-ego, not ego-less, it's my favourite religion, but that doesn't mean that there's no such thing as Buddhist claptrap.

For scientific purposes this split between evolutionary altruism (ultimate) and everyday altruism (proximate) is important, and it seems as though the use of these two separate terms are long overdue, instead of the present situation where we tend to use the same word 'altruism' for both. Meanwhile for you and I it is enough to know which of our acquaintances tend to be selfless (everyday altruists) and which are selfish egoists, it is more than enough.

It is everything.

Of course egotists often try to masquerade as altruists, but the sniffing out of such people is a different day-to-day matter from the question of whether or not there is in the final analysis such a thing as 'genuine altruism', by which is meant evolutionary altruism.

So back to our main topic here, Game Theory is much more than a game, the game is an experiment, an attempt to see how real human beings react to the series of mini moral dilemmas they are presented with as they interface with those around them.

How they really react mark you, not how they talk, not how they say they will react, talk is cheap. This is how they do react. Tit for two tats, tit for three tats at a stretch, and when the behaviour of others starts to push us beyond this we begin to suspect … here is an egotist, one of the selfish, taking the piss. Taking advantage of my easygoing nature.

LIONS

You're still a bit doubtful? How about a little example illustrating that 'the experts' can often miss out the bit that's important to the rest of us, in their concentration on scientific theory?

You will have heard wildlife commentators say something along the lines of: "the new male lion kills the existing cubs so that the female will come into heat again, and the cubs that then result from their union will propagate his line not her former mates". No doubt this statement is biologically correct, but there's a mistake hidden in it. A step they miss out, unintentionally gloss over, call it what you will, but it's an important step, when dealing with everyday matters, and it's an omission repeated for many creatures.

The male lion does not kill the cubs so that he can propagate his lineage, he kills the cubs so that she will come into heat and he can have the Pleasure of sex with his new partner.

If we were talking about humans, his new girl would have sex with him even though she had a baby already, because human females have no in-heat season. With many other creatures though she will not be sexually receptive until the young are either weaned, which takes time, or off the breast due to 'sudden infant death syndrome'. The new male lion kills the cubs for sexual gratification, for the Pleasure of having sex with her (a proximate cause). This is his immediate, indeed is only purpose, and it 'just happens' that due to the biological construction of life upon this planet, this also procreates his lineage (ultimate cause).

'Here, give me your hand, sit down, let me help you with that. One day years from now...'

32. Can't help it...

When young it seemed to me that Nurture was more influential in bringing up a child than was that child's original Nature at birth. I believed that my own efforts could mould and change into something different what the mix of genes had presented me with at birth. Oh there were many things, many aspects of myself to tackle. Many things about myself that were far from satisfactory, and that would be changed and changed forever. Later I found out that it's not quite as easy as that.

Some people tell us every wrong is a response to a previous wrong e.g. a delinquent son has previously been bullied by his father, or by Capitalist Society, which has bullied him into being a member of the underclass. In other words every bully has been bullied, every perpetrator of a crime has also been a victim of some kind, and therefore it is society who is 'to blame', not individuals.

As mentioned in Chapter 18 if they go too far in that direction others call them the loony left, but as we've seen they have a point, regarding upper castes condemning lower castes having first made sure of, and sure of maintaining, their position of privilege. Now that's hypocrisy.

There is maybe a lot of truth in the position that 'every bully has been bullied', but is it the whole story? The opposing rough-justice-right wing view would say the proposition that 'every bully has been bullied' is beloved of do-gooders, and is idealistic nonsense. That on the contrary there are some amongst us who would from the make up of their character at birth, have always been prone to being bullies, no matter what.

NURTURE or NATURE

This every bully has been bullied hypothesis would only be true if Nurture (the way we're brought up) was totally responsible for our attitudes and actions in the world, without any contribution whatsoever from our Nature (the mix of our genes at birth). And though the Nurture versus Nature issue is by no means settled, it seems clear that neither one is solely and wholly responsible for the development of our personalities.

We are a mixture...

Evolutionary biologists say that at bottom we are all selfish, and our trawl through the struggle Morality has had and still has with Power suggests that they have a point. This struggle is why Morality has arisen amongst us, as a response to the misuse of Power, and if this is true then a tendency for the Alpha Male and Female to bully others must be inherent in our genes, to some extent. Surely the Alpha doesn't want to be 'leader of the pack' because someone has bullied him into it? Surely he and she want to be top dog in order to have the best chance of eating well and the best chance of a satisfying sex life. If they were not born with a tendency to assert themselves as animals in the wild, they wouldn't have lasted long enough to survive at all, let alone form groups to aid that survival.

We see around us assertive men and 'feisty' women, as we seem to like to call them nowadays, and if they are assertive not aggressive then we admire them for it, and rightly so, they are positive people who often take the lead in various of our enterprises. We don't suggest that these people are assertive solely because their parents/ nurture was assertive with them and so this is the one and only factor causing them to be positive assertive leaders of those around them. Instead we do the opposite and give them credit for their 'feisty' nature, good for you, well done we say, you've earned it – 'it' being a place of prominence in the group.

How odd then that if one of the people in question is just a touch more than assertive, is what we would define as aggressive, some of us want to find a cause of that behaviour, that is wholly and solely down to other factors than their own efforts. That is down to something other than their Nature. Is down to something that is the opposite of their fine admirable selves of a moment ago, and is instead all due to their Nurture.

Surely as we look around at our fellows, are not some more selfish than others? And are not some more inclined to be aggressive with other members of the group? Are not some then, by dint of their Nature from a young age, more inclined to bully? So Nature, this having an instinctive inclination to bully at birth, or at least a tendency to be very assertive, should be set alongside Nurture, people bullying because they themselves have been bullied. I put it to you that what we each are and how we behave is a mixture of our Nature at birth and how we have been Nurtured, a mixture of genetic factors and how we have been brought up and in what circumstances.

Isn't it logical that those of us born of aggressive parents (Nature) are more likely to be inclined to be aggressive, more inclined to bully, than those born of parents who are less aggressive themselves? If we are also born into a tough neighbourhood in tough economic times (Nurture), we may become even more of a bully to survive, a double dose, Nature-bully plus Nurture-bully. Even if one is 90% and the other 10%, and whichever way round?

BLAME
Historically and still today: the element born in us is that which we designate as less forgiveable (Nature-bully). Let's clarify this, it seems to me that all humans consciously or unconsciously designate Nature-bully as immoral automatically with little hesitation. Whereas we consider that

Nurture-bully is less blameworthy, and is dependent on the circumstances, of the crime that has been committed, and of the life and upbringing of the accused. In other words with them we are willing to hang fire and judge more slowly, instead of rushing to judgement as we do with those we consider to be Nature-bullies.

What we humans consider unforgivable behaviour is the amount of blame we apportion to others for their tendency towards the unprovoked aggression we designate as bullying. And in particular the tendency to bully they were born with via their inherited genes, since clearly this is always unprovoked by them being bullied first, because it is the way they were made. They will thus tend to be aggressive without any provocation, or with virtually no provocation, and thus their case is easier to judge, the odds are that this act of theirs is an act of bullying.

Which is where the Nature versus Nurture arguments rests, with the forgiving left saying such people are a myth, and the rough justice right claiming the opposite. And those of us in between? When courts ask for 'reports' before sentencing, they are trying to assess the circumstances (Nurture) which have contributed to the defendant doing whatever it was he did. All of us in fact ask constantly for 'reports' on those around us (via gossip), so as to be fair in our assessment of their actions towards us. 'To be fair', is to judge how much circumstances have contributed to an act, and how much is due to unprovoked bullying. We blame others much less, or sometimes not at all for their tendency to bully caused by their environment.

And like it or not, this is how we make our moral judgements. If the judge asks for psychological or psychiatric reports as well, then in addition there is a query over sanity, and in particular whether or not this person understands the difference between Right and Wrong. Provided the accused does know Right from Wrong, then the next consideration is how much his circumstances (acts of bullying committed against him) should be taken into account in deciding sentence, in deciding how Bad/Wrong he is. Which brings us back to the 'reports' the judge requests, and the gossip we listen to for lesser 'crimes' amongst our social group.

By an accident of birth some of our number are born with more of an inclination to be aggressive in order to survive in the world than others of us, and this aggression, when directed without provocation towards one's fellow group members, we call bullying (derived from Disloyalty). These we designate anti-social, or when taken to further extremes immoral.

We see carefully bred, cattle, horses and many other domesticated animals, including fighting dogs and accept that these qualities that we breed for so carefully are genetic. Yet we shy away from accepting that characteristics are genetically transmitted when it comes to innate aggression in some humans, even though it is there for all to see in aggressive dogs and other creatures. Actually illegal fighting dogs are a good comparison because they are bred for aggression, but are also no doubt kept in foul conditions that induce aggression in them.

Completely genetically transmitted or only partially so, either way we tend to avoid social contact with such people, because we know that sooner or later they will hurt us, they are selfish-plus-aggressive and cannot be trusted to be fair towards others. They will unhesitatingly push us down as they pull themselves up in what they consider to be the rough and tumble of the race called life.

Incidentally these are not by any means always 'street bullies', there are wealthy and respectable 'Capitalists' whom it suits to believe that life is a jungle, conveniently forgetting that the whole purpose of us humans banding together in the first place was to combat that jungle. What they do now is to import that jungle back inside the human group, back into the very place created by early humans to offer some protection from its pain and rigour. And think when they say life is "the survival of the fittest" that they are telling us a great truth! They tell us this having received support and a leg up from the group they now condemn as weak. Now that's hypocrisy.

Remember the example in Chapter 18? A young boy of 15 comes out from the big city slums one night with a couple of older men, to break into a house out beyond the edge of town. A wealthy country house, where he gets himself shot and killed by the householder.

Is he Nature-bully or Nurture-bully?

We judge less harshly when they treat us roughly those we consider have been badly bullied themselves. We are more inclined to forgive the boy than the men who bring him with them, to forgive those we think have 'never had a chance in life' due to their social circumstances. And it makes it easier for us if we believe that those we designate as 'bullies we do not feel inclined to forgive' are nature-bullies, otherwise the water gets very muddy, the decisions get very tough.

It is the ones born with an inclination to bully, those who give free rein to their innate aggression that we condemn. It is these we reserve our anger for, these we are pleased to see get what 'they deserve' in books, plays and films, as well as in real life. Sometimes it is argued that 'they cannot help it' or 'it is their nature', and this is true, but it doesn't take us very far. The fact is that it is these traits, the in-born tendency to bully, that humans judge and have always judged to be immoral, to be Wrong. Whether it is the hard fisted, hard drinking husband, the thief, the murderer, the cruel torturer or the merciless dictator, all are condemned.

All are judged immoral, irrespective of whether they can 'help it' or not. That some of us are born more inclined to be more aggressive than others is just a fact of life, a fact of evolution. And remember that these are looking out mainly, usually only, for themselves ... themselves ... themselves ... themselves alone. The rest of us, having formed co-operative groups, have to try and protect ourselves against freeloaders. Protect ourselves from those who are worse than freeloaders, those who do not just do less than their fair share of work, but instead actively hurt other members of the group.

We must protect ourselves against the ravages of individuals born so selfish that they treat others of the group as though there is no group. No group which offers them a protective umbrella. These bullies-from-birth violate the code, and whether they can 'help it' or not is immaterial, it is still this behaviour which we automatically designate immoral.

In fact it is because they can't help it that they stand condemned.

We don't care if they can't help it.

If you happen to be born an aggressive bully and claim therefore you can't help it, the rest of us don't care, we never have, and we never will.

It's in your genes?

It's in your genes and so you say that you can't help it.

So what, society still doesn't care.

We don't care, nor should we – you have been born with a tendency to look-after-yourself-at-the-expense-of-others.

The first Ancient Groups were created to share the burdens of life and thereby all would have a better life. The rest of us have to keep an eye on you, because you have a tendency to take more than your fair share (you were born that way and can change it only a little), you have an in-born tendency to bully.

We have to accept the way you are, and make allowance in our dealings with you.

Is it really such tough luck to be born a bully? Generally most of them seem to get by pretty well, the Nature-Bullies, the bullies from birth, get by in this world pretty well I think.

But with societies now so large, some say that in practise there is no longer a group that offers a protective umbrella. Society now looks after its higher castes and does little or nothing for its under employed and unemployed lower castes. Except condemn them when they 'step out of line', they're quick enough and hypocritical enough to do that. And on this basis the forgiving-left forgives them all. Forgives all offenders a darn sight too readily, the rough-justice-right wing say

Another difficulty in our huge modern societies is that of telling which of the many people we don't know intimately are those who are bullies-due-to-circumstances and which are the bullies-from-birth. The bigger the society the greater the difficulty of having to decide: "has another bully previously made this one who's bullying me now, the way he is now?". Or, "has he been like this from birth, born with an aggressive gene?". And with neither credible 'reports' nor village gossip available, the forgiving-left tends to give them the benefit of the doubt – and forgives these cases also.

Either way that which we humans call immoral behaviour is the amount of blame we apportion to others for their tendency towards unprovoked bullying, and in particular therefore the bullying they were born with via their inherited genes, since this is thus by definition, always unprovoked.

Most bullies-from-birth get by pretty well in life.

They do so very often at the expense of the rest of us.

Let's not be too soft on them – let's not get too misty eyed.

33. Unlimited Forgiveness

We have come full circle and can now see why, as was said in Chapter 2, we are all guilty of hypocrisy, except a few Saints, and we must be aware of this when we accuse others. We are all attempting to be selfish enough to look after ourselves and our own health while at the same time trying to fulfil, or appear to others to fulfil, our obligations to those others, our fellow group members. Nature and Nurture, wherever you stand on it 50/50, 75/25 or 90/10 and whichever way round, is a live issue, because it is how we judge, it is part of why we instinctively condemn or forgive, the actions of others.

My proposal is that limited forgiveness is the basic building block of Morality, it is the fundamental response we use in our relationships with others. And it has been those responses, and the responses in return to those responses, for generation after generation that have built in us these feelings we have of Right and Wrong. Including forgiveness, of those we deem worthy of forgiveness, and reciprocity against those we see as not worthy of our forgiveness.

We can see how that which starts with those who make petty spiteful comments in our social group, ends at the opposite extreme, with those who take us into a dark dungeon in the dead of night, and at the behest of a powerful dictator apply electrodes to our genitalia. It is all a question of degree regarding the same phenomenon, and thus we can also see a little more clearly which of those around us are manipulating us, as opposed to those we can trust. Well I hope you can.

The members of the troop learn forgiveness and the withholding of forgiveness, and those who master this art most adeptly, flourish more than others because their mix of characteristics is suited better to group life than is the character of others. They learn to stand in judgement. This troop member, he's OK, he's tough, but fair, he never shirks his duties, or hangs back when danger threatens – he can be trusted. This other one though hurts those who're weaker than himself, he eats all he can, is lazy and hangs back in times of trouble – he is trusted and forgiven less. If you forgive him he'll only take advantage rather than repay you like for like. I do not trust him. He's quick, oh so quick to claim his rights, but slow so very slow to undertake his duties.

As they learn to judge during the squabbles round the carcass, they form the early bonds of Loyalty, especially to those less selfish members of the group. These they come to feel they will do anything for, and from now on strength alone is not enough, though still necessary, you have to also be unselfish, you have to be Loyal, to earn the group's respect.

But...

Not once in all this time do humans ever think to grant unlimited forgiveness, even to fellow group members. No one until the Buddha and 'soon after him' another, Jesus Christ, ever thinks to go so far as to advocate unlimited forgiveness.

Except a parent, a parent does, and a lover, but not average group members, it is relationships between typical members of the group that we're interested in here, because it is these relationships that hold the group together, and which we come to call Morality. Although the fact that we do grant unlimited forgiveness to certain categories of our fellows shows that it is there inside us as a possible response.

Game Theory has shown that it seems highly likely that during the thousands of years during which the Ancient Groups form and coalesce there is no such thing as unlimited forgiveness, except between very close blood relatives and lovers. Forgive once, maybe twice, certainly not more than thrice, this is Morality, because this is how the early human groups were formed. By the evolutionary result of co-operation amongst partially competitive individuals; it seems highly unlikely to have developed other than by the gradual iterative process that Game Theory illustrates.

Unlimited forgiveness, extended to other group members than our closest friends, unconditional trust as we now know to call it, is something other than Morality. Is something beyond another of the boundaries that are part of an accurate definition of the word we bandy about with such gay and confusing abandon, that little word Morality. Whether it is Jesus, the Buddha and other religious leaders who present it to us, or psychologists speaking in terms of soaking up the insults, barbs and pain, until the one dishing it out begins to heal themselves – I whisper again, 'something different, something different, than Morality' ... something beyond it.

Does the soaking up of the pain of others always work, do the hurt and bullied always heal themselves?

Does this indisputably powerful technique work without exceptions, in each and every case?

And if it does work sometimes, but not others, what are the limitations of its successful use?

There seems to have been a limit to Morality during its derivation, a boundary. After you have forgiven someone one or two times, and decide to keep on forgiving rather than lashing out, then you have gone beyond Morality. Game Theory shows us Morality probably stops at tit for two tats, because that seems likely to have been a stable evolutionary survival strategy.

We have been using the terms forgiving-left and rough-justice-right, and while these are crude labels, they are far more accurate than talking in terms of Muslims, Christians, Hindus and Atheists, etc. Because as we have seen and see around us each day every religion, indeed every human institution has its left and right wings, its forgiving and retributive wings, its doves and hawks. Why is this so? Because our anger at Disloyalty and the B/A-b morality derived from it stretches across all human religions and lies behind all our institutions.

I'm not belittling the contribution religious belief can make to the quality of society. Do we see anyone other than those with such, or similar beliefs, being capable of unlimited forgiveness? Here though is something I've pondered over.

"You have heard that it was said, An eye for an eye and a tooth for a tooth. But I say to you, Do not resist one who is evil. But if anyone strikes you on the right cheek, turn to him the other also."

I remember looking that up in Matthew 5, expecting to see the turning of the cheek, and expecting to be able to say: he turns the other cheek once, maybe twice, three, four, five, six, seven or more times, maybe 77 times … but not forever. But it doesn't say that, it says *"Do not resist one who is evil"*. Full stop.

Can that be right?

Are those words really what he said?

Is *"Do not resist one who is evil"* a correct translation? Elsewhere, in Matthew 18, he does say: *I do not say to you 7 times, but 77 times.*

That's a limit, it's a lot of forgiveness, a hell of a lot, it's a mountain of perseverance and patience, but it's a limit too, and that is what makes the big difference between these two seemingly similar statements.

'Do not resist one who is evil', is endless unlimited forgiveness, whereas 'I do not say to you 7 times, but 77 times', is I suppose an extension of limited forgiveness, albeit an incredible extension.

It seems to me that there is a problem with unlimited compared to even 7 times. If everyone knows your forgiveness is endless, then they can take it as a given, they can in effect do what they like to you, knowing you will always forgive. Whereas with 3, 4, 5, 6 or 7 times, your forgiveness has to be earned, the offender has to put in effort, even if it is only a promise to do better, to try harder next time.

Otherwise what?

We should grant our forgiveness, as a matter of course? As a given, provide our answer long before the question has been asked? Before the circumstances are known? Pacifism for example can be seen as giving your answer in advance for all time, that you will never respond with violence no matter what is done to you.

Don't rush to give your answer, make them guess, make them wait, that would be my advice, for what it is worth, next to these great teachers and prophets. Stop, don't allow them to take you for granted. Forgiveness is a sliding scale. Should we really grant it in the same degree to someone we don't really trust, as we would to a long time close friend or lover? This is the core of the famous reply from Confucius.

"Master Confucius, should one repay hatred with kindness?"
"And what will you repay kindness with?" came the old one's answer.
(Confucius, 400BCE)

At its best unlimited forgiveness sends a message of trust, it says I forgive you because I believe you are a person of worth, and your bad behaviour can be reformed, with a little help from me, but mainly ... by your own efforts. Now, go and ... live up to my expectations, which I'm sure you will.

A moment ago I asked if unlimited forgiveness does work sometimes but not others, then what are its limitations? Well here is one, a massive modern state compared to a small ancient group of hunter-gatherers. Even if unlimited forgiveness works well amongst a tightly knit band of 50, 100 or even a couple of hundred people, is it as effective in huge societies where we don't know everyone so well?

When their Big Man (or Big Woman) is in close touch with the whole group he or she commands respect from bullies along with everyone else, his/her opinion of them is important, without it they will have a reduced status within the group. When the Big Man and/or Big Woman frowns everyone reacts, even bullies take note, they want to impress, and are willing to an extent to modify their behaviour to do so.

No one wants to gain the respect of a faceless state, and so one means of coercing bullies into improved conduct is lost, or at least curtailed in effectiveness. When the Big Man slaps you down it's personal, when he forgives you once, or twice, or again and again, it means something – it means he believes in your potential, believes in you.

"I forgive you because I think you will make something of yourself, will when you grow older you young pup, be a worthwhile member of our group. I forgive you, not because I forgive everyone as a matter of course, but because I think you are worth my time and trouble. What do you say to me, how do you respond, what do you have to say? Speak sonny boy speak, respond daughter respond."

This is lost in a large scale society with a faceless justice system.

Is unlimited depersonalised forgiveness effective?

Is it as effective as the unlimited personalised forgiveness of those we respect?

One would think not, the anonymity of the state helps to stop personal vendettas between rival males and their families, it has the advantage of administering justice in a neutral and disinterested way. As is common though, something is also lost in return for this gain, the forbearance of the Big Man and/or Woman – the forgiveness and trust of those whose respect is sought. In a large scale state unlimited forgiveness can be taken instead as a sign of weakness, a sign of state sponsored stupidity. Or so the right wingers amongst us think.

Forgiveness, and especially unlimited forgiveness, is tied into personal relationships. A faceless state doesn't grant unlimited forgiveness, often all that is granted is a let-off, to be laughed at and taken advantage of. Let's admit that this is one of the disadvantages of large scale societies to be set against the advantages.

Extending limited forgiveness beyond morality to 4, 5, 6 or 7 times is what we sometimes do in large societies, to give people the benefit of the doubt, and in an effort perhaps to try to make it up to those born in the underclass, for ignoring them. For the rest of us turning a blind eye and doing nothing about it, paying them no attention until it's too late and they have already become criminals. It seems to me that extending forgiveness in this way is not always appropriate in every case, in particular because it is unlikely to be effective with a Nature-bully, and even if they represent only 10% of criminal cases, that means it will not be effective in at least some cases, and so it is not a 100% solution. The trouble is that we find it very difficult to tell which 10% exactly.

To believe that it will always work is an illusion of the forgiving-left, understandable perhaps, because we humans are prone to seek and believe in solutions that solve everything. We don't like 90% solutions, we're all like that I think, for example many on the right wing seem to believe that by some magical means, hidden from the rest of us, rampant unrestrained capitalism will somehow solve all the problems and ills of large societies. Whereas in practise, as we have been discussing, the problems of huge societies are just that, problems created by the way we have scaled them up from those Ancient Groups of our beginnings.

Talking of the illusion of 100% answers brings us to the Death Penalty, and the ultimate case of those who society has not forgiven.

34. Death Row

We've come through the whole of our moral history and in doing so have returned to our beginnings. We have returned to the statement, 'that action is morally wrong, shall I hit back or hold off, for the moment, or hold off for longer still?' Let's look at those who have been condemned to death to illustrate: appropriate, inappropriate and 'not inappropriate' responses to cases of Disloyalty-bullying. We usually call society's moral response to bullying within the group by the name punishment.

Is punishment aversion therapy for the offender? A warning to others? Or a comfort to the one offended against? Or all three – and if all three, how weighted? It's probably all three and the weighting and success of the policy varies with different situations, but I'm not going to digress, the subject is a book in itself, and one I'm not qualified to write. We are focussed instead on digging into every last corner of the phenomenon we humans call morality.

Any punishment is 'not inappropriate' as long as it does not break the rule of tit for one or two tats that created human morality. In other words that is not disproportionate to the offending act and is withheld a time or two as a warning before responding. The term 'not inappropriate' is used because we are entitled, some would say even obligated, to forgive more times than twice, at our discretion. Provided we forgive once or twice at least though, and when we do respond we do so reciprocally, with an eye for an eye, then our responding or punishing actions are morally 'not inappropriate' because they are not bullying responses.

Tit for two tats may be appropriate, but for many of us tit for three tats is more appropriate, or some may want to forgive 7 or 77 times and would consider this appropriate. So because we differ, we can only ever say 'not inappropriate' with any certainty, to say appropriate is to give no latitude for additional forgiveness.

As we said in Chapter 24…

When a thief grabs your handbag it is not inappropriate for you and your friend to chase after him, catch him and dish out a little physical chastisement to encourage him to hand your bag back. This giving him a thick ear is clearly not forgiveness, but neither is it inappropriate, if you are only as rough with him as he was at the theft.

It's simple stuff that we're all familiar with – the concept of sufficient or reasonable force and a proportionate response, because a disproportionate response is itself a bullying response.

174

MISUSE of CAPITAL PUNISHMENT

Before we take the step of looking at whether there really are instances where capital punishment may be morally 'not inappropriate' we must first recognise the vile and grossly unjust ways in which the death penalty is totally inappropriate. In essence these are instances of bullying by the State, and which are therefore immoral, as follows.

1. Firstly crimes other than murder.

At one time sheep stealing was a hanging offence, but that is bullying by the State because it is clearly nothing like an eye for an eye. In China citizens can and frequently do receive the death penalty for such things as tax evasion. Like our own sheep stealing era, this policy is immoral because it is bullying by the State.

Some other countries also use the death penalty for crimes other than murder, and all such cases are clearly immoral. The death penalty can only come under consideration as a non-bullying response for repeated murders, or for torture-unto-death, for all other lesser crimes it is clearly bullying by the State, and therefore immoral.

2. Secondly the social circumstances of those who commit the murder.

One could argue that the death penalty is always unjust in large scale stratified societies because of the privileges of the upper castes, and the lack of such of the lowest caste, the underclass without jobs or education. Thus we often see and say, like that boy thief, that such things 'are not right' because the person condemned, 'never had a chance in life'.

For example there is something immoral afoot if a country consists of say 10% black and 90% white people, and yet its death row consists of 90% blacks and only 10% whites. When the USA, or any other country, consists of such glaring disparities between sections of the population, it is clearly immoral to use the simple rule of 'reciprocity', you've killed so the State will kill you. Those in the lower caste have been bullied into and then kept in their deprived position by the rest of the (270 million strong) group. So maybe reciprocity should only be used for the wealthy and privileged sections of that society?

In existing small forager societies, of a similar size to the Ancient Groups, there are few in-built injustices, but in our large ones we see vast inequalities, some of which are themselves bullying by the State, let alone following it up with State sanctioned murder.

Those are the two categories under which there can be no doubt that the death penalty is inappropriate. And there is a strong left wing argument that says they cover virtually every case in the book, so much so that it is simpler and more effective to campaign against the death penalty in its entirety worldwide, than to split hairs over a handful of cases.

Well yes, but that's practicalities not philosophy, and it is philosophy we're here to discuss, not what may or may not be politically most effective, we are striving to grasp things as they truly are.

3. Thirdly the issue of the finality of the death penalty.
Is it really morally sufficient to use tit for one or two tats as our guide when the punishment is so final? This issue includes the not infrequent cases where the wrong person is convicted, with the death penalty there is no going back. The rough-justice-right counter this by pointing out that imprisoned murderers are constantly coming up for review, and they then seem to receive a lot of publicity and sympathy, things not afforded to their victims. The case is raked over again and again, and all the relatives of the victim can do is listen to never ending claims regarding the rights of murderers.

Both sides have a point, but it would seem that to avoid miscarriages of justice that can never be reversed we should ban the use of the death penalty.

However that's enough about arguments against the death penalty, we are here for something else, the moral philosophy behind the subject. We are attempting to look behind these arguments, at some befuddled thinking that lurks there.

An introduction to which follows now.

It is sometimes said that the death penalty is the violation of a human right, 'the right to life', but this is philosophical nonsense. Every human right a society grants is 'earned' by the individual member of the group concerned fulfilling a certain duty, the single one all encompassing duty not to bully other members of the group. When an individual breaks this contract, by murdering, there is then no automatic 'right' that somehow absolves the murderer from the death penalty.

There may well be mitigating circumstances, some as listed above, that do absolve the murderer, but the asinine repetition, by rote, of a clause of human rights legislation demeans our intelligence and the importance of many aspects of that legislation. It is akin to saying that all wives are supposed to obey their husbands, why, because it says so in the marriage vows. The 'right to life' is another example of us being fooled by our own shorthand. The 'right to life' is actually the right not-to-be-bullied into an early grave, it is the right not to have your life taken away by a bully, and in particular by that most terrible bully of all, the bully called the State. The State when it takes your life without provocation or justification, which is what bullying always is – unprovoked.

Thus the State must prove, beyond the shadow of a doubt, that this person who has come up for judgement as a result of an especially cruel murder, or murders, or the torture-unto-death of another human being, has been given during his life up to now, a 'fair crack of the whip' by the group he is part of, and that we now call society. If he has been so fairly treated by the rest of us then society has at least addressed the first two of the three major objections above, philosophically, if not practically...

We now approach the circumstance for which the death penalty may be considered appropriate, or rather not inappropriate, the case of those who have tortured others unto death. We approach it not to advocate the death penalty, but to pick a hole in something people say, something that is a philosophical mistake.

THE 'STATE NO BETTER THAN' ARGUMENT

As philosophers we have no truck with vague phrases like "the death penalty is not what a civilised society does" or "the death penalty makes the State no better than the murderer". Our immediate response to such phrases is, what do you actually mean by that? And if now, towards the end of our long discussion, the answer comes "because to do so is an act of bullying by the State", that's fine, we accept it – when it is bullying by the State.

But, is it true that to execute those who commit endless-torture, those who torture-unto-death, makes the State no better than the offender? State inflicted murder, as some people argue?

No better than this grossest of offenders?

What no better than he who tortures-unto-death, and particularly he who does this many times?

That can't be correct?

It's just not logical.

If the State inflicts on one of these purveyors of endless-torture a quick fairly pain free death, isn't it difficult to argue that the State is now as bad as he is? They have let him off with a speedy end – how many of us will plead and pray for the same before we're done?

Once you define a civilised society as one that does not bully its own citizens, fine, that surely is what we mean when we say a civilised society doesn't do this that and the other, now we're getting somewhere. Where we are getting is that on this definition it is nonsense to say that a society is uncivilised if it grants a quick death to a foul dictator who has had thousands murdered and hundreds tortured-unto-death.

Hitler had 5 to 10 million killed, including the mechanised horror of the Holocaust, Stalin upwards of 10 million and Mao more than 20 million human beings, starved, tortured and murdered. Are we saying that the mark of a civilised society is that it would not condemn such monsters to death? That it would be uncivilised, unjust and most important of all immoral to execute these mass murderers? Or in fact are there some of us, just a few, who do deserve the death penalty, some of us for whom the death penalty is actually too good?

And are we saying that these three were, and the others like them are, all Nurture-bullies? All bullies created 100% by they themselves being bullied? Are we saying that 'society' is entirely to blame for creating these ultra-selfish brutal maniacs? Or are they in fact, and those like them, in large part bullies-from-birth, Alpha Males gone exponential, given an opening in a vast society and gone utterly, totally, completely berserk.

I ask you, is each Alpha Male and Alpha Female, as they scramble to the position of top dog, driven by something society has done to them or by something born inside them at their birth? That is all, this is not an argument for the death penalty, it is an exploration of some fallacious arguments that if we allow them to stand unchallenged cause confusion in our attempts to grasp the will-o-the-wisp called morality. Yes we should ban the death penalty worldwide because in practise we cannot meet the three objections regarding misuse raised above. As long as when we do we don't back it up by the claim that judicial killing, of those who have tortured many unto death makes the State no better than the perpetrator. We should ban it because it is misused so often by all kinds of murderous regimes, that the only way to stop them is to ban it too for those few cases where it is morally 'not inappropriate'.

It's fine by me to get rid of the death penalty, but I'm not going to tell a lie to do it – because philosophy is a search for truth. And the truth is that the right wing are correct when they say that some (very few) people do deserve the death penalty. But because so many others who do receive it don't deserve it, we should ban it nonetheless. Morality stops at tit for two or three tats at most, because that is how it was formed in us, as a tit for tat compromise between competing egos, a compromise that formed us into groups.

As soon as we go beyond tit for two or three tats, we are in the land of Unlimited forgiveness, or no, to be more accurate we are in the land of Additional forgiveness and following it Unlimited forgiveness. Maybe these two combined, wrapped close together as they are, is the seventh great thread that runs through human life? I don't know. But whatever it is it's time to stop calling it Morality. Let's stop, along with all those other mistakes we've encountered, confusing ourselves by the misuse of words.

In the name of accuracy let's stop calling them all Morality, the sex-in-public prohibition, self-governance, Metaphysical-religious beliefs, those things we designate unnatural-and-therefore-immoral, Utilitarianism and

Unlimited forgiveness, none of these things are Morality, none of these entities are the phenomenon of the-compromise-that-forms the group and later controls and governs the tensions within it. As with so many words – love being one, and obscenity another, we use them carelessly to cover a whole host of different topics that happen to be closely related. Morality starts as Loyalty-within-the-Group, which is I propose why loyalty is still to this day so important to us, even though we cannot personally extend it to the millions upon millions that now make up a typical group.

Morality is the emotional response engendered in us by Group Loyalty, by the Rights and Wrongs of group life, and that is the whole story...

35. In its entirety –

These observations are a good place to stop. Remember A. J. Ayer, the Professor and his Boo/Hooray being all there is to Morality? Well thanks Professor, yes hip hip hooray for all those actions and responses that are non-bullying, because these are moral actions and responses. Whereas boo hiss boo, against any action or response that is bullying or bullying-manipulation because these are immoral. It is one of these two opposites we point at as we cheer or condemn.

Morality, or B/A-b morality as we should call it to remind ourselves and others of what we speak, based originally upon Disloyalty/Loyalty, represents the largest part of the Contract between us. The only other part being the sex-in-public prohibition and any pornography so graphic that it amounts to live sex in public.

As for the rest, there is no rest, all else is error and delusion.

We've come a long way from the groups that morality was first formed in. It strikes me that it is surprising how well we do, how well some of us do anyway. We manage to just about organise massive societies of 20, 50, 60, 100, 200 million and more by the use of an instinct bred into us when we lived in small groups of 20, 50, 100 or 200 individuals at most. The main thing we have lost is immediacy, and by enlarging the group it has become so stratified that it now seems ridiculous to call it a group at all anymore. I don't suppose for one moment that Morality worked like a well oiled machine in the Ancient Groups of its origin, but at least access to everyone, from the Big Man down, was there to hand to be had.

There is a tension between our innate selfishness and our willingness to sometimes be selfless too. This tension, and how it plays out within the group, and later also between groups, under the labels fair, unfair, justice, injustice, dominance, hypocrisy and a host of other words, is what we call Morality. We carry these feelings with us from a half million years ago and more, and inevitably, when applied to huge countries, there are many defects in the societies we thus produce. What else can we do though, but with the true derivation of Morality as our constant guide continue to try to improve society along moral lines. What else but try to come as close as we can to the central underlying principle of thou shalt not bully.

At least a society so governed, messy unjust and argumentative as it often is, is nonetheless based directly on Morality. The others, those that put themselves forward as alternatives to democracy and the Open Society, are based on Power, the naked greed of Power claimed by a minority. Sometimes this Power is claimed as an aristocratic birthright, sometimes crudely as the right of the strong, and sometimes as a direct gift from God to those who obey said God, via those special persons who are especially close to him.

I see a thief, or do I?

Is this stealing from the seed store a venal act of individual greed, or are 'the Council' and their wives keeping all the best and most food for themselves? In which case that which has the surface appearance of theft is in fact an act of liberation against a ruling elite. And that which appears to be democracy is really aristocracy – a dictatorship of certain wealthy families.

Is he stealing from or for the people?

Is this act that of a thief or a liberator?

An act of political hegemony in a struggle between rivals for Power, or a blow against tyranny?

Is he a terrorist, or a freedom fighter?

A criminal or a political activist?

Is he a Disloyal bully or an Anti-bully, loyal to the underlying ethos of the Group?

Is he Al Capone or Robin Hood?

I see our thief, he leaves the grain store, but I still cannot tell from this brief glimpse, which he is, thief or liberator? More facts, we need more facts on which to base our judgement, we sit upon a never-ending jury all our lives, we gather facts, information, gossip, more, more information, our thirst seemingly insatiable. Who is the bully here and who the victim? Then I'll cast my vote.

A vote we never ever change, we always vote the same. Never changing parties, we vote the Disloyal bully is immoral, in this court oppression's always wrong. All that changes out there are the circumstances of who it is we think is being Disloyal, who it is who's bullying whom. The factory junior bullied all day long goes home, and once there rules his wife and children with his fist, his boot, his belt upon their backs. All that changes is our view of who the bully is, and who's the victim now.

Some people look for a pattern in history, well this is the pattern, the Disloyal and the Loyal, the bully and the bullied, the tyrant and the freedom fighter, the upstanding citizen and the thief. The king and his barons, the feudal lord and his subjects, the landowner and his tenants, the capitalist and the proletariat, the husband and his wife, the business man and his workers, the army and the people, the Party and the peasants, the father and his children, the masters and the slaves.

Morality, the single principle of thou shalt not be a disloyal bully, as we have seen is not just the backbone of society, is not just the main driving force of each and every human society there has ever been or ever will be, but is in fact the whole of society, is the very stuff of which it is made.

This one principle is the bottom, top, middle and furthest flung corner of the mechanism by which we co-operate one with the other, this one single principle is the basis of every relationship between each person on this planet and the person next to them, the whole of it, the whole world of human relationships, in its entirety – period.

And so I rest my case and repeat to you my previous refrain. To attempt to analyse moral questions without any reference back to the Ancient Groups in which morality first appeared amongst us is doomed to either complete, and sometimes catastrophic, failure or at best to only partial success.

Appendices

Appendix 1
Green Issues and Terms of Trade

There has been no mention of Green Issues thus far because living in a green way is conservation of the planet, rather than morality. But it does deserve a mention because in international terms there are two parts to 'being green', and the second part is a moral issue. The first part is good husbandry, a term we use for the farming habit of care for the soil and what grows out of it so that it will yield food over and over again in an efficient and sustainable manner. By which we mean both now and for an unspecified almost limitless number of years to come.

This is not a moral attribute, it is closer to the way a big cat or bird of prey carefully cleans itself, or takes care and preens its feathers. Many creatures if they aren't in their best clean and most efficient hunting condition will starve to death, and it is the same with good husbandry. Without the habit of collecting, and planting, and growing, or historically without us using every bit of the carcasses of the wild animals we had worked hard to hunt and kill, we would not have survived.

Good husbandry, on a farm for example, is a habit of careful efficiency, a thrifty care in husbanding and re-using our resources, rather than being profligate and wasteful. And the same goes worldwide, to husband our resources in a careful and sustainable manner is to be 'green' in the modern parlance. Good husbandry is a matter of self-governance then, not a moral question.

Note that it is thus a Utilitarian habit, in so much as good husbandry is about the future greatest happiness of the greatest number of the group – by the avoidance of starvation. This is a study though of morality, and thus of contractural relationships between individuals and how this then becomes extended also to relationships between groups.

Green Issues become moral, and international, when developed countries use up the earth's resources for themselves and then dictate to others, in particular under-developed countries, how they must limit their industrial output to 'save the planet'. It is clearly immoral for developed countries to burn up all the world's resources and deny them to third world countries, because this is to take more than our 'fair share', and we have long since extended the same moral rules to the rest of the world (other groups) that we use at home amongst 'our group'. All the same as a political philosophy groupism is by no means unpopular, just the opposite. George W. Bush and others have used it very successfully to appeal to domestic audiences, and all the cheers they have received from those audiences, regarding putting the USA first, serve as evidence of the existence of the continuing ancient and not so ancient boundaries between groups.

It nonetheless also highlights the kind of pressures that must have led us into compromises with other groups as soon as we first started to acknowledge that these others too, understood and were governed by the same feelings of loyalty and B/A-b as we in 'Our Group' were. But the compromises we make within-Group are inevitably much quicker to reach than compromises between groups. This is because two individuals are capable of striking a deal much more adroitly than can two groups, each of whom must consult, discuss and take soundings from many people, (hawks/right and doves/left wingers) inside their group, before signing a deal.

This aspect of the Green Issue argument is analogous to relationships between 'have and have nots', both within groups and between groups worldwide, as touched on at the end of Chapter 21. Rich western countries invoke and inveigle terms of trade that are more favourable to themselves and less favourable to the third world countries who supply them with foodstuffs. They also have been known to send aid to those countries, frequently tied into further trade deals, wherein the poor country buys the rich country's industrial products.

Lately even this aid is being questioned considering the mess of debt that 'rich' western countries have got themselves into. The people who ask those questions are demonstrating yet again that in many respects morality still stops at the group boundaries of old, no matter how big the groups called countries have now become. Terms of trade are a moral matter, in which the subtle bullying of one party by another occurs, worldwide on an industrial scale, so the old group boundaries are still in place. As demonstrated by the asylum question that we will come to next, we feel sorry for the poverty stricken of other countries, but the vast majority of us, though willing to be charitable, are not willing to go so far as to impoverish ourselves to help them out.

Now that the groups we live in are so big, we don't even need to look outwards to see such iniquities, we can see them all too clearly 'within group'. Many women, who engage in what is euphemistically called the sex industry, would not do so if they could obtain a decent wage elsewhere. The terms of trade between such working class women and middle class men are so slanted as to be a bullying relationship in itself, irrespective of other aspects of prostitution (discussed in Chapter 13). One doesn't have to be an anthropologist to figure out that such terms of trade between classes inside a group are extremely unlikely to have been present in Ancient (human and pre-human) Groups of 50 to 100 persons.

And thus in the modern mega-groups we call countries, we can see that 'the group' is so large that it has become, due to its numerous sub-groups, a copy in miniature of the international scene between groups. Thus we can for instance see international compromises are the same phenomenon, but between countries, as once long ago compromises were first made between the selfish egotism of individuals, in order to be able to form the first human groups. Formed on the basis of the greatest good/happiness of the greatest number, formed despite the inevitable tensions between the various egos of those who make up The Group. A tension the governing principle of which, we later come to call morality – and which is now still in the process of being transferred from between individuals to between the mega-groups we call countries.

While even as it is, the countries/groups are themselves becoming, and have in fact already become, so large that they render the concept of the group virtually meaningless. In its place we often see instead, greater loyalty to the sub-group, than to vast amorphous groups of however many millions that now represent the Ancient Groups of our beginnings.

Appendix 2
Sub-groups and Asylum Seekers

What did they do I wonder, back in those Ancient Groups, when they noticed stronger members of the pack next door bullying others of that group? Probably nothing much, perhaps they just reminded themselves to steer clear of the bullies from that group, as we would ourselves today. But what if one of the neighbours came over and asked to be taken in because of this bullying – would they send him back? Would they turn on such persons, or would they welcome them?

We'll never know, it would probably depend in part on how many mouths they had to feed, and also on whether the asylum seeker was male, or a young female, and which category they were short of. If they had not witnessed the bullying, and knew the group next door was having a hard time making ends meet, they might consider her to be an economic migrant, not a genuine asylum seeker at all. And, again just as today, they would probably, and a little strangely, have less sympathy for one fleeing hunger than they would one fleeing ill treatment at the hands of a bully.

"We can't take them all in" they would say, "what if more come, we'll run out of food for ourselves." Perhaps another would say, "no, she's been bullied, I stayed over there a couple of days trading last summer, their leader and his crew are brutes, it's not like it is here. Every one of them, especially those in the smaller families, are running scared."

Our natural sympathies for the bullied and against the bully are so strong that they cross the boundary between groups, and yet our feelings do not seem as strong towards those suffering from economic deprivation. A curious difference, but less so perhaps when seen in the light of the derivation and group orientated continuation of our moral feelings. It looks as though we hate to see bullying even more than we hate to see poverty, disease and the human misery caused by starvation – that seems to be the way we're made.

We are sympathetic to economic migrants.

We all flinch in horror at the sight of starving people in third world countries, but we are even more sympathetic to those being bullied by the ruling cliques in those countries.

It is a mistake, even a lie I think, to be so idealistic as to pretend that we are capable of having sympathy enough to take in everyone. Having said that we can see that there are those on the right wing of our modern groups, who play on our fears, who play, in the same way that out and out racists do, on those old boundaries, between 'our Group' and other groups.

Nevertheless there is some kind of boundary still in existence, however old, rotten and misused. What we are doing here then, is identifying that there is therefore a genuine dilemma between our acceptance of asylum seekers compared to economic migrants. However difficult and however complex societies have become we still try to weigh the evidence. Is this person attempting to manipulate us, or has their own government bullied them?

Are they a bully or a bullied?

Are they migrants coming here to take advantage of our system, our relative wealth and better way of life, or are they asylum seekers running from the bully of bullies, a foul murderous dictatorship. Are they victims of poverty, or victims of torture?

Torture – the epitome of evil.

It must surely have been easier to decide back when our group was small. If in doubt, which we usually are, we cannot say 'well we're short of young breeding females and we have plenty of food this season, so let's give her the benefit of the doubt'. Apart from anything else this is because despite all our gathering of statistics, despite all the claims and counter claims that the country is or is not full, due to the size and complexity of modern society we actually haven't got a clue whether we really have or have not got sufficient space and affluence to soak up these economic migrants.

This dilemma is the same now as it was for the Ancient Group members, it is a question of relationships between groups. Now as back then, when asylum/migrants come knocking on our door we ask ourselves – should we send back those running from poverty and allow in only those running from bullying?

Before we go on we should notice two important matters here. Firstly that the concept of human rights has helped to push forward the, what seems to us now, obvious necessity of other countries and individuals within those countries watching and criticising the human rights record of governments everywhere towards their own citizens. Or as we now know to call it, the record of bullying by governments of countries (groups) towards members of their group whom they don't like. Because if other countries don't criticise and complain, who else is powerful enough to do so and be heard?

Secondly the question of jobs, in view of the argument over whether or not there are enough of them available in our group even before we also include the employment of immigrants of either kind. There can be no meaningful group if some supposed members of it have no employment or hope of having any. This lowest caste of long term unemployed are being ignored by the rest of the group, and are thereby excluded from the group. The solution? Have you ever seen how third world countries sometimes undertake quite large projects with labour intensive methods? We should do the same, by building, using spades, wheelbarrows and unemployed labour, roads and other schemes that we can't otherwise afford. If this is a slow way of working so much the better, with proper supervision it would still achieve its main purpose, training for future full time work while making a contribution to group endeavours. They would then be members of the group, instead of what they are now, non-members, or rather members of an unemployed sub-group.

OH YOU'RE SO RIGHT WING, BUT I LIKE YOU

Groups within groups, so many groups, so many groups to interface with, no wonder morality has become so complicated, it's not just us and our neighbour across the river any more. After some kind of border check, a group, for all kinds of reasons, lets some people in. See how quickly, in the space of a just a generation or two, that which starts out with the best of intentions can morph into something else, when people emigrate and form a new sub-group inside another group.

Some from similar, as well as different, cultures to the host country, assimilate and intermarry to such an extent that, apart from a few non-British sounding surnames you can't see the join. When this happens there is still only one group, but when the immigrants don't assimilate quite so much, it is then that a sub-group has in effect been imported into the larger original group. This is in addition to the many sub-groups that the large society has itself already fractured into. Such things though matter only a little as long as there are but a few of them, their funny foreign ways add a certain colour and variety to the surrounding host nation – and the host nation does not feel threatened. Rather the opposite, there is a certain pleasure, a certain massaging of their egos to think that the country they have built is so worthwhile that others come from many foreign lands to live in it.

But then more and more immigrants come, until in certain parts of some towns and cities they outnumber their hosts. And so it becomes the case that it is the few hosts who remain in an area who now add a little colour to the sea of immigrants. Either way there is now a part of one group imported inside a different and larger host group. Some of those who come don't learn the language of their new home, in fact they do the opposite and attempt as much as possible to recreate their own country in miniature, as a comfort no doubt to replace that which they have left behind. And to an extent this is the colour they add to their adopted country, and this is a fine thing, up until there is a clash say between the religious laws and values of the host nation and those of the immigrant people. When such a clash comes, there is a danger that, due in part to this lack of assimilation in some areas, these two sets of people revert to, or is that continue to be, two separate groups. Groups in the originating sense, groups that form a borderline, that form a stumbling block, groups that represent an ancient boundary.

This is the same stumbling block we have been trying to overcome ever since that ancestor of ours gave that apology to his trading partner in the group next door, all those thousands upon thousands of years ago. Let's not kid ourselves that it is a boundary we've crossed and can comfortably forget about and leave behind. We are trying and we must continue to try, we can't give up as some right wingers would have us do, and all get back in our bunkers and stare balefully through its peepholes at our neighbour. But equally what we must not do is underestimate the difficulty, this is not just any old obstacle, this stumbling block is the boundary that formed morality within-groups. It stopped at this boundary you will recall, not just as some archaic limitation due to distance and poor communications, but because it was at this boundary that all loyalty stopped. It was precisely because you could do whatever you had to do in order to survive, to any humans and animals beyond this boundary, that loyalty within the group was so important, so strong and so sacrosanct.

To betray it made us then, and makes us still today, very angry. It is thus still very much with us, it is the place jobless young men go to when they join the gang culture of many large cities and find comfort, comradeship and satisfaction. Maybe for the first time in their lives – they find a purpose in ancient Loyalty-to-the-Group.

This boundary is not some kind of bigoted aberration, some fiction, or figment of the imagination – ironically it is that which made us moral, (Bowles & Gintis, 2011). It is that which formed all human morality, the whole emotional reaction of it. In fact it is because of this boundary that we feel loyalty at all, and it is because we feel loyalty that we feel 'thou shalt not bully' others of the group. The boundary made us, it formed us, we cannot and must not make the mistake of underestimating it. We can get past it, we already are doing so to a considerable extent, but to try to brush it aside as if it were nothing is a foolish mistake, a mistake that will hinder rather than help us. To succeed in this difficult endeavour we must acknowledge the boundary, along with its historical importance in human development, instead of pretending it is nothing but a prejudice of the right wing.

Amongst the next generation some of the children of the immigrants feel that certain things are wrong in the host society – and rightly so, things are wrong, there are abuses, iniquities and deficiencies in every large society. Nothing unusual about that, it is their proposed solution that is the backward step. They blame these inadequacies on the host's religion, or lack of it. Some of the young firebrands have either held onto or reverted back to their parent country's religion, and so have not changed at all in order to accommodate the ways of their new home.

Now we all get angry over injustices, over wrongs that need putting right, but these are moral feelings and as such have very little to do with the different religions of the host country and the incoming group. We are back again then, back at those ancient group boundaries.

Remember those angry young people with placards in London and many other places, inciting death to those who they deemed had "insulted" their special Prophet? Those who they accused of being blasphemous – that meaningless word? Yes it's just the usual extremists, and they're all the same, whether they're Communist, Fascist, Atheist, Christian, Islamic, Hindu, Sikh or Jewish. They represent disaffected youth, mainly angry young men who can't find a fit in the society around them, whereas the vast majority of us moderates get on with each other with a minimum of racism and friction most of the time. Leave it alone and it will soon die away, and things settle down, but on the other hand there is something else here too. This is more than youthful bigotry; these placards are an attack by Metaphysics-religion upon Morality, by aggressive religiosity upon the Open Society.

The generation before us, including my father and grandfather, all those people whose sacrifice in the two World Wars we commemorate at the Cenotaph each November, fought for something permanent.

They fought fascism, and they thus extended the Open Society.

They fought for freedom from tyranny. They fought and died to defeat Hitler, but they also sacrificed themselves for a principle, for the very core of the Contract, they fought for freedom from oppression and thus for freedom of speech. They died for more than just one (very big two part) War, they died to defeat a terrible Dictator, and in particular a fascist dictator, the worst kind, the kind who actually professes a belief in inequality, in some humans being less than equal, and even less than human, when compared to others. At least Communist Dictators espouse that we're all equal, even though they don't act upon it.

For your tomorrows these gave their today.

They sacrificed themselves for the survival of something bigger than themselves – the survival of the Open Society. This isn't something to shrug off, something to condone or appease, this is everything the generation before me, my father and his veneration of Winston Churchill and the achievement of 1939 – 45 was all about. This isn't some old-fashioned nothing, for old folks every November, no this is everything.

When you go home, tell them of us and say, 'For your tomorrows these gave their today'.

The generation before me gave and gave so that I could have freedom of speech, and if I were ever invited to walk those lines at the Cenotaph I would feel I should do so on my hands and knees. Should kneel as not being worthy to stand in their presence.

There is a need for sensitivity towards other people's feelings, but I am not willing to spit in the faces of the few that remain of the few. Just so as not to offend a few over-sensitive Islamic fundamentalists. In the Open Society all viewpoints are scrutinised and questioned, and can be held up for satire and ridicule. And those that survive this, those that weather the storm well, do so because they are worth keeping.

In this form of Society nothing is too sacred to question – that is how the Open Society was formed, it is its *raison d'être*, the basis of its being. In our huge mega-Groups only the Open Society has any chance of delivering a moral society, because it and it alone is based upon the founding principle of the Basic Morality, on Disloyalty/Loyalty and upon Bully/Anti-bully. The rest offer this or that Grand Solution to all society's ills, the only difference between them being the different illusions their beliefs are based upon.

They all share one thing.

They seek perfection.

They seek perfection in a world where evolution, and especially the evolution of human morality we have been tracing, shows us it can never exist, never has existed and never will exist. Let's be content instead with telling the truth and making a realistic 'best of a bad job'. We hear talk in recent days about aggressive secularism, but it is those responsible for aggressive religiosity that we hear it from.

PERFECTION, AND THE LACK OF IT

We have these strong feelings of right and wrong, bequeathed to us from a half million years ago and more, and we are often not sure where to direct them. It's as confusing when we are enmeshed in matters of international relations as when we are arguing over minor domestic matters.

A footballer requests a transfer, and deserts the club to whom he has been apprenticed from a young age, in favour of more money with a bigger club. The fans feel angry, but the lad justifies it by taking the usual line of 'big wages but short career, got to think of my family'. The fans are angry because they feel he has been Disloyal to the club that has nurtured him for so long. We need guidance even for a case as simple as this; yes he is being disloyal and this strikes an ancient chord amongst the group he deserts. On the other hand it is true that his career and earning potential will probably be short, and the fans will not pay his wages once he's over the hill.

So on the face of it the loyalty he owes to his wife and children does outweigh the loyalty to the group we shall call 'the fans'. They are only one group of many that he will belong to during his life, unlike the way things were for us 500,000 years ago, when we belonged to one group for the whole of our lives – and we stuck with them like glue. We stuck with them, and if we were never disloyal and never bullied any member of the group, then we were behaving morally – and that was all there was to it. In the good old days, the simple old days that is, when it was all for one and one for all – and no exceptions.

The list is endless, we are rightly angered and object to the outrageous salaries of some company directors because in the original groups all are part of the same team. Now though due to the size of modern groups our ability to redress such imbalances are limited. All our groups, no matter how big are co-operatives, and in the Ancient Groups though those contributing more were probably rewarded more, they were still likely to have always been within touching distance of those rewarded less. Despite its limitations of size and wealth the Ancient Groups were probably never an egalitarian society, but the imbalances were minimal, and to stray beyond these slight imbalances is thus immoral.

Capitalists think such gross imbalances are fine, and in fact that we need more of them in order to 'perfect society', whereas Socialists want to revert to the originating moral principle of the group – egalitarianism, as they see it. From the size of groups today, it seems clear that there is no cure-all, and the sooner we realise this the better chance we will have of making a continuous and never ending series of slow incremental adjustments. These have to be made, amongst other reasons in the face of bullying on this side, and then when that is corrected, the sway and balance of power results in bullying on the other side, and that needs correcting. All this, tricky as it is, is better than living the illusion called 'a perfect society'.

In the face of all we have been discussing it seems to me that one of the biggest mistakes we make when addressing our many social problems is the error of perfection. Even if we could, with more knowledge, have 'perfected' the original small group societies of half a million years ago, there is clearly little chance to in some way 'perfect' the monster societies of more recent creation. We do have a chance though of continuing to improve them, as long as we understand what they are, and what it is that makes them tick.

THE FABLE OF ISLAM VERSUS THE WEST
Despite these group within group issues there is no clash of fundamental values, as some like to portray, between Islam and 'the West'. How could there be when we all share the same common human values? The same values of Disloyalty and Loyalty, expanded with the expansion of the size of 'our group' into Bully/Anti-bully. There are for example many persons in 'the West', Christians as well as others who share Islam's stance on homosexuality. There are many also, on the right wing, in 'the West' who share an enthusiasm for much harsher punishments – these things are largely questions of degree.

Similarly with public drunkenness, didn't we conclude on the last page of Chapter 18 that *'the Open Society should live by its principles and not do as it does at present, pay woolly minded lip service to its own values'*? As to 'female dress codes', didn't we also draw an initial conclusion on this in point 15 of our reasoned discussion in Chapter 12. We left this as *'Any woman dressed in a sexually arousing way is entitled to do so, both for her own Pleasure and the Pleasure of others, but she is being foolish if she is not also aware of her personal security. The more explicitly you are dressed the more attention you are likely to receive, and the more potential there is for 'trouble'.*

I don't propose to debate this matter in detail here, except to say that obviously the enforcement of a ridiculously restrictive Islamic dress code onto women by men is clearly bullying and therefore immoral. The above italicised tentative conclusion does illustrate though that the dress code issue is a concern of 'the West' just as it is within Islam. It is an issue we understand and it is therefore not a clash of values, but as with the rest of the above, the same values taken to different extremes.

This also raises the issue of governmental paternalism (last discussed at the end of Chapter 9), which Islam believes in, and which we do too in 'the West' to 'an extent', otherwise why would we legislate that all persons riding motor bikes should wear crash helmets, and all persons in cars should wear seat belts. Allowing Sikh males to be an exception to the helmets rule because of their religious turbans is an example of secular tolerance, it is an accommodation. The exception is made because the risk of injury, and therefore the only person affected, is to the religious observer concerned. If for example we were discussing wearing the full face all encompassing Moslem female veil with gauze even over the eye slit while riding a motor cycle, we wouldn't allow it because it would affect vision and could result in the death of someone else. (The subject of such full face veils is discussed in Chapter 12.)

The reason for these kinds of laws, and the legislation against the use of certain drugs that 'we' think society is better not to be awash with, is because we do share the same values, we do see the same need (for some limited) governmental paternalism, for 'our own good' and for the greatest good of the greatest number. The only part of this that religious fundamentalists don't share with us is the caution that both the secular and religious majority feel regarding the great danger of the Prohibition or Religious Police becoming such terrible bullies, and doing so with such complete impunity, that they become far worse than the perceived evil they are allegedly protecting us from. Oh we share the same values all right, and they are moral values based upon Disloyalty/Loyalty and its corollary Bully/Anti-bully.

Meanwhile 'the West' and the USA in particular allies itself with the ruling elite in countries such as Pakistan, and then seem to be astounded and mystified when many young men of the poverty stricken class of that country revert to fundamentalist Islam and paint the USA as the 'Great Satan'. We should note that this issue too, despite the religious labels applied, is nonetheless nothing other than Bully/Anti-bully morality. And is related again to the issues of 'terms of trade' and vast inequalities between the sub-groups inside modern countries, as briefly mentioned in Appendix 1.

If you were a member of a poverty stricken underclass hemmed in by the wealth, inertia and corruption of those in power you to would turn somewhere, to some movement that you saw as less corrupt than the venal hypocrites in Power. It is no coincidence that during the Cold War the churches of Eastern Europe were full, but are now a lot less full, because the bullying Communist Dictators have been vanquished in large part. In Moslem countries it is natural to turn to Islam, same thing, the same phenomenon – morality, B/A-b moral issues over and over and over again.

No there is no clash of so called 'Islamic values' compared to so called 'Western values', all are really just a range of human moral values, on some items of which we disagree. Just as the left wing and right wing disagree inside every society. If 'they' didn't share the same values as 'us' we would have no basis for discussion. Human moral values are the values we all share, the differences, resentments and confrontations are frequently between the downtrodden and the bullies that tread them down. And because they are really a range of human values then by talking about Islam and the West we won't be leaving out the followers of Hinduism, Buddhism, Confucianism, Communism, Fascism and all the other 'isms'.

There is no clash of values, but we must be mindful of something, it has taken us a slow two hundred years or more to move our society towards an encompassing secular basis, and further away from a

Christian one. It has been a considered, painful for some people, inch by inch process, but it has been the correct course to follow, especially for what has now become a multicultural society. Correct that is as long as we implement the true basis of the Open moral Society, namely Bully /Anti-bully, instead of slipping into as we have in recent times 'paying woolly minded lip service' to it, in the name of political correctness.

We must therefore be careful not to give any religious faction the idea that our society is or ever will be based upon the backward step of what for want of a better expression we can call non-secularism. It is hardly surprising that (mentioned in Chapter 22) there was an incredulous outcry when my old boss the Archbishop suggested the introduction of Sharia Law might be a good idea for certain parts of our society. I wish him no harm, but it serves to illustrate how misguided and confused we can become in these matters. It should also alert us to how out of touch with the reality of morality, well meaning, and not so well meaning, religious persons can become. It is a worry that a so-called religious thinker such as the former Archbishop seems to totally misunderstands the place of religion in a secular society – which is to encourage moral behaviour, but never to define it.

We must be careful, while welcoming all contributions from every sector of our modern mega-group not to give certain religious zealots the impression that their way of looking at the world has more relevance than it really does. We must be careful not to give them an inch and then stand back and watch in horror while they take a mile. To do otherwise is to lend them support in their confused belief that they are fighting for the 'moral high ground', whereas in reality they are not even fighting for morality. How could they be? How could they represent morality, when they don't fully understand what it is.

Glossary

Basic Morality, the – is the morality of all human beings, based upon the emotional reaction of Disloyalty/Loyalty and Bully/Anti-bully, which is derived from it, and is the basis of every human moral system no matter what various religious and other 'add ons' societies worldwide have subsequently attached to it.

Contract, the – is the agreement first made between the members of the Ancient Groups and then carried forward to all modern contracts in the present day. Moral philosophers tend to call it the moral contract, but that seems to me to be confusing because it conflates entities from different sources. Firstly the very ancient one of incest (see chapter 7), common to most animals, followed secondly by the peculiar and relatively recent **sex-in-public prohibition** (chapter 8) found only in humans. Then thirdly and separately by the real foundation of what we should properly call morality – by Disloyalty/Loyalty, and its extension Bully/Anti-bully itself.

Common Rights or common minimum rights – an alternative term to 'equal rights' used because in fact, although the concept of equal rights is a legal necessity, in terms of moral philosophy it is misleading. We don't have equal rights within the Group because we earn our rights by doing our duties, thus in theory and in the Ancient Groups, some of us earn more rights than others by doing more work for the good of the Group than others do.

Complications – this term is used to cover the complications that arise and occur to the originating Loyalty-to-the-Group B/A-b principle due to and during the passage of time. The first being the cross over of the principle from 'within Group' to apply also 'between groups' as well. This is followed by the massive increase in the size of groups and the introduction of religious ideas 'explaining' the derivation of morality.

Confusions – these are matters that sit closely along the boundaries of morality, and so are often mistakenly classed as moral issues. The main ones listed very roughly in the order in which they appear in this book are: Utilitarianism, Incest, the **Sex-in-Public prohibition** and Self-governance (or Buddhist Skilfulness) based on autonomy. Plus in addition 'unnatural' sexual deviations such as bestiality, and last but not least the many religious pronouncements upon what is and is not moral.

Note that religion, much as my own off beat version of it is dear to me, falls into both categories, because it causes both complications and confusions.

Duty-cripple – is a human being so crippled in some way as to be unable to fulfil his or her duties as a member of a human group, but is given the benefit of the doubt by us assuming that they would do so if able. As a result we treat them as fully paid up members of the Group.

Duty-future – is the status of the children of the group, we are naturally charmed by them and assume that when they are old enough and able, (different levels of responsibility will be given to them as they grow up), they will undertake all the duties expected of a fully grown up member of the group.

Duty-history – their duty-history is how we assess other members of the group in our dealings with them, we ask ourselves 'how well are they, and have they, fulfilled their obligations towards the rest of the team?'. We make these judgements, and constantly update them, via what we see for ourselves as well as the information others give us. This information may stretch (in the form of gossip) from concerns about minor insults and slights all the way up to torture-unto-death. In the latter case, or when other crimes are committed, we ask for 'reports' on previous behaviour and other mitigating factors before we sentence those we judge to be guilty.

Everyday altruism – covers cases where we do something for others without expecting or wanting anything in return.

Evolutionary altruism – is if some creature were to do something for another that benefits another's capability and opportunity to breed, while reducing its own.

Group, the – is the archetype of the many Ancient Groups that each of our ancestors belonged to during former times. 'Within group' refers to the feelings of Loyalty-to-the-group that are the precursor of what today we call B/A-b morality. 'Between group' refers to the way we have extended these same 'within group' principles to our dealings with other groups, to treat them 'fairly', as we consider it, and to limit and reduce the tendency to otherwise be in a constant state of war with neighbouring groups around us.

LOYALTY AND DISLOYALTY

The terms within group and between group are essentially the same as in-group and out-group used by Samuel Bowles (Bowles and Gintis, 2011)

Half-moral – is a categorisation of Utilitarianism, this is because the first half of the famous greatest happiness of the greatest number, is a pleasure-pain calculation. A calculation which is common to every life form on earth, even plants prefer and therefore flourish in some conditions as opposed to others, thus it cannot be morality. The second part is though, to give consideration to the pleasure-pain of others, and so Utilitarianism is half-moral.

Limited forgiveness – is the forbearance members of the group show to other members, and that we still show to each other today, it is the basic building block of 'the Group', and it is thus that which actually creates morality. It is the glue that first binds the Group into a group and then continues to hold it together.

Mega-groups – are the giant countries we have created, but that we still are forced by our moral feelings, to organise, rule, legislate and conduct on the same basis as we did our original small 50 to 100 person groups. How could we do otherwise? These moral feelings are all we've got.

Moral-response dilemmas – are our responses, and the range of possible responses available to us, towards what we take to be acts of bullying made against us. In the judicial system we often designate such responses as 'punishments' of various kinds..

Reciprocal rights – all our rights (our one Right-not-to-be-bullied) are earned by us being honest, fair dealing members of our group, in other words by us doing our Duty towards others in the group. Therefore when we encounter other groups what we have are reciprocal rights between groups, there is no such entity as international rights, that exist somehow somewhere out there in the ether.

Self-governance – is also referred to by the Buddhist term Skilfulness and is based upon the parts of our lives that are autonomous, ie that are our own business, our sphere of independence from others in the group.

Sex-in-public prohibition – is a peculiar facet of the sex lives of humans that along with us having no 'in heat' season and the way we continue to have sex after the female's loss of fertility, separates us from the vast majority of other animals.

Tit for two tats – is a term used for the most successful strategy revealed by the computer simulations of Game Theory, and thus is the means by which the B/A-b response was built within the Ancient Groups.

Titillation – is whatever level of soft pornography a society considers is legally acceptable for transmission via the various media outlets available in that society. In other words these are all images that are considered to be NOT so graphic that they break the sex-in-public prohibition.

Note that hard core pornography, which is either extreme actual sex or graphic simulation, will therefore usually be considered to be illegal and condemned on the grounds of it being either a 'direct contravention of the sex-in-public prohibition', or a contravention via a 'graphic simulation of the sex-in-public prohibition', so realistic as to be tantamount to sex-in-public.

Torture-unto-death – is to torture someone without end, endless torture with no hope or possibility of escape, and ending only in their death, it is thus the ultimate wrong and therefore the definition of what we call evil.

Unlimited forgiveness – turning the other cheek as promulgated by Jesus and the Buddha, and which is sometimes called 'unconditional love', and which is therefore also in effect the love and forbearance shown by many parents for their offspring.

My proposition is that this should be classified as something that is beyond the boundaries of morality (it can therefore be considered as a '**Confusion**' as defined above), because morality was built amongst us by the giving and withholding of limited forgiveness. The amount of the limitation usually being no more than tit for tat, or tit for two tats, maybe conceivably tit for three tats at most.

We could speculate that it might possibly encompass four or five tats, but even if we do stretch it that far, it is limited, and thus a long way short of unlimited forgiveness. Thus Unlimited forgiveness is beyond morality.

Bibliography

Alcock, J. 2001, *The Triumph of Sociobiology,* Oxford, Oxford University Press

Axelrod, R. 1984, *The Evolution of Co-operation,* New York, Basic Books

Ayer, A. J. [1936] 1971, *Language, Truth and Logic,* Hamondsworth, Penguin Books

Bagemihl, B. 1999, *Biological Exuberance: Animal Homosexuality and Natural Diversity,* Stonewall Inn Edition

Balcombe, J. P. 2011, *The Exultant Ark: A Pictorial Tour of Animal Pleasure,* Los Angeles, University of California Press

Berlin, I. 1995, *Liberty,* Oxford, Oxford University Press

Bentham, J. [1789] 2010, *An Introduction to the Principles of Morals and Legislation,* Virginia USA, White Dog Publishing

Boehm, C. 1984, *Blood Revenge,* Kansas, University Press of Kansas

Boehm, C. 1999, *Hierarchy in the Forest,* Cambridge Mass, First Harvard University Press

Bowles, S. and Gintis, H. 2011, *A Co-operative Species,* Princeton New Jersey, Princeton University Press

Confucius, [400BCE] (Tr. Leys, S. 1997) *Analects,* New York, Norton & Co

Darwin, C. [1859] 1985, *On the Origin of Species,* London, Penguin Classics

Darwin, C. [1871] 1981, *The Descent of Man,* Princeton New Jersey, Princeton University Press

Dawkins, R. [1976] 1989, *The Selfish Gene,* Oxford, Oxford University Press

Dawkins, R. 1996, *Climbing Mount Improbable,* London, Penguin Books

Dawkins, R. 2005, *The Ancestors Tale,* London, Phoenix Orion Books

de Waal, F. 1982, *Chimpanzee Politics,* London, Jonathan Cape

de Waal, F. 1997, *Bonobo: The Forgotten Ape,* Los Angeles, University of California Press

Diamond, J. 1992, *The Rise and Fall of the Third Chimpanzee,* London, Vintage

Diamond, J. 1997, *Why Sex is Fun,* New York, Basic Books

Diamond, J. 1998, *Guns, Germs and Steel,* London, Vintage

Durant, W. 1963, *The Story of Philosophy,* New York, Simon and Schuster

Dworkin, R. [1986] 1998, *Law's Empire,* Oxford, Hart Publishing

Emerson, R. W. [1836-1862] 1982, *Selected Essays,* London, Penguin American Library

Hume, D. [1777] 1975, *Enquiries concerning Human Understanding and Concerning the Principles of Morals,* Oxford, Oxford University Press

Harris, S. 2010, *The Moral Landscape,* London, Transworld Publishers

Kant, I. [1785] 1998, *Groundwork of the Metaphysics of Morals,* Cambridge, Cambridge University Press

Kant, I. [1788] 2004, *Critique of Practical Reason,* Mineola New York, Dover Publications

Katz, L. D. (Ed.) 2000, *Evolutionary Origins of Morality,* Thorverton, Imprint Academic

Kinsey, A. C. 1948, *Sexual Behaviour in the Human Male,* Philadelphia, W. B. Saunders

Kittler, R. et al 2003, *Molecular Evolution of Pediculus humanus and the Origin of Clothing,* Leipzig, Max Plank Institute Current Biology Vol. 13 1414 - 1417

Leaman, O. (Ed.) 1998, *The Future of Philosophy,* London, Routledge

Locke, J. [1690] 1964, *Two Treatises of Government,* London, Everyman Paperbacks

Machiavelli, N. [1516] 1999, *The Prince,* London, Penguin Classics

Mascaro, J. (Trans.) [500BCE] 1962, *The Bhagavad Gita,* London, Penguin Classics

Marx, K. [1867] 1995, *Capital,* Oxford, Oxford World Classics

Mill, J. S. [1863] 1972, *Utilitarianism and On Liberty,* London, Everyman Paperbacks

Mill, J. S. [1869] 1970, *The Subjection of Women,* Cambridge Mass, MIT Press

Nagel, T. 1979, *Mortal Questions,* Cambridge, Cambridge University Press

Neitzche, F. [1885] 1969, *Thus Spoke Zarathustra,* London, Penguin Classics

Norman, R. 1998, *The Moral Philosophers,* Oxford, Oxford University Press

Paine, T. [1791] 1989, *Rights of Man,* Oxford, Oxford World Classics

Pirsig, R. M. 1974, *Zen and the Art of Motorcycle Maintenance,* London, Corgi

Plato, [375BCE] 1987, *The Republic,* London, Penguin Classics Edition

Popper, K. R. [1945] 1966, *The Open Society and Its Enemies,* London, Routledge

Rawls, J. [1971] 1999, *A Theory of Justice,* Oxford, Oxford University Press

Ridley, M. [1993] 2003, *The Red Queen,* London, Harper Perennial

Ridley, M. 1997, *The Origins of Virtue,* London, Penguin Books

Rousseau, J. J. [1762] 1968, *The Social Contract,* London, Penguin Classics

Scanlon, T. M. 2000, *What We Owe to Each Other,* Cambridge Mass, First Harvard University Press

Sen, A. 2009, *The Idea of Justice,* London, Penguin Books

Sober, E. and Wilson, D. 1998, *Unto Others,* Cambridge Mass, First Harvard University Press

Sommer, V. and Vasey, P. L. (Ed.) 2010, *Homosexual Behaviour in Animals: An Evolutionary Perspective,* Cambridge, Cambridge University Press

Thoreau, H. D. [1854] 1983, *Walden and Civil Disobedience,* London, Penguin Classics

Wolf, A. P. and Durham W. H. (Ed.) 2004, *Inbreeding Incest and the Incest Taboo: The State of Knowledge at the Turn of the Century,* Stanford, Stanford University Press

Wright, R. 1994, *The Moral Animal,* New York, Vintage Books

also from

ARENA BOOKS

A Childhood in BOHEMIA
and the flight to the West
by Erika Storey

Erika, a small girl, growing up in the picturesque town of Saaz in Bohemia (Czechoslovakia) discovers the way of the world and her own nature amidst the turmoil of WWII. In 1945, just after the war ends, she and her family, together with at least 17 million other Germans from the Eastern European countries and with the consent of the Allies, are expelled into the devastated Germany.

Always accompanied by her mother, she feels safe in spite of the family's sudden loss of all their possessions at the same time as their homeland of hundreds of years. As many as 2 million, mainly mothers and children die on the long flight into the unknown.

Erika, her sick sister Elisabeth and her mother Josefine find themselves in a camp in East Germany (occupied by the Russians) and later in one room on a starvation diet. Her father, Ferdinand, a POW is released in West Germany, finds his family through the Red Cross and after 2 years of separation the family is re-united in West Germany, but only after the ordeal of being shot at, while crossing the East German border. Many more hurdles have to be overcome before life finally becomes less "life-threatening". The dramatic attempts of other close relations to escape the chaos are interwoven into the main story, while the background is the roller coaster of political events and history in the making.

284 pages   **Original Paperback**

ISBN 978-1-906791-34-6   Retail Price £15.99 / US$ 27.18

Lightning Source UK Ltd.
Milton Keynes UK
UKOW03f0928100913

216895UK00001B/17/P

9 781909 421219